WORKING WITH CHILDREN'S LANGUAGE

JACKIE COOKE &
DIANA WILLIAMS

EDITED BY CLARE LATHAM

Speechmark

Published by
Speechmark Publishing Ltd, Telford Road, Bicester, Oxon OX26 4LQ
United Kingdom
www.speechmark.net

© Jackie Cooke & Diana Williams, 1985
Revised 1991
Reprinted 1992, 1993, 1994, 1995, 1997, 1999, 2000, 2001, 2003, 2005, 2006

002-0103/Printed in the United Kingdom/1010

British Library Cataloguing in Publication Data
Cooke, Jackie
   Working with children's language. – Rev. ed.
   1. Language arts (Elementary) 2. Language acquisition
   I. Title II. Williams, Diana, 1957– III. Latham, Clare
   372.6

ISBN 0 86388 374 5
ISBN 978 086388 374 3
(Previously published by Winslow Press Ltd under ISBN 0 86388 025 8)

CONTENTS

ACKNOWLEDGEMENTS

We would like to thank the following people for their kind and considerable help in the compilation of this book: Janet Gompertz (Dip.CST); Dierdre Pacey (Specialist Speech Therapist for Language Disordered Children; I.L.E.A.); Jane Stokes (B.A. Hons, Dip.CST); April Winstock (Dip.CST); Rachel Steadman (Dip.CST), for their welcome contributions of practical ideas and activities; Dr Joan Reynell and MTP Press Ltd, for kindly allowing us to use her work on the developmental stages of attention control in Chapter 2; the Principal and teaching staff at the Centre for Clinical Communication Studies, City University, London, for their advice and encouragement; Debbie Death for patiently and efficiently typing the script; and David Doorley for his help in reading the manuscript, as well as in numerous other ways.

We would also like to thank all the therapists, teachers and children we have had the pleasure to work with and who helped frame the experience from which this book has grown.

EDITOR'S NOTE

For the sake of clarity alone, in this text we have used he to refer to the child and she to refer to the adult.

FOREWORD

This book has two main virtues rarely found in practical guides to language intervention. Firstly, it attempts explicitly to relate theory to practice; and secondly, it contains a wealth of practical suggestions —many more than one could ever use in a particular instance.

There are many conflicting opinions about the way in which young children acquire language and the extent to which it can be taught or deliberately programmed. The authors of this book skilfully achieve their aim of making their practice consistent with their understanding, and students and practitioners alike will follow the theory more clearly because it is related to a set of intervention strategies.

At the same time the user of the book is not constrained by theoretical considerations because the organisation of the book makes it easy to take what is required for the needs of a particular child. Anyone working with children's language will find this volume an indispensable handbook to practice.

Bill Gillham,
Department of Psychology
University of Strathclyde

INTRODUCTION

This book is designed primarily to stimulate language in children whose language is delayed, but who are otherwise developing normally. These children develop language in a normal pattern but are delayed in their rate of acquisition. Many of them have difficulty learning language in an incidental fashion and may need specific remediation. This is reflected in the book's fairly structured approach to language-teaching. However the activities can easily be adapted for more informal use in playgroups, nursery and infant schools.

In producing *Working with Children's Language* we aim to provide a range of activities based on a developmental theory of language acquisition, which will stimulate the reader and help him to create his own ideas. The book is intended to encompass ideas and information that will be helpful to speech therapists, playgroup leaders and teachers, in fact anyone involved in the care of young children. Wherever the word 'therapist' has been used this is intended to cover anyone who is involved in the child's remedial language programme. However, we strongly advise that any child with a suspected speech or language problem should be initially referred to a speech therapist for a comprehensive assessment.

There are six chapters. Each one examines a different aspect of language and language-related skills and is divided into three parts: theory; guidelines to remediation; activities. Chapter 1 describes the development of the infant's early language skills from birth to the appearance of his first words. It also covers the growth of symbolic awareness. Chapter 2 outlines the stages of attention control as defined by Dr Joan Reynell, and examines its importance to language learning. Chapter 3 explains the role of different types of play in language development and stresses the importance of play to the child and the therapist. Chapter 4 looks at the comprehension of spoken language, beginning with the first verbal labels. Chapter 5 describes the growth of expressive language, from the child's first words to complex utterances, taking into account the functions, meanings and form of language. Chapter 6 defines some of the terminology commonly used with reference to the child's perceptual skills, and discusses the importance of perception to language acquisition.

The chapters are inter-related: the concept of separating the different areas of a child's development is only possible in theory; in practice we are faced with the whole child, developing along a number of parallel lines. For this reason there is considerable cross-referencing between chapters and certain skills have been included in more than one chapter. Throughout the book, activities are repeated, because one activity can be used to develop many abilities.

We do not pretend that all the activities in this book are original, but we hope it is useful to bring together ideas from many different sources—and to link treatment to theory in a pragmatic way.

Considerations of Therapy
1. Management
There is a current trend towards carrying out language-teaching in groups. In principle, this is desirable as the advantages of *small* groups are many (Fawcus et al). However we should not forget that they also have their drawbacks, and that individual teaching can have positive advantages. It is worthwhile giving considerable thought to the issues of membership, environment, aims, objectives, leadership, methods, and group dynamics when planning a group. Some advantages of group-work are:

(i) It provides a more natural communication situation (Fawcus et al).
(ii) It provides more opportunity for learning social skills and conventions.
(iii) It eases the pressure on individual children.
(iv) It makes healthy use of children's competitive instincts.
(v) It allows a wider range of games and activities to be used.
(vi) It helps the child to practise and generalise skills he has learnt in individual sessions.

Some advantages of individual work are:

(i) It enables more time and concentration to be given to specific tasks.
(ii) It provides the child with undivided attention.
(iii) It reduces environmental distractions and allows the child to focus on the task.
(iv) It may be more suitable for teaching attention control, and the comprehension of difficult concepts.

The optimum situation is a combination of group and individual teaching, to reinforce each other.

2. Guidelines to Remediation
Certain therapeutic principles have been stressed throughout the book. It is important to remember these when designing an individual remediation programme. Each chapter contains a set of principles relevant to that aspect of language; however, some factors are common to all language teaching and we would like to highlight them by listing them here.

(i) Teaching should be based on careful assessment.
(ii) Take account of all the variables that may affect the child's competence, eg his attention control, memory and dexterity.
(iii) Activities should be at the child's developmental level.
(iv) Use materials that interest the child.
(v) Materials and activities can be adapted to serve a variety of purposes.
(vi) The adult's language should be modified according to the child's level of comprehension.
(vii) The child needs to feel secure and comfortable to be able to make progress.

(viii) Children should play freely with new equipment before they are asked to perform specified activities with it.

(ix) Children should proceed at their own pace—some may need carefully graded levels of teaching, while others will not.

(x) Repetition and practice are essential for consolidation of learning.

(xi) Generalisation activities and carry-over into school and home must be built into the child's remediation programme.

(xii) Parents and other significant people must be included in the treatment programme wherever possible.

3. Techniques of Teaching

We do not intend to discuss different teaching philosophies, but only to mention a few more commonly used techniques.

(i) **Elicited Imitation:** the adult models the required behaviour, eg the use of the past tense, and the child must imitate him immediately or after a calculated delay.

(ii) **Modelling:** the adult gives many examples of the required behaviour, intending that the child will assimilate and later spontaneously reproduce them.

(iii) **Role Reversal:** as the name suggests, the adult and child swap roles, eg the adult models a word by naming a picture for the child to find, and then the child names a picture for the adult to find.

(iv) **Sentence Closure:** the adult models a word or structure and then elicits it, by requiring the child to finish her sentence, eg 'I'm drinking *milk*. Mary's drinking *milk*. You're drinking . . .'.

(v) **Forward-Chaining:** the child starts off an activity and the adult completes it. Gradually he is expected to do more and more.

(vi) **Back-Chaining:** the adult shows the child an activity and leaves him to carry out the last step, eg she builds up a sequence of blue and yellow beads, and helps him to place the final bead, to complete the sequence. She repeats the activity, gradually leaving more and more for the child to do. This has the advantage of giving the child the satisfaction of completing a task.

(vii) **Reinforcement:** the adult reinforces the child by rewarding his appropriate behaviour, and ignoring inappropriate behaviour. This may be done systematically, with a carefully worked out system of rewards and 'time-out', or on an informal basis.

4. Coping with Errors

It is best to decide beforehand upon a strategy for coping with a child's errors, so that they can be dealt with swiftly and consistently by everyone involved in the teaching programme.

Here are some suggestions for responding to errors:

(i) **Failure to attend:** get the child's *full* attention and repeat the question or command.

(ii) **No response:** repeat the stimulus, and if there is still no response, give him as much help as he needs to carry out the activity, and then praise him for his effort.

(iii) **Unclear response:** ask the child to repeat his response with some modification, eg to speak more slowly. Then model the behaviour for him.

(iv) **Incorrect response:** model the correct response, making sure he is aware of what you are doing, and then repeat the stimulus.

Until the child has fully consolidated a new skill, errors are to be expected. In the early stages of learning every appropriate effort should be rewarded as you gradually shape the correct responses. Slowly reduce the rewards and reinforcement as the child becomes more proficient.

How to Use this Book

The practical activities have been kept separate from the developmental theory, to allow the reader easy access. The activities are subdivided according to the particular skill that they develop, eg *Activities to Encourage the Child to Listen*. The user can thus look up the goal that he is intending to achieve and find suitable games and ideas listed there.

CHAPTER 1
EARLY LANGUAGE SKILLS

Introduction

This chapter does not try to cover the whole of child development but sets out to describe those areas that can loosely be termed 'early language skills'. The skills described are not just basic to language, however, but are fundamental to the development of good cognitive, social and communicative skills. We have divided early language skills into five topics: early communication; early vocalisations; early concepts; early speech perception and early verbal understanding.

This chapter is closely related to the chapters on Attention Control and Play, and should be read in conjunction with these to give a wider view of the developing child.

Factors Affecting Early Language Skills

1. Mental handicap. A mental handicap can delay or even prevent the development of fundamental skills, such as the concept of object-permanence.
2. Physical handicap. A gross disability such as quadriplegia is quite obviously handicapping, as it prevents the child from moving about and exploring his world. A relatively minor handicap, such as cleft palate, can have subtle consequences; for instance it may interfere with normal babbling, which can impair both language development and the quality of communicative exchanges between mother and infant.
3. Sensory handicap. Deafness and blindness obliterate a whole range of experiences which are important to early language and cognitive development. Impairments of smell, taste and touch also deprive the child of a rich source of sensations, and consequently, of knowledge.
4. Emotional deprivation. Whether the roots are in a withdrawn child or an uncaring parent, emotional deprivation impairs the bonding between infant and parent, which is vital for the development of social and communicative skills, and for the sense of security that a child needs in order to explore and experiment with his environment.
5. Material deprivation. If the baby has no suitable playthings and little in his environment to interest him, his development may be slow.
6. Lack of stimulation. Despite many beautiful toys some children are under-stimulated because they are left to their own devices too often. Babies need adults to show them things, play games with them, and talk to them.
7. Frequent illnesses. Serious illnesses may have a debilitating effect on the baby, making him tired and under-responsive. Hospitalisation and separations from his family can delay his development. Even minor illnesses have their effect, eg, frequent colds can impair

a child's hearing and consequently his early speech perception and production.

Assessment

Health visitors, doctors and mothers keep a watchful eye on growing babies. There are regular routine health checks on young babies that assess motor, visual and hearing development, and test reflexes, physical well-being and important performance milestones. If there is concern about a baby's development he can be referred to a regional paediatric assessment centre for a more detailed examination.

There are several developmental scales that are widely available. Many professionals also design their own checklists to focus more closely on early language and related skills.

Some of these developmental scales are:

1. Sheridan M, *Children's Developmental Progress. From Birth to Five Years. The Stycar Sequences*; NFER-Nelson, 1973.

2. White M and East K, *The Wessex Revised Portage Language Checklist*; NFER-Nelson, 1983.

For the slightly older child, there are formal tests:

1. Sheridan M, *Stycar Language Test*; NFER-Nelson.

2. Lowe M and Costello A J, *Symbolic Play Test*, Experimental Edition; NFER-Nelson, 1976.

3. Hedrich D L, Prather E M and Tobin A R, *Sequenced Inventory of Communicative Development (SICD)*; NFER-Nelson.

Informal assessment is an essential part of the assessment process. This includes a good case history, detailed observation of the child's interactions in a free situation in his own environment, parents' observations and informal performance testing.

Early Communication

Although the child is communicating from the moment of his first cry there is a fundamental difference between his behaviour before he is six months and after about nine months. For the younger child, vocalising is not purposeful; it is a reflex action, reflecting feelings of hunger, discomfort and pleasure (Bloom, 1978). The older child however does communicate with intention (Halliday, 1975). Intention develops as the child becomes aware that his behaviour has an effect on his environment and that movements and sounds can stand for feelings, needs and desires. Both these realisations are helped by the parents' responsiveness to the baby's behaviour.

Early actions and vocalisations are reflexive but parents give them meaning and respond to them (Cole, 1982). This is the beginning of a social interaction, eg the child smiles, so the parent smiles back and probably also talks and plays with the child, which leads to further smiling. The form of these communicative episodes gradually changes over time as the child matures and is able to take a more active part.

Attention to a Common Referent

This is a necessary prerequisite to communication and to language learning. Until 3 to 4 months of age the infant's attention is restricted mainly to his own body and its movements, and therefore parents concentrate upon the child, playing with his toes, tickling his hands, imitating his mouth movements and facial expressions and so on. Once mutual attention to the child's object of interest is established, the adult gains the infant's attention by using a high-pitched voice, exaggerated intonation, facial expression and eye contact; bringing the face close to the child's line of regard and smiling (Bruner, 1975; Stern, 1977).

After four months the infant can recognise and follow another person's line of regard which means that the parents can direct the child's attention to objects and events in the environment (Cole, 1982).

Co-Actions

Co-actions are activities that the child and adult engage in simultaneously. They begin at about 3 months and include mutual gaze, sustained eye contact, synchronised head movements, making faces, smiling and co-vocalisations, all incorporated into play routines (Stern, 1974). Either the parent or the child may initiate the activity and the other joins in. At 3 months vocalisations will increase when an adult responds to the child, especially by talking, cooing or making other sounds (Weisburg, 1963). Mutual feedback is essential to maintain the interaction and if a child does not join in with his parents, or vice versa, instances of communication begin to decline in frequency and intensity.

Mutual gaze and co-vocalisations are particularly common and provide experiences that can be shared by both parent and child. These behaviours are available to the baby almost immediately and are exploited by the parents, who adapt their own behaviour to the changing capacity of their infant's.

Alternate Actions

Gradually, at about 4 to 6 months, co-actions give way to alternate exchanges as the infant develops his imitative skills. Initially the parent imitates the child immediately he ceases an activity to encourage him to repeat it. The child repeats the activity and an alternate exchange is established. If the infant doesn't respond then the parent takes both turns, leaving a pause for the child's response until he does join in appropriately (Snow, 1977; Stern, 1977). Parents also hold two-way conversations with their children, taking both speaking parts, but leaving appropriate pauses for the baby's coos and gurgles. Later, the parents initiate an exchange by imitating a sound or facial expression they know the child can do, and encouraging the child to join in (Cole, 1982).

Co-vocalisations still take place and tend to predominate during times of high excitement and emotion while alternate exchanges occur at mid-levels of arousal (Stern, 1977). Stern believes that this pattern has a parallel in adulthood; for instance, people tend to wait their turn in a rational discussion, but all shout together when angry or excited.

From 4 to 6 months parents can differentiate between the child's varied vocalisations and impute different intentions to them. If the parents consistently respond to the child's calls he will soon learn to expect a response. This is the beginning of his appreciation of cause and effect, and of his intentional behaviour, as he learns that vocalising can bring about social interaction and the satisfaction of his needs.

At 8 to 10 months infants show a significant increase in intentional behaviours, especially those oriented towards achieving goals. This marks the beginning of the means-end distinction (Cole, 1982). The child will repeat actions that evoke an interesting response from adults.

From 8 to 12 months infants begin to indulge in other kinds of alternate actions, such as 'give and take' games, when the child demands a toy, gives it back and demands it again, or puts it down and asks for another one (Bruner, 1975). The child is learning many things during this game. He is taking turns, which is vital for later reciprocal exchanges, including conversation and games with rules. He is actively experiencing agent-action-object relations. Role-reversal teaches him the effects of his own actions and those of others on himself, and enables him to regulate the behaviour of other people.

Early Vocalisations

Functions

Children use vocalisations to perform many functions from an early age. Halliday identified the following functions:

   (i) the interactional function (from 3 to 4 months): to maintain social exchanges.
   (ii) the personal function (from 9 months): to express feelings and states.
   (iii) the instrumental function (from 10½ months): to satisfy needs and desires.
   (iv) the regulatory function (from 10½ months): to control the actions of specific people.
   (v) the heuristic function (by 15 months): to obtain information.
   (vi) the informative function (by 18 months): to give information.
   (vii) the imaginative function (by 18 months): to play and create.
  (viii) the dialogue function (by 2 years): to maintain social communication.

Halliday states that the interactional, instrumental and regulatory functions develop into the pragmatic function, while the personal, heuristic and interactional functions develop into the mathetic function (see Chapter 5, page 58).

Halliday's list describes the intentional behaviours of the child, but even before these functions are established the child's vocalisations are reflections of his different feelings and states, eg hunger, pain, discomfort, pleasure and excitement.

Form

The first sound a baby makes is usually a loud cry. During the next few weeks he will also yawn, sneeze, belch and cough, which are mainly due to physiological activities such as breathing and feeding. Even these sounds may be interpreted as communication by many mothers who respond with speech and play (Snow, 1977).

Between 8 and 20 weeks, cooing, laughter and other sounds of pleasure are heard (Stark, 1979). These sounds need more modification by the vocal tract than crying, which decreases as pleasurable sounds increase.

Soon the first vowel sounds appear, usually front vowels followed by middle vowels (Rutter and Martin, 1972), and from 12 to 24 weeks the first consonants are heard. It used to be thought that front consonants such as [p] and [b] appeared first, probably because they are produced earlier in meaningful words, but recent research suggests that the child produces back consonants, [k] and [g], very early on. These become less and less frequent in later babble and early words and must be relearned at a later date. Nasal sounds [m] and [n] appear very early and by 12 months nearly all the vowel sounds have been produced (de Villiers and de Villiers, 1978). The child discovers these sounds on his own; they are not learnt by imitation, but through self-exploration.

Between 16 and 20 weeks the child engages in vocal play, ie playing with sounds for their own sake (Fry, 1977). To begin with there is no intention to communicate and sounds are produced for pleasure and curiosity. The frequency and intensity of the infant's vocalisations are influenced by whether or not he is comfortable (Delack, 1976), stimulated, or gets a response (Weisburg, 1963). This stage of vocal play may also be called babbling.

Babbling

The child's repertoire of sounds during this phase may include many non-English sounds but not necessarily all the English ones (Fry, 1977). Babbling sounds change as the child matures, eg back consonants are relatively frequent early on but are infrequent in later babble. Although an adult's attention can increase the frequency of early babbling it probably does not affect which sounds are produced, as the child cannot imitate until he is older (Dodd, 1972).

Early babbling:

1. Stimulates the child and brings him pleasure; (Nakazima, 1975, found that babies actually babble more when they are alone).
2. Practises sound production and perception, as the baby experiments with moving his lips, tongue, soft palate and larynx, while listening to the results.
3. Attracts adult attention and brings reponses and material needs.

Later babbling also:

4. Maintains social interaction.
5. Communicates feelings and needs, mainly through the nature of the intonation pattern.

From about 25 to 50 weeks the child produces reduplicative babbling. This is a repetitive consonant-vowel (CV) sequence, consisting of an unchanging consonant although the vowel may vary, eg 'ernerner' or 'dudada' (Stark, 1979).

At 9 months non-reduplicated babble occurs and may persist up to 18 months. This consists of a single CVC or VCV sequence, eg 'merm'; 'ubih', with the consonants differing from one syllable to the next (Stark, 1979). This may also be called expressive jargon as the child uses a rise-fall intonation and sentence-like structures. When the first words appear they may be embedded in strings of expressive jargon.

Deaf children also babble at the same age and in the same form as hearing children but they tend to develop less intonation, and cease babbling much earlier.

Vocables

There is increasing evidence to suggest the existence of sound-sequences, occurring between babbling and the first true words, that are not an attempt at adult words, but are used consistently and frequently to signal different meanings. They normally stand for functions rather than objects or people, eg requests, rejection, frustration, achievements, and are accompanied by gestures and actions which convey the gist of the message, eg a child consistently says 'der' whenever he asks for an object and points to the one he wants (Carter, 1979).

These sound-sequences have various names, including 'vocables', which is used by several researchers and will be used here. Vocables may consist of only a consonant and vowel, or even a single vowel, and can be difficult to distinguish from the first attempts at true words. At 12 months a child may use about a dozen vocables and one or two attempts at real words. Little is known about the development of babble into speech, but it appears that vocables may influence the acquisition of the first real words, in two ways:

(i) The child's first words may be words that begin with the same phoneme as the vocables.
(ii) The vocables themselves may actively evolve into real words (Carter, 1979).

First Words

At 10 to 15 months the first recognisable words are heard, often reduplicated syllables such as 'dada' and 'mama', or single syllables such as 'da' for dog. Babbling continues but declines as more words are learnt. There may be a period of near silence between the last of the babbling and the first of the real words but more usually elaborated babbled sentences continue (de Villiers and de Villiers, 1978).

The child now has to relearn the sounds that he babbled in his first year, as meaningful phonemic contrasts (Jakobson, 1968). This time front consonants are usually produced before back ones, but there are individual differences in order of acquisition (Menyuk and Menn, 1979).

Chapter 5 contains a more detailed appraisal of the child's early words.

Gesture

The development of gesture will not be detailed here, but the reader must not forget that the child's use and comprehension of gesture develops alongside verbal language. A baby responds to waving 'bye-bye' at about 7 or 8 months. At 9 months he uses gross gestures such as pointing and holding up an object, and, when he is able to get about, he will take a person to an object he wants. From 12 to 18 months a child's play is dominated by imitative gestural games, such as peek-a-boo and pat-a-cake.

Early Concepts

The child's early learning is dominated by the acquisition of the object concept (ie information about the properties and functions of objects) and relational concepts (ie information about the ways in which objects relate to each other).

The Object Concept

This has three basic elements: object constancy, object permanence and object identity (Bee, 1981).

1. Object Constancy

This has to do with perception; the child must be able to perceive that an object is the same object, despite changes in distance, orientation, the child's viewpoint and the effects of light and shadow etc. This begins in the very young child but is not fully-developed until he is 2 to 3 years old (Bee, 1981).

2. Object Permanence

This refers to the realisation that an object exists in time and space even though it can no longer be seen or acted upon. This concept develops in well-defined stages (Piaget, 1973) although there is some disagreement about the ages that children progress through them. The very young child acts as though an object that is out of sight is also out of mind. At 1 month a baby shows no response when an object is removed from his sight. At 2 months he may look surprised if a toy is hidden but doesn't try to find it.

At 6 months he looks for a dropped toy but if it doesn't reappear quickly he will forget it. Also at this age he will remove an obstacle to uncover a partially-hidden toy, but does not attempt to uncover or search for a completely hidden one. This suggests that he recognises that part of an object represents the whole object (Bloom, 1978).

At 8 to 12 months the child is capable of reaching and searching for a fully hidden object if he sees it being hidden. This implies that he realises the object exists even though he can no longer see it and therefore has become aware of the permanence of objects. At this stage the location of an object seems to exert a stronger pull on the memory than the object itself. If a child succeeds in finding an object at place (A) he will continue to look for it there, even if he watches it being taken out and re-hidden at place (B). At 12 to 18 months a child will look for the object at (B) as long as he saw it being hidden there. However, if he did not see it being hidden he will continue to search for it at place (A) and will not look for it at place (B) even when he cannot find it!

At 18 months a child will search for an object in any place, even if he has not seen it being hidden. He is now said to have the full concept of object permanence. He has processed, coded and stored information about the object, can hold it in his memory and continue to look for it in successive places (Bloom, 1978).

Object permanence develops as a discrete concept regardless of the object involved, so the child does not have to learn about the permanence of each new object he encounters. The achievement of object permanence means that the child has separated the object from its context and from his own actions (Bloom, 1978). The object concept can now evolve, ie the child can proceed to recognise the similarities and differences between objects, and form them into categories.

Object permanence is important to language development, as the child must first learn that objects do not shift and change, before he can understand that words are symbols, used to represent objects (Bloom, 1973). Before this stage a child may use words, but they are confined to specific items in specific contexts, eg his family and familiar toys, and are not used symbolically.

3. Object Identity

This is the ability to recognise that an object is the same from one day to the next and from one situation to another. This ability depends on the development and interaction of object permanence, memory and internal schemata (Bee, 1981). It begins with situational understanding in the same way as early verbal understanding begins.

At 8 to 9 months the child recognises an object only in its familiar context with all cues present, eg he knows his own cup at mealtimes but he neither recognises it in other contexts, nor does he recognise that other cups are also cups (*see page* 7). He is not yet aware of a class of cups (Bloom, 1978).

At 9 to 10 months the child will recognise his own cup in different contexts as long as there are familiar clues present, eg it contains his usual milk or orange juice.

At 10 to 11 months he can recognise it in any situation and by 12 months he is aware that other cups of the same size are also cups, and can use them appropriately.

All the above developments add up to the achievement of the object concept, or what Reynell calls 'object recognition' and Piaget, 'internal schemata', ie the child can recognise all real cups in any situation. He has become aware of a class of cups (Bloom, 1978). Thus object recognition stems from a gradual reduction in situational cues and is essential for the development of symbolic understanding (Reynell, 1980) (*see also page* 7).

The acquisition of the object concept involves the processes of generalisation and discrimination. The child first recognises one instance of an object, 'his cup'; later realises it is an example of a category of 'cups'; and lastly learns to discriminate between members of the same category, eg 'plastic cups' and 'china cups', and between different categories, eg 'cups' and 'saucers' (Bloom, 1978).

Relational Concepts

Relational concepts are a second major factor contributing to the content of later language. They are important as knowledge in themselves and also contribute to what the child knows about objects.

Bloom found a relatively stable order of emergence of relational concepts:

    (i)   reference
   (ii) actor, action and object relations
  (iii) attribution
  (iv) location
   (v) possession (Bloom, Lightbown and Hood, 1978).
       See also Chapter 5.

Children learn these by looking, touching, listening and doing.

The early relational concepts that children learn about are existence, disappearance and recurrence. Movement and change are dominant forces in their development, as objects come in and out of sight, backgrounds change and persons reappear. As children learn which objects tend to stay put, eg bath, bed and house, and which move, eg mummy, cat and ball, they learn about action relations. They also identify which objects move by themselves and which need to be propelled, thus becoming aware of agents and objects of actions.

The child discovers the effects of his own movements on objects, eg he can bang his spoon on a hard surface or shake his rattle; and the effects of other people's movements upon himself, eg how it feels to be swung, pushed and stroked. It takes time for the child to sort out all the different aspects of these movement events (Bloom, 1978). Movement also brings about a change in the location of the people and objects being moved, which teaches the child about locative-action relations.*

Although location may be learnt initially through the movements of objects, the child soon becomes aware of static locations, through associating an immovable object with a specific place; for example that the bath is always to be found in the bathroom (in most houses!) At 10 to 18 months children can respond appropriately to a 'Where?' question when the object is not in view, as long as it is in its usual place, eg fish in a tank. After about 18 months, they can locate an object out of view, that is in a temporary place, such as the fish tipped into a bucket for tank cleaning.

Up to 16 months the child is not aware of instrumental relations. He may use object (A) to reach object (B) or to perform an action upon it, such as banging a brick with a spoon, but his attention is fixed upon the second object and object (A) is almost regarded as an extension of his own body.

From about 13 to 19 months, the child begins to use one object in an appropriate way, but not necessarily in relation to the second object, eg he may use a broom to sweep a doll's face.

From 18 to 24 months, as symbolic representation develops, he learns to use both objects appropriately in relation to each other, eg he washes his doll's face with a toy flannel (Bloom, 1978).

Cause and Effect

The newborn baby is prompted by innate reflexes which are soon modified by his experiences. Things happen to the baby; he is picked up, fed, bathed, cuddled and rocked etc. At the same time he discovers he has certain abilities of his own, eg he can look and notice things; listen and hear sounds; touch and feel his blanket and his mother's body; move his arms, legs, head and body; cry and make interesting noises.

Between 1 and 4 months the baby is very concerned with his own body and he begins to repeat physical movements—an early attempt to make things happen again. At this stage he does not distinguish himself from his environment, or from his actions and the effects of his actions (Piaget).

The child's reflex movements sometimes cause enjoyable things to happen, eg as he waves his hand, a brightly coloured mobile twists and turns. Through constant repetition of such 'accidental' activities, the child learns that his movements have an effect and he begins to separate himself from his environment. Piaget calls these events 'Magical Phenomalists': 'magical' because they are centred upon the actions of the child without his being aware of the connection between the cause and its effect; and 'phenomenal' because the link between the two events is enough to make them appear related. Between 4 and 10 months the child begins to repeat activities to make interesting things in the environment happen again. The child is beginning to co-ordinate information from two senses at once (Bee, 1981) and is paying increased attention to objects and

events in his immediate environment. The parents help to develop this awareness by directing their child's attention to toys placed near his line of vision, and maintaining his attention by moving the toys, talking about them and helping him to manipulate them (*see also Chapter 2*). As the child develops object permanence and object constancy, his visual and tactile explorations become more systematic. He begins to recognise the connection between his own action and the interesting outcome; for example, he realises that grasping a dangling string swings a mobile or toy into view.

From 10 to 12 months the child's actions become more purposeful as he develops the understanding of cause and effect. He now acts with an end or goal in mind, eg he pulls the string because he wants the toy that is on the end of it. The subtle difference between this child and one who is still at the 'Magical-Phenomalist' stage is that the latter would pull the string even if there were no toy on the end. The year-old child is able to combine two behaviours in order to achieve specific ends, eg he can employ both gesture and vocalisation to gain somebody's attention and direct it to an external event. He uses people to achieve his goals and satisfy his needs, thus developing his understanding of instrumental relations.

At 12 to 18 months, when the child can manoeuvre himself around more freely, he becomes more exploratory and experimental, trying out new activities with familiar objects and old activities with new objects (Piaget, 1973). Up to about 12 to 15 months, the infant's exploratory behaviours consist of non-specific actions, including sucking, dropping, shaking, banging and throwing, regardless of the specific properties and functions of the object. In this way he extracts a great deal of useful information about objects and action-relations. From 16 to 19 months, his activities become more object-specific, eg he rolls a ball and shakes a rattle (Bloom, 1978).

Through these operations the infant of 18 months ultimately distinguishes actor from the object being acted upon, and learns cause and effect and means-end relations (Piaget, 1973; Gratch, 1975). The child first learns these concepts with himself as an active participant and only later in relation to other people.

The concept of cause and effect and its association with appropriate language forms the basis of verbal reasoning (Piaget, 1973). The child will later use language to seek causes and reasons for why things are as they are, and to work through problems by anticipating the effect of one action upon another.

Early Speech Perception

The perception of speech sounds is usually in advance of production (Edwards, 1974), but the two develop together and may not follow identical paths (Stark, 1979). Indeed, early perceptions may well be inaccurate (Edwards, 1974; Garnica, 1973).

To comprehend verbal language the child must be able to do three things (de Villiers and de Villiers, 1978):
1. Discriminate the human voice from other environmental sounds.
2. Discriminate speech from other human sounds.
3. Discriminate between different speech sounds.

Very early on, perhaps even from birth, infants can distinguish and respond to the human voice. Neonates are responsive to sound frequencies that are in the same range as adult speech, and can be quieted or stimulated

---

* This is Bloom's terminology: locative-action refers to the place that an object is moving to; while locative-state refers to the place that a stationary object is in.

by the sound as well as the rhythm of speech. At 2 months a baby can respond differentially to a rising or falling intonation, and at 4 months can distinguish between stop consonants, such as [p] and [b], on the basis of Voice Onset Time (VOT) as adults do (Eimas, 1974 and 1975). Like adults they do not distinguish between different sounds that fall in the range of one phoneme, which suggests that babies are born with an inbuilt system of 'linguistic feature detectors' (Eimas and Corbit, 1973). However, although babies can discriminate instinctively between phonemes, they must consciously learn that different phonemes signal differences in meaning, as their phonological system develops.

Recent evidence has shown that sounds are perceived in the context of the word or phrase, and not as discrete phonemes, ie the perception of a sound varies according to how it is affected by its neighbouring sounds. Children probably acquire the full phonological system through learning new vocabulary, for as they learn new words they become aware that different sounds produce different meanings.

Theories of speech perception and the development of phonological contrasts are intricate and many and the subject is too vast to do justice to here; however it is obviously an important aspect of language acquisition, and the reader is urged to explore some of the books and papers on the subject.

Early Verbal Understanding

The exploration of real objects in the real world gradually leads on to the symbolic representation of objects. We use symbols, such as toys, pictures and words, to stand for objects, ideas and events. The use of symbols is basic to true language, which is a system of symbols that allows man to transcend the here and now in his communication and thought. The child must have reached at least the early stages of concept formation before meaningful language is possible, because words are symbols and symbols must be related to concepts and not to specific objects.

Symbolic understanding develops gradually through consistent stages, from about 9 to 27 months of age (Reynell, 1980).

Situational Understanding (from 9 months)

Through the child's experiences with the real environment he comes to understand a good deal. Mothers often feel that their 1-year-olds understand everything that is said to them. The child uses all the available contextual clues such as the parents' gesture and intonation, and his familiarity with the situation to interpret what is going on. In fact, the child understands few of the actual words, and perceives them merely as part of the total situation. For example, if a mother asks her child to sit down for dinner while pulling out the highchair and tying on his bib as food smells waft from the kitchen, he would be unlikely not to understand what she wanted.

Talking is part of the whole situation but gradually the child becomes aware of a familiar phrase emphasised by the parent's clear intonation and stress pattern. Soon the phrase heralds the event that is associated with it, and the child of 9 to 11 months shows anticipation and an appropriate response, which may themselves become part of the familiar routine

(Reynell, 1980). Gradually, the situational clues become redundant so that the child of 12 months can recognise the situation by the linguistic clues alone.

Between 11 and 13 months the key words in the phrase are identified as the most significant, eg 'cup' signals the arrival of orange juice or milk; later it is associated with the action of drinking, and finally with the object itself (Reynell, 1980). The phrase is associated with a specific action or situation, however, and does not yet represent true verbal understanding.

With the development of the object concept at about 13 to 15 months, the child is ready for early symbol recognition.

Symbolic Understanding

'Readiness for true language can be seen by the child's spontaneous meaningful play with toys, showing awareness of symbolic representation' (Sleigh, 1972).

At 12 months the child understands real, familiar objects in relation to himself and can demonstrate knowledge of their function by using them appropriately, eg drinking from a cup. This is sometimes referred to as definition by use.

At 13 to 15 months he can play meaningfully with large dolls and toys. At this stage he may use some single words, usually situational ones such as 'bye bye' (Reynell, 1980).

At 15 to 18 months he will use real objects appropriately in relation to large dolls and to people other than himself. This is the beginning of symbolic play (Sleigh, 1972).

From 18 months he can relate two familiar symbols, such as feeding a large doll from a large toy cup.

From 18 to 20 months the child recognises small and miniature toys and relates them to each other, eg feeding a small doll with a miniature bottle, although he may also use the objects on himself. At this stage true verbal labels appear (Reynell, 1980).

Between 20 and 24 months he begins to recognise clear coloured single-object pictures and can match the picture to a real object.

Between 24 and 27 months he can relate two different kinds of symbol, eg matching a toy to a picture. He can also match one object to a picture showing two objects.

From 2½ years the child acts out meaningful sequences with small toys, such as a dolls' tea party. At 2½ to 3 years he can match two or more pictures to a multi-object picture (Sleigh, 1972).

The 3-year-old begins to understand composite pictures with the help of toys and objects that he can manipulate according to the relationships shown in the picture. At 3½ he can understand and try to describe a composite picture (Sleigh, 1972) and at 4 and over, he will put together picture sequences and comic strips and understand them (Reynell, 1977).

Toy and picture recognition is important to the child's development and seems to be very closely related to language acquisition. Sleigh's study showed that the ability to relate two symbols is correlated to the use of two-concept phrases, and that after 3 years of age, the child who is able to assimilate many toy and picture symbols also becomes more fluent in his speech, producing multi-concept sentences. Her work suggested that the use of toys and pictures, or other symbolic forms, in the treatment of a child with language impairment, may facilitate his awareness of symbols and so help him towards greater fluency in language (Sleigh, 1972).

Guidelines to Remediation

1. Therapy for these early pre-language activities must be regular and consistent.
2. Therapy must be reinforced at home.
3. Advice and practical suggestions to the parents, and other people who are closely involved with the child, are of vital importance.
4. Therapy should be enjoyable; make games out of these early activities.
5. Never try to make the child 'perform'. Activities should be as natural as possible.
6. Take every opportunity that naturally presents itself to reinforce the concepts you are trying to teach.
7. Give the child as much practice as he needs.
8. Make sure the child has a quiet environment some of the time, so that he can listen to his own sounds and those of his natural environment. Always have quiet when carrying out sound-work.
9. Ensure that all toys and materials used are hard-wearing, safe and hygienic.

ACTIVITIES TO PROMOTE EARLY LANGUAGE SKILLS

Early Communication Activities

Attention Sharing

At first, follow the child's line of regard and attend to whatever he is attending to. Establish a mutual interest in whatever interests him by looking at it, listening to it, manipulating it, talking about it, demonstrating how it works or what can be done with it and so on. Sustain his interest for as long as possible (*see also Chapter 2*). Use any situation that presents itself, for example, the child playing with his toes, watching a moving or dangling toy, listening to music or the sound of rain, looking out of the window, playing with a toy or building with bricks, looking at a book or picture, eating food or sweets, and so on.

Gradually establish a connection between yourself and the activity. The child will become aware of this association as you make things happen to him, eg hug, stroke, turn and rock him; or to the object of his regard, eg tickle his toes, swing the mobile, shake the rattle and knock down the bricks. Be sure to call the child's attention to your face from time to time or he may just see you as an extension of the object.

Place the child where he can see you and watch what you are doing so that you become the object of his regard. Talk to him about what you are doing.

Synchronised Routines

Join in whatever the child is doing and imitate his actions. Use any activity that stimulates the child, preferably age-appropriate and purposeful, but if the child is very delayed and has few interests almost any of his behaviours can be utilised.

Examples are smiling and looking, rocking, babbling, humming, laughing and crying, rolling, crawling, dancing, singing, pretending to be trains, cars and animals etc, and playing with toys.

When the child is fully aware of the adult's participation, the adult should try to initiate another activity that she knows the child can do. Initially, this change of activity should be similar in kind so that the child need not make too large a leap in his 'thinking', eg start clapping while the child is singing, or stamping feet when he is dancing.

Once the adult and child can play happily together the adult can begin to initiate games, or try to turn what the child is doing into a game. For instance, if he is running around they can play 'chase' or 'galloping horses'; if he wants to be lifted up, they can play 'piggy backs'; if he is turning in circles, this can become 'Ring-a-ring-a-roses'.

Alternate Exchanges

During play sessions the adult should sometimes try to trigger off an alternate exchange by imitating the child as soon as he pauses. The adult may imitate a sound, a facial expression or a movement, and continue long enough for the child to become aware of what he is doing, and then pause for the child to take his turn. If he does not do so then the adult must stand in for him (Cole, 1982). If the adult must take both parts it is essential to continue to leave pauses for the child to join in. Related language such as 'your turn' can be incorporated into the sequence.

Once an exchange has been established, the adult can try to introduce another familiar activity into the routine, eg if adult and child are smiling at each other the adult can start a peek-a-boo game.

Pre-Conversational Routines

Incorporate into baby games, such as 'peek-a-boo' and 'I'm coming' (when the adult builds up the child's suspense by saying 'I'm coming' and pretending to catch or tickle the child), behaviours that are a normal part of conversation. These behaviours include eye contact, head and body movements, facial expression, such as smiling and raising the eyebrows, exaggerated intonation and pitch changes, and liberal use of gestures. All these are usually a natural part of baby games but may have to be more exaggerated for language-delayed children.

If the child breaks eye contact the adult should cease the game and resume when eye contact is regained. You may try to actively regain his attention by calling his name or turning his head, but if there is no response from the child leave him for a few moments before trying again.

Face-to-face games are the most useful; the child can be sat on your knee while you play tickling games, finger plays and bouncing games, in which you make the child bounce up and down and suddenly fall down. Singing songs and nursery rhymes can also take place in this position. The child should be encouraged to take a more and more active part.

Later Exchange Activities

1. Games of Give and Take
The adult gives the child a toy and holds out her hand for it back, using accompanying language such as 'here y'are' and 'give it to me'. She encourages the child to hold out his hand or reach for the toy. These games can become more purposeful, eg the child hands the adult an object to post. She then takes it out of a box and gives it back to the child to do the same.

Give the child a toy and let him play with it. Hold out a second toy but don't let him have it until he has given you the first one back (Jeffree, McConkey and Hewson, 1977).

2. Games of Back-and-Forth
The adult and child roll balls and marbles* to each other; push cars, trains and toys on wheels between each other, throw beanbags, cushions and balls, roll pastry together, push a swinging toy backwards and forwards; make clockwork toys and walking dolls walk between them, and snakes slither past, and so on.

3. Peek-a-Boo Games
Adult and child take turns to hide their faces in their hands and peek out, or to pull hats down over their eyes, or hide behind doors. You can also play 'peek-a-boo' with different parts of the body when the child is getting

---

* Do not use marbles and small objects if the child is mouthing all objects, and make sure all toys are safe.

---

dressed, eg make a big fuss when a hand reappears from a pyjama sleeve.

4. Hand Games and Finger Plays
These include clapping routines, 'pat-a-cake', piling up hands, 'This little piggy', 'Walkie round the garden' and other tickling games.

5. Physical Games
Rowing boats (where two people sit opposite each other on the floor, join hands and rock back and forth); chase and relays are all examples of exchange routines.

6. Nursery Rhymes and Stories
When the child is very familiar with nursery rhymes or stories, you can leave a pause for him to join in at key moments, by making the appropriate action, sound or word. Rhymes with repetitive choruses are best for this. As the child gets older you can introduce language in the form of questions, such as 'and *what* did the Big Bad Wolf do *then*?'.

7. Symbolic Play and Real-Life Sequences
Adult and child take turns to carry out specific actions while they are either making a real cup of tea, or pretending to do so. For instance the teacher may pour the tea, then the child puts in the sugar, the teacher adds the milk and the child stirs it. This teaches the child to wait for another person's action and to act upon it accordingly. It also teaches him to assume some responsibility.

Other routines can also be employed, such as cleaning teeth, but they must be familiar ones, as the objective here is to teach turn-taking, not sequencing, although this can be a useful by-product.

Activities for Eliciting Early Vocalisations

Making Sounds and Babbling

1. Tongue and lip games: games such as licking jam and ice cream off the lips, tongue-waggling, and blowing and sucking games are useful in helping the child to become familiar with his tongue, lips and soft palate.

2. Feeding habits: good feeding habits are important for strengthening and exercising the muscles that are used in speech. The child should be chewing solids as soon as he is ready to.*

3. Use exciting toys and games to elicit sounds. Toys that provide an element of surprise eg *Humpty Dumpty* [3] are the most likely to make the child vocalise. Whenever he does so, whether accidentally or intentionally, reward him immediately. Suitable rewards for young children are cuddles and physical contact, bobbing toys, wind-up toys, buzzers and flashing lights such as lanterns and Christmas tree lights. Accompany these with verbal praise.

It is best to keep a few objects especially as rewards so that the child learns to make the association between vocalising and being rewarded (Jeffree and McConkey, 1976).

4. *Worm-in-the-Apple* [4]: this is a toy apple with a microphone inside; when the child vocalises or blows into the apple a worm rises up out of the top. If he maintains the voice or airflow the worm's eyes eventually light up. Other similar gadgets can be

---

* If in any doubt refer mother and child to their GP.

manipulated so that they only 'perform' when the child makes a sound, eg a monkey on a stick that climbs up as the child vocalises and stops when he stops. There is also a clown whose eyes light up, *Magic Man*[4].

5. Make a windy snake out of plasticine, pastry, wool or cardboard, and encourage the child to join in hissing with you (Jeffree and McConkey, 1976).

6. Make the appropriate noises when playing with toy animals, cars, trains and aeroplanes etc, and encourage the child to join in and copy you.

7. Do the same when showing the child pictures, once he is showing an interest in them. The book *Old MacDonald had a Farm* is a large book with a hole on each page that reveals a different animal; this helps the child to focus on particular animal sounds.

8. Use a mirror large enough for two people to see themselves in and make silly faces and noises together, eg blow raspberries, hold your nose and try to talk, and make lip-smacking noises. Imitate any sounds the child makes.

9. Make sounds that are associated with feelings and states, in the appropriate situations, eg say 'ah' when bubbles and fireworks go up; 'oh' when you hurt yourself or are surprised; 'grr' when pretending to be angry, and so on. Accompany these sounds with the appropriate gestures, facial expression and exaggerated intonation. These are the kinds of things that many people do spontaneously, but the language-delayed child may need more deliberate exposure to these situations.

10. Make onomatopoeic sounds to accompany actions, eg say 'bang bang' as you or the child hit pegs with a hammer; 'splash' during bath-time or sand-and-water play; make blowing noises on a windy day.

Later on these sounds can be incorporated into a short story and the child can help you make them.

11. Sing to the child in babble-sounds, eg 'la-la-la', 'mmm' and nonsense sounds, and encourage him to join in.

12. Associate sounds with musical instruments, eg a trumpet goes 'oompah-oompah', a triangle says 'ting-a-ling', 'crash' go the cymbals. These sounds, too, can be put together into a story or into a song, 'I am the Music Man'.

13. Read rhymes and stories with nonsense words in and encourage the child to say the word at the right time.

14. Observe the child in his daily routines; note which situations lead him to 'talk' and then exploit them (Hastings and Hayes, 1981).

Using Sounds to Achieve Ends

When the child can make some sounds, help him to use them in a purposeful way. The child must be relaxed and happy with the adult before he can be expected to use sounds to communicate (Derbyshire Language Programme). A language-delayed child may be used to people anticipating his needs and he may be frustrated at first by having to make them known. Other children may have learned to suppress their own wants and needs as a result of constantly being misunderstood, and their confidence must be carefully built up.

Once the child has accepted the adult she can use play situations and familiar routines to elicit spontaneous vocalisations. Withhold toys or games until the child vocalises and then reward him with the object and with liberal praise. Offering the child forced alternatives may also prompt him to attempt to 'talk', eg 'Would you like milk or orange?'

The success of this exercise depends upon consistently and regularly (but not necessarily constantly) rewarding vocalisations, while *not* reinforcing inappropriate behaviour. The objective is not to turn the situation into a battleground, however, so be lighthearted and give the child lots of good examples and encouragement. The sensitive use of other children as models can be useful.

Suitable situations include rough-and-tumble, peek-a-boo, being tickled, cuddled, stroked and having the hair brushed, blowing bubbles, chasing and hiding games, and asking for toys, games and sweets. In fact almost any situation where the child must ask for something, or more of something. It is probably not a good idea to start with things the child needs, such as food, being washed, or going to the toilet, as you cannot refuse him these things should he be unwilling or unable to vocalise.

Once the child is using sounds to communicate his needs, start differentiating between the different noises, eg if he says [m] associate it with 'Mum' so that he begins to understand that language is meaningful. If he says [ku] show him a car and see if he can imitate 'car'.

A ringing toy telephone may be useful; the child attempts 'brr-brr', 'pip-pip', 'ring-ring' or similar, to get the adult to turn the dial or speak into the receiver. There are several interesting varieties available in shops and catalogues.

Word Shaping

Use activities that involve small steps, repetitions or sequences. For example, early graded pull-out puzzles can be useful to encourage word shaping in a child who is slow to respond, eg:

(i) to get the first piece the child must make eye contact.
(ii) to get the second piece he must attempt oral movement.
(iii) to get the third piece he must vocalise.
(iv) to get the fourth piece he must imitate the word.
(v) to get the fifth piece he must spontaneously use the word, although an approximation of it is sufficient at this stage.

Other activities that can be used in a similar fashion include:

1. building up a tower of bricks.
2. putting together a cone made up of plastic rings.
3. stacking a nest of barrels or beakers.
4. connecting up carriages to a train, eg *Brio Passenger Train*[3] by the Early Learning Centres.
5. hammering different coloured balls through holes, eg *Hammer and ball set.*[3]
6. threading large beads or cotton reels.
7. loading miniature cars on to a trailer; the child gets closer to the word 'car' each time he puts on a car.
8. graded objects and pictures can be used in a similar way.
9. hole-in-the-wall: make a hole in a large piece of cardboard. Push a ball or toy through the hole to the child when he imitates a word (Jeffree and McConkey, 1976).

Activities for Early Conceptual Understanding

Object Permanence

Start with games where the object does not actually disappear from sight although it may go out of the child's line of vision.

1. Roll a ball, favourite toy or sweet along a table top and encourage the child to track the moving object. As it falls off the end of the table bring his gaze down and show him where the object lies. Let the child pick it up and then repeat the activity. When you have his total interest let the child roll the object along the table, continuing to show him where it has landed if necessary.

2. Sit on the floor and roll a ball behind the child a little way; help him to turn around and find it. Later you can roll the ball behind yourself and if necessary keep moving so that he can see where the ball is, until he begins to look for it.

3. Drop toys out of the child's cot, highchair or pram and help him look to see where they have gone.

4. Hide yourself and help the child by peeping out and calling his name until he comes to look for you, if he is mobile, or looks expectantly towards where you are hiding, if he is not.

Games where a person or object disappears and reappears are suitable. Proceed in small steps as follows:

1. The object disappears and reappears quite quickly in the child's immediate gaze, while the adult draws his attention to it with much exaggerated surprise and comment.

2. The object disappears and partially reappears in the child's immediate gaze. Again the adult makes much of the toy's reappearance and encourages the child to reach for it and reveal the whole object.

3. The object disappears but keeps peeping out until the child is stimulated to look for it.

4. The object disappears in the child's immediate gaze but does not reappear. If the child does not look surprised and show some searching behaviour, make a big show of looking for it before it reappears.

5. Repeat step 4 actively guiding the child to search if he does not do so spontaneously.

Suitable games are: pushing a train into a tunnel; putting a car into a toy garage, a doll into a box or house; a Jack-in-theBox; Weather dolls; *Hammer –Balls*[4]; hiding glove or finger puppets behind the back; bouncing a dangling toy or string puppet in and out of the child's sight; hiding a sweet or toy in your hands, or the child's hands, and playing peek-a-boo games.

Hiding games. Use a favourite toy or sweet, or an object the child has just shown some interest in and a plain cover, and again proceed in small steps (adapted from Kiernan, Jordan and Saunders, 1978):

1. Place the object immediately in front of the child so that he has to reach for it, let him take it and play with it once or twice.

2. Help the child to cover the edge of the object with the cloth and then encourage him to remove it again. Make a big show of surprise at seeing the whole object once more.

3. Help him cover more and more of the object and again prompt him to remove the cover.

4. Move on to partially covering the toy yourself, while the child watches you.

5. Present the object already partly hidden and repeat the procedure if necessary. At all stages act surprised and pleased to see the hidden object again. Don't feel embarrassed to exaggerate your behaviour.

6. When the child can consistently remove the cover from a partially hidden object, take one of two pathways: either use a variety of different covers to ensure the child does not only associate one object with one cover, or completely hide the object.

7. Once the child can reliably retrieve a completely hidden toy from under a variety of covers, introduce a time delay by stopping him for five seconds as he is reaching for the object. This teaches him to remember the objective.

8. Use different types of hiding devices, eg screens, boxes, beakers and cartons. Make sure the child sees where you put the object. Gradually increase the number of hiding places for the child to choose from.

9. Hide the object in different places around the room, while the child watches you. At first leave it wholly in view, then partly hidden, and finally completely hidden. Take the child to the object if necessary and gradually reduce your help.

10. Repeat step 9 but this time don't let the child watch where you put the toy or sweet. Encourage him to keep looking and if he seems about to give up, take him to the toy. As he gains in confidence he will persist until he finds the toy.

Suitable games include: hiding toy money in a piggy-bank, coin-box or purse; placing a toy in a pocket (if you have many robust pockets); putting a sweet under a hanky, doll's blanket or inside a box, beaker or postbox; hiding a toy in a cupboard, drawer, box or shelf. Do not make things too difficult for the child.

11. Introduce a five-second delay between hiding and searching and gradually increase the delay.

12. Play hide-and-seek with other adults and children.

Use all naturally occurring situations to encourage the child's awareness that an object continues to exist even when it can't be seen, eg comment upon people leaving the room and coming back again; help the child to anticipate somebody's reappearance, eg Daddy coming home from work; Mummy coming to the clinic room. Remark upon things in the environment that the child sees regularly, such as the toy shop that he passes by to get to school!

Cause and Effect
(see also Chapter 3 on Play)

Learning about cause and effect is a continuous process which becomes more complex as time goes on. Lots of the child's spontaneous activities teach him cause and effect, but there are certain toys and everyday objects that do something as the result of an action upon them, which are excellent for highlighting the relationship between action and object, and cause and effect. Some of the toys already mentioned, eg the *Worm-in-the Apple*[4] are such examples. Toys which make a noise, produce a picture or light, have movement, or open and close, are very useful.

Always give plenty of demonstrations and when the child is attentive and enjoying the result, help him to manipulate the toys for himself, eg hold his hand around a string or handle to pull a toy towards him.

Examples of Useful Toys

1. Sound makers

Rattles, shakers, squeaky dolls and toys, crying dolls, animal-noisemakers, musical instruments — especially woodwind, which changes its sound according to the holes covered — alarm clocks, music boxes, door bells, balls with bells inside, loud-hailers; the volume control on radios, record-players and television and *Roll and See*.[3]

These all make a noise as a result of some action by the child. Making sounds with the lips, cheeks, feet and hands also helps understanding of cause and effect. Many pull-along toys also make interesting noises and extend the child's understanding of causality, eg *Musical Turtle*[3] and *Clatterpillar*[4].

2. Toys that have movement

Wind-up toys, walking dolls, blow-windmills, spinning tops, push-and-pull toys such as *Webster*[3]; toys on strings, such as the *Musical Bear*[3]; clockwork train sets, Scalectrix car sets, bubble-blowers, hoovers, food mixers, lawn mower, toy cash register, hammer and pegs, rocking horse, see-saw, swing, car, *Musical Rabbit*[3], *Super Helta Skelta*[3], *Water-Pump*[4], *Sand Wheel*[4], *Elephount*[3] and *Play Boat*[4].

3. Toys that produce visual effects

Kaleidoscopes, *Bubble Balls*[3], magic lanterns, slide-viewers, *Jack-in-the-Ball*[1], large rolling dice, picture-cubes with different colours or pictures on, *Humpty Dumpty*[3], television, electric light, water-taps, showers, hoses, spinning-tops, mobiles, jig-saws, *Etch-a-Sketch* (by Peter Pan Playthings; available from most toyshops), painting and colouring, face make-up, potato-printing (and other kinds of printing), squeezing toothpaste and other tubes, making a lather, looking through a microscope.

4. Toys that open and close

Doors, drawers, cupboards, tins, boxes, beakers, jars, cannisters, books, envelopes, bags, cases, purses, pots, pop-up books, windows, Advent calendars, shape-posting boxes, Russian dolls, 'Crocodile's jaws'.

5. Toys that fit together

Screw-top jars, nuts and bolts (large plastic ones are made by Galt Toys), nesting boxes, beakers and barrels, *Chunky Wooden Inset Boards*[4], stacking toys, eg *Stack Caterpillars/Clowns*[4], *Lego*[4], boxes, *Unifix* bricks, *Duplo* sets[4], *Playmobile*[4], *Pegmen*[4], *pegs and pegboards*[2], Russian dolls.

6. Other types of cause and effect

Putting things into the fridge makes them cold, putting them in the oven makes them hot; sitting by the fire makes you warm; bumping heads, playing pat-a-cake and other clapping games produce physical contact; putting things in and out of containers and sand-and-water play.

Appropriate language should be incorporated into these games and real-life situations: words such as 'on', 'off', 'it's going', 'it's stopped', etc.

When the child can appreciate that an action produces a result, introduce an accumulative effect, eg add a rattle to a mobile so that there is sound as well as movement. Activity centres such as the Fisher-Price one and the *Activity Bear*[3] can be valuable once this stage has been reached. Some electronic activity centres produce different visual and sound effects as different buttons are pressed and can be suitable for children with poor manipulative ability.

Object Concept

The child gradually develops the object concept as new experiences are fitted into existing ideas. If a new experience is too novel, the baby reacts by ignoring it or becoming defensive and crying. Therefore introduce new objects and experiences gradually and cautiously. Infants tend to respond to people and objects first, actions next, and events last.

1. Gradually reduce the contextual clues that are present when you give the child an object, eg don't put the child in his chair or tie on his bib before showing him his dinner or drink.

2. Expect the child to take more responsibility, eg instead of placing a cup in his hands, put it in front of him and encourage him to reach for it. Increase the child's active participation as his motor skills and understanding of objects increase, eg send him to fetch his own cup.

3. Object constancy: first, present the child's own well-known possessions to him at different unfamiliar angles and help him to use them appropriately. Move on to placing them in unexpected places around the room and helping the child to recognise them and respond to them with appropriate actions.

An unexpected place?

4. When the child consistently shows recognition of his own possessions by responding appropriately in any situation, gradually introduce a number of similar objects, eg different-coloured cups at meal-times and different-patterned flannels at bath-time.

5. Join in with what the child is doing, eg both drink orange juice from similar cups, or play with toys, so that the child becomes aware that there is more than one cup, one teddy, and so on.

6. Carry out lots of matching and sorting activities in a natural situation, such as helping Mummy lay the table, putting things away, stacking up similar objects and doing the washing-up (*see also Chapter 6 on Perception*).

7. Carry out structured matching and sorting activities with real objects. This can be done both verbally, eg by telling the child to 'get all the forks out' or non-verbally, eg by starting to sort all the forks out of the cutlery tray and seeing if the child can copy you (*see also Chapter 6*).

8. Object-object matching can also be carried out as a game or table-top activity. Several pairs of objects, eg cups, socks, balls etc can be put on the table. The child is shown one of a pair and asked to find the one that looks the same.

Objects should be identical at first and gradually made less and less alike; ie vary one dimension, such as colour, to begin with, then two dimensions, eg colour and shape, then three, and so on.

Relational Concepts

1. Reference (Existence, Disappearance and Recurrence)
Take every opportunity to point out objects and events in the environment and to show the child new objects and toys, making sure to alert him first, by saying, 'Look', 'Listen', 'What's that?' and so on. Go beyond naming to describe what the toy can do, or comment upon what is happening. This should not be a structured situation, any time or place is suitable as long as the child is paying attention.

Remember also to comment when objects go out of sight, or reappear, such as a bird flying in and out of view. Give lots of models of the vocabulary being used, eg 'It's gone'; 'Where is it?'; 'There it is again' etc.

2. Action
Nearly all activities teach the child about actor, action and object relations, and there are plenty distributed throughout the book so we will not reiterate them here. Encourage the child to explore and experiment with objects and movements, and discover actions and effects at first hand. Always accompany with suitable language, commenting upon what the child is doing, seeing and hearing. A child who is left sitting in a pushchair all day will not have his natural curiosity stimulated, or have the first-hand experiences upon which cognitive and language developments are based.

3. Location
Help the child to get to know places by letting him find things and do simple errands, instead of putting everything in front of him. For example, you can say, 'Let's have a biscuit' and give him the tin or box to open. Later, when he is more mobile, you can ask him to get the biscuits and see if he can find the right cupboard. The same can be done with his clothes, toys and eating utensils. Help him as much as he needs to prevent unnecessary frustration but not so much that he never encounters a challenge. It is in overcoming challenges that we all experience learning and achievement.

The child can be helped initially by putting pictures of the food, toys and objects on the doors and lids of the respective cupboards and boxes where they can be found. He can also be given pictures of what he is to fetch, as an aid to his memory (Jeffree and McConkey, 1976).

4. Instrumental

Relating Two Objects
Suitable ideas include: banging cymbals together, hitting a drum with a stick, banging a spoon on a cup, taking toys and jigsaws apart and putting them back together again, playing with stacking and nesting toys, and shape-posting boxes and pagodas (*see Chapter 2 for more ideas*).

Ideas for True Instrumental Relations
  (i) drinking through a straw.
  (ii) using a hammer to bang pegs or *Tap 'n Turn Bench* [4].
  (iii) playing musical instruments, such as glocken-spiel, drums and triangle, where a tool is an integral feature.
  (iv) hitting balls with croquet or golf sticks.
  (v) hitting stones with sticks.
  (vi) all bat and ball games.
  (vii) drawing, colouring and painting.
  (viii) making plasticine and pastry shapes with pastry cutters and wheel.
  (ix) eating with a spoon, knife or fork.
  (x) sweeping the floor with a broom.
  (xi) using a steering-wheel, eg on a go-kart, pedal-car or tricycle.
  (xii) transporting toys in pull-and-push trucks and trailers.
  (xiii) using real or toy fishing rods.
  (xiv) tiddly winks; toy Snooker.
  (xv) building sand-castles with a bucket and spade.
  (xvi) carrying earth in a *Digger* [3] or *Loddy* [1].
  (xvii) symbolic play activities where one object is used appropriately in relation to another, eg brushing a doll's hair with a brush; washing her face with a flannel, cleaning the dolls' house with a toy duster, washing toy cars with a tiny bucket and cloth, and so on (*see also Chapter 3 on Play*).

Encouraging Awareness of Sounds

1. Interest the child in toys that combine auditory and visual stimuli, such as a music box, wind chimes, activity centres, *Baby's First Car* [4] and so on (Derbyshire Language Programme). Move on to toys and objects with a predominantly auditory effect. See Chapter 2 for ideas to maintain the child's attention to sound.

2. Imitate the sounds made by the toys and encourage the child to join in.

3. Encourage the child to associate the object with its sound. Ask him to fetch toys or instruments by describing the sound, eg 'Where's the one that goes squeak squeak?' Perform the appropriate actions to help the child, and gradually fade this clue.

4. Show the child a variety of sound-makers and ask him 'How does a drum go?' 'What noise does a train make?' If he doesn't respond, demonstrate the sound and ask him again. Help him to perform the real action, eg bang the drum as you say 'bang bang'.

5. Help the child to anticipate and respond to events that are normally heralded by a particular sound, eg Daddy's car in the drive means that Daddy's home; when the bath taps are running it must be time for a bath. Talk about the event, drawing attention to the sound, and then take him to see what is happening.

6. Teach the child to respond to his own name (*see* Chapter 2). See also Chapter 2 for activities to develop listening skills and auditory attention; and Chapter 6 for more complex activities.

Activities to Encourage Early Understanding

Situational Understanding

Start by consistently using the same phrase or two in association with a particular, well known situation, eg while putting on the radio, record or cassette player, say 'Let's listen to some music', or 'Turn the music on'. Other phrases that can be attached to familiar routines are: 'It's dinner-time', 'Wash hands for dinner', 'Daddy's home now', 'Time to get up', 'Playschool's on now' etc. At this stage the phrase must accompany the actions. The child needs lots of repetition before he can begin to understand the link between the language and the situation.

Gradually move towards using the phrase slightly ahead of the event so that the child learns to anticipate a situation in response to specific language cues. If the related language is too far removed from the event it will of course become meaningless.

Do not discourage the child from carrying out actions that show his anticipation, but praise and help him, for this is a sign that he has understood your words. For example, if you tell him that you will take him shopping soon and he rushes to fetch his coat, show him how delighted you are.

Gradually reduce the number of gestural and contextual clues that accompany your language until the child can show true understanding of the words alone (*see* page 7). See Chapter 4 for advice on verbal input to very young children.

Symbolic Understanding

1. Large Doll Play

1. Help the child to recognise large dolls as symbols by using them in the same ways that you interact with the child himself; for instance when you bath him, give him his dinner and play with him, include the doll in these activities. At first you will probably have to perform actions on the doll yourself, telling the child what you are doing all the while, eg 'Now we wash *your** face, then we wash *dolly's* face'. Encourage the child to take his turn at washing dolly, always using real objects at this stage.

2. Include the doll in games with the child, first as an 'observer', and then as a participant. Suitable games include rolling balls between you, giving dolly a ride in a pull-along truck or train, dressing-up, doing housework, looking out of the window, looking at picture books etc.

3. Let the child's routines become dolly's routines, eg dolly has breakfast, orange juice, bath-time, bed-time and goes to playgroup, just like the child. This also helps the child's understanding of his own day.

4. Gradually introduce doll-sized accessories, sticking initially to those possessions that the child is familiar with, such as dolly's 'own' cup, flannel and toothbrush. Continue to include the doll, now with his or her own things, in the child's routines.

*Use the child's name if it is more appropriate to do so.

5. Slowly distance the doll's day from the child's day, and help the child to carry out meaningful sequences with the doll whenever you suggest it. At this stage you will probably still need to be very involved with the child's play, taking the lead and making suggestions.

6. Introduce more dolls and give them roles to play in the games, eg Mummy, Daddy, Grandma and baby.

7. Introduce more possessions, including less familiar ones such as dolly's handbag, umbrella, horse and so on. It may be a good idea to give dolly her own 'home' to live in; perhaps a large box or a special shelf or corner of the child's room.

8. Encourage the child to play alone with the dolls and carry out the sequences you have played together. You can start off by incorporating your absence into the game, eg 'I'll go to the shops. You get the children to bed.' Make the periods of non-participation brief to begin with but gradually fade your involvement. However, do not expect any pre-school child to amuse himself for long periods, because even the most imaginative child must run out of ideas, and no dolly, however well-loved, can offer the communication and companionship of a real-life playfellow.

2. Small Doll Play

1. You may repeat the above procedure with smaller and smaller dolls, or start to include slightly smaller dolls into the large doll play. Gradually decrease the size of the dolls and when they reach a certain smallness it may seem only too obvious to the child that the doll needs its own set of small furniture and possessions. If it is not obvious to the child then exaggerate the absurdity of the little doll wearing big shoes and clothes. Encourage miniature doll recognition as soon as the child is ready, as it allows for much more flexibility in symbolic play and other games. However, large dolls and home-corner play is still very important to the child and will continue to be for some time and should not be discouraged.

2. Use a variety of small toys such as *Playmobile* [4], *Pegmen* [4], *Duplo World People* [1], *Miniature doctors and nurses* [4], zoo and farm animals, to extend the variety of the play situations.

3. If the child does not demonstrate an understanding of miniature toys through play, the more direct approach of object-miniature matching may be used. This can also be used to augment symbolic play activities.

Make active comparisons between real and miniature objects. Demonstrate the similarities between the two, starting with very familiar objects, such as chair, table and shoe. The difference in size between the real object and the miniature should be great, but not so great that the child ceases to perceive the visual likeness.

To begin with it may be best to verbally differentiate between the two objects in terms of size, eg show the child a toy table and ask him to find the 'big' table. Later he can be taught the words 'real' and 'toy'.

It is easier for the child to take the toy object to the real one at first; then reverse the procedure. If this is impossible, point to the real object and ask him to find the toy one. Start with only one or two clearly visible miniature toys, and gradually extend the choice. Increase the complexity by introducing the memory factor and figure-ground discrimination skills, eg place the miniatures in a toy box, so that the child has to remember his objective as he searches through the box.

4. When object-miniature matching is fairly well established, vary the activity by putting two miniature toys into a feelie-box or bag, point to a real object and have the child find the copy by feel.

To practise object-miniature matching, think up new and interesting ways to present the miniatures, eg put them in a series of boxes so the child must open the boxes to find the correct toy: hide them around the room; wrap them up in parcels; incorporate the matching activity in a play sequence, eg build a doll's room to look like the one that the child is in.

3. Picture Recognition

(i) Object-Picture Matching

Coloured photographs tend to be understood first, colourful drawings before black-and-white ones, and lastly more abstract line drawings. Pictures should first be presented to the child in relation to real objects.

When playing matching games it is useful to start off with photos of the actual objects involved, and then gradually make the pictures less and less like the original. It may be best to avoid perceptually or functionally similar objects which may confuse the child, eg knife and fork, plate and saucer, until the child has a good grasp of the rules of the game.

1. Paste pictures on to cupboards, tins and drawers, depicting their contents, so that the child learns to associate the picture on the outside with the real objects within (Jeffree and McConkey, 1976).

2. Take photographs of the child's family and favourite toys, then match the photo back to the toy or person.

3. Show the child three photos of his toys and bring him the one he points to (Jeffree and McConkey, 1976).

4. Take turns to place photographs on the appropriate matching objects around the room.

5. Hide objects and toys in boxes with the corresponding pictures on the lids. The child has to recognise the picture to find the toy (Jeffree and McConkey, 1976). Start with only one box so that the child cannot fail. Then have two boxes but only one has a picture on the outside and contains a toy, eg a small car, so that the child comes to realise that he must choose the box with the picture. At this stage introduce another picture and gradually increase to six boxes, each with a different picture. Only one box should contain a toy so that the child is not rewarded by finding a toy in whichever box he opens. When he can consistently choose the correct box you can begin to introduce other toys into the game.

6. Match objects to pictures, naming each one as you go. Make sure that the object and picture are in the same orientation from the child's point of view. Place the objects in a bag or box, again naming each one, and then ask the child to find the object as you point to its picture (Derbyshire Language Programme).

7. Show the child a picture and ask him to fetch the correct toy or object. He can take the picture with him to aid memory at first.

(ii) Miniature-Picture Matching

Start off as for object-picture matching with photographs or exact copies of the miniature toys, and then gradually make the pictures more abstract, eg proceed from colour photos to black-and-white photos, to colour pictures, to shaded pictures, to line drawings, to cartoon-type drawings.

1. Follow some of the ideas suggested above.

2. Place a number of miniature toys and pictures in front of the child and help him match them. Increase the number gradually from one to six.

3. Show the child one picture and name it. Then show him two to three miniature toys, also naming them, and place them into a feelie bag. Ask him to find the toy that corresponds to the picture, by feeling in the bag. When he can do this, show him the picture after you have placed the toys inside the bag. The next step is to give him the feelie bag with the toys already inside and then show him the picture of the one he must find.

4. Place two to three miniature toys on matching pictures, naming each one. While the child shuts his eyes remove one of the pictures, replacing it in a small pile beside the child. Draw his attention to the missing picture and ask him to find it (Derbyshire Language Programme). Increase the number to six pairs.

5. Lotto: the child has a Lotto picture-card in front of him; the adult holds up a toy and if the child can find the right picture he covers it with the toy. To practise miniature-picture matching, vary the presentation so the child does not become bored, eg

   (i) Set up a room with dolls' furniture and ask the child to find matching pictures.
   (ii) The child picks a picture-card from a pack and finds the correct toy.
   (iii) The child finds pictures of his toys in a picture book.
   (iv) Lay large sturdy pictures on the floor—the child throws a bean-bag and finds the toy that matches the picture it lands on.
   (v) Stick large pictures on to skittles: the child aims to knock down the one that corresponds to a small toy held up by the teacher.
   (vi) Put the pictures into 'mystery' envelopes for the child to open.

6. The child rolls a picture-cube and finds the toy shown by the picture which falls uppermost (*see Chapter 5 for instructions on how to make a picture-cube*).

7. The child matches toys and miniature objects to a composite picture (from the age of about 3 years).

8. The child is shown action pictures, such as a boy kicking a ball and acts out the situations with toys (from 3 to 3½ years).

All these games can be adapted for two children, eg one rolls the picture-cube and the other finds the toy, then they change over.

(iii) Picture-Picture Matching

1. The child matches two identical pictures. Gradually increase the number of pairs of pictures. When the child can do this efficiently make the pictures less and less alike.

2. Spin-an-arrow: the child has to find the picture to match the one the arrow points to.

3. The teacher and child have identical packs of picture-cards and take turns to pick a card for the other person to match.

4. Make a scrapbook and a set of matching pictures.

5. Place pictures around the room and give the child duplicates of the ones he has to find.

6. Make a picture-roundabout by putting a knitting-needle through a picture-cube. Find the picture that matches the one the roundabout lands on.

7. Play picture-matching games such as Snap, Dominoes, Lotto and Pelmanism.

8. Make small pictures to match a large composite picture, and after discussing the picture with the child, help him to match them to it (from about 3 years).

9. Have the child sort through a pack of cards, making two piles—one for identical pairs and one for non-identical pairs. An example of a non-identical pair could be a red dog and a blue dog. The differences should be fairly obvious.

10. Adapt the activities in the two previous sections.

(iv) Picture-Action Matching

Carry out the same sort of games as above but the child must match an action-picture to the real action or mime. Use the actual utensils shown in the photograph if this helps the child, and if necessary keep to the same sex. Lay two to three pictures on the table. The child chooses one to mime and the adult guesses.

When the child can select and act out an action-picture using objects as props, gradually omit these clues until he can simply mime or gesture the actions. See Chapter 5 for further activities for the child of 3 and above.

CHAPTER 2
ATTENTION CONTROL AND LISTENING SKILLS

CHAPTER 2
ATTENTION CONTROL AND LISTENING SKILLS

Introduction

The ability to attend to a stimulus and to sustain that attention is essential for all forms of learning. It is particularly relevant to language learning which requires a fairly mature level of attention control (Reynell, 1980). A child who cannot maintain his attention or who becomes fixated will be unable to process the complex stimuli of language (Berry, 1980). Social communication is greatly hampered if a child cannot attend to people, by looking, smiling and reaching for them. Concept formation will not develop if a baby does not attend to an object for long enough to extract meaning from it.

Cooper et al (1974) found that many language-delayed children manifested attention problems and that therapy directed to these also helped their language development. It is clear therefore that certain children must be taught a measure of attention control as part of their language therapy.

Factors Affecting Attention

1. There may be a neurological component, such as electrical or metabolic disturbances in the central nervous system, which causes interruptions of attention (Berry).

2. The child's home or school may have led him to ignore certain stimuli, eg he has accommodated to a noisy environment.

3. Physical illness, tiredness and medication may cause the child to lack concentration.

4. Emotional and behavioural disturbances may produce attention problems.

5. Environmental distractions can be too strong for the child to attend to the task in hand.

6. The child's ability to recall may not match up to the task he has been given.

7. The child may be lacking in motivation, for many reasons, eg:
   (i) the task is developmentally too complex or too simple so that he is either confused or bored
   (ii) he fails to understand the verbal instructions accompanying the task
   (iii) the materials are uninteresting or the task without purpose
   (iv) he feels no sense of achievement upon completion of the task.

Assessment

The child's level of attention and the exact nature of the problem must be accurately assessed, by observing and recording his actual behaviour in a variety of situations, at home and in school. These include free play, interacting with children, parents and other adults, taking part in classroom activities and engaging in solitary tasks. Parents' and teachers' observations are invaluable.

Levels of Attention

In 1977 Joan Reynell conducted a study of non-handicapped children, and discovered clear stages in the normal development of attention control. Within each stage there is considerable variability because attention depends upon the situation and the nature of the task, and is influenced by a multiplicity of factors. These levels may be used to measure the child's behaviour for assessment purposes.

Level 1 (0 to 1 Year): This is characterised by extreme distractibility, when the child's attention flits from one object, person or event to another. Any new event, such as someone walking by, will immediately distract him.

Level 2 (1 to 2 Years): The child can concentrate on a concrete task of his own choosing, but will not tolerate any intervention by an adult, whether verbal or visual. He may appear obstinate or 'wilful', but in fact his attention is single-channelled and he must ignore all extraneous stimuli in order to concentrate upon what he is doing.

Level 3 (2 to 3 Years): Attention is still single-channelled in that the child cannot attend to auditory and visual stimuli from different sources. He cannot therefore listen to an adult's directions while he is playing, but he can shift his whole attention to the speaker and back to the game, with the adult's help.

Level 4 (3 to 4 Years): The child must still alternate his full attention, visual and auditory, between the speaker and the task, but he now does this spontaneously without the adult needing to focus his attention.

Level 5 (4 to 5 Years): The child's attention is now two-channelled, ie he understands verbal instructions related to the task without interrupting his activity to look at the speaker. His concentration span may still be short but he can be taught in a group.

Level 6 (5 to 6 Years): Auditory, visual and manipulative channels are fully integrated and attention is well established and sustained.

Transfer of Attention Control

From the age of 4 to 5 years, children are expected to be able to listen to verbal instructions and attend to individual and group activities in a classroom that is often noisy, full of children and has dozens of competing, distracting stimuli. However, many language-delayed children are not at a mature enough level of attention to cope with these demands. Although in such cases individual work on attention control is necessary, the majority of the child's time is spent in the classroom, and it is therefore essential to ensure that he can use his new skills in his normal environment. The therapist should also recognise that his peers are an important influence on a child's learning and social development and he must learn to attend to, and interact with, other children (Berry, 1980).

Guidelines to Remediation

1. There must be carry-over into home and school for optimum effects.

2. Attention therapy should be initiated in a distraction-free environment to allow the child to concentrate on the presented stimulus (Reynell, 1980).*

3. Some constraints on the child's behaviour are necessary for learning to take place.

4. The child should be physically comfortable and at ease for therapy to be successful.

5. The child must experience success. The purpose is primarily to teach him to *attend* to a task, therefore initial activities must be short, simple and within his ability.

6. Materials must be interesting to the child.

7. Rewards should be inherent in the game or task itself, eg the joy of discovery; the satisfaction of completion.

8. If intrinsic rewards are insufficient, then other rewards, whether material, eg sweets and crisps, or social, eg smiles and praise, must be immediate and consistent, so that the child learns to associate them with the task.

9. Progress should be carefully recorded, in a form that the child can appreciate.

10. The task must be developmentally appropriate for the child, taking into account his level of functioning in other areas, such as symbolic understanding and performance skills.

11. Verbal instructions should be modified to the child's level of comprehension.

12. Memory constraints must be taken into consideration.

13. Materials should be age appropriate but the child's interests are the guiding factors; some language-delayed children may prefer toys usually associated with a younger age group.

14. Teaching should normally proceed in small steps; gradually extend the duration and complexity of the stimuli the child is expected to attend to, and move towards a more normal environment.

15. Regular re-evaluation of therapy is essential.

Where they are felt to be particularly pertinent, further principles are listed above the activities for each stage of attention control.

---

* M F Berry takes a different approach. She believes attention therapy should take place in the child's normal environment and distractions should not be removed. Instead the dominant stimulus, ie the task in hand, should be made much more intense or interesting to maintain the child's involvement. A situation somewhere between the two is probably the most feasible.

ACTIVITIES TO PROMOTE ATTENTION CONTROL AND LISTENING SKILLS

The aim is to consolidate the child's skills at his level of attention and to take him into the next stage. The materials listed are suitable for children in that age group; for older children, it is best to use age-appropriate materials if possible. For example, with a 3 to 4-year-old at Level 1 of attention control, glove puppets, small cars and miniature dolls could be used to attract and sustain his interest.

Level 1 (0 to 1 Year)

Aim

To attract and sustain the child's attention to people, objects and events in his environment, in order to promote sensori-motor exploration and social inter-action.

Principles

1. For the very young child his parents are the best teachers.

2. The stimulus must be in the child's sight and hearing and be intense enough to evoke a response (Berry, 1980).

3. Sustain attention for as long as possible to the original stimulus, investigating all its properties and stimulating all the child's senses as far as possible (Berry, 1980).

4. Do not continue with something the child has lost interest in, but wait a while before introducing another object.

5. If extrinsic rewards are used they must be given *before* the child's attention lapses.

Suitable Materials

Mobiles, flashing lights, windmills, bouncing toys, pop-up toys, bells, rattles, wind chimes, music boxes, squeaky toys, soap bubbles; anything that catches the child's interest.

Activities for Catching and Sustaining Attention

1. Small children are attracted by moving objects so hang a mobile or swinging toy just to one side of them at face-level. Keep it moving and twirling, eg *Musical Mobile* [3].

2. Twirl a patterned disc on string so that its pattern revolves and changes.

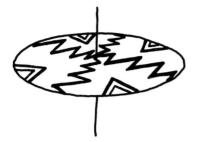

3. Hang wind chimes that jingle as they move. When the child turns to these toys, repeat the action so that he is rewarded and move the toy to his other side; make it a little higher, lower or nearer.

4. Use a flashing light in the same way, but vary the sequence of flashes to sustain interest. Move it around his full field of vision. Say, 'On! Off!' to accompany the actions.

5. Shake a rattle to one side of his face; vary the intensity of sound and movements; bring it closer; shake it on the other side and when he turns place it in his hand, bring his hand into vision and help him to shake it.

6. Carry out similar activities with a variety of sound-makers, preferably ones that the child can manipulate easily himself.

When you get to know the child better try these activities:—

7. Place your face close to the child's and make very exaggerated lip shapes; pull faces; poke your tongue in and out; zoom your face in and out; chatter or sing to him with exaggerated intonation; kiss his cheeks, nose etc; encourage him to explore your face with his fingers.

8. Use your fingers to attract the child's attention by indulging in finger-plays and rhymes; stroke his cheeks; place his own fingers where he can see them and play 'This Little Piggy went to Market', 'Walkie round the Garden' and so on.

9. Find out what sort of voice he responds to: Mum's, Dad's, a child's voice, a pet; crooning, humming, nursery rhymes; pick the child up so his head is close to yours while you sing or chat to him with lots of melody and vocal inflection; swing him round.

10. At bath-time use bubble bath (eg *Matey*) and dab it on the child's nose, mouth and tummy; blow it about; make patterns in the water; splash the water.

Hang a brightly coloured soap on a rope and swing it; rub it on the skin and make it lather; drop it into the water with a splash and make a game out of looking for it.

Use talcum powder and put some on the child's palm; show him how soft it is; rub it in and blow some off (avoiding his face).

11. Blow bubbles, watch them rise and fall; burst them and pretend to catch them; let some burst on the child. (Giant bubble blowers can be bought in toy shops.)

Activities to Encourage Visual Tracking

Once the child is attending to a toy, encourage him to track its movements, so that he has to turn more and more. The best toys to use are both visually and auditorily exciting. If he doesn't do this spontaneously he may have to be gently turned so that he learns he can keep the object in his sight.

1. Shake a rattle, bell or other sound-maker to one side and gradually move it across his field of vision. When he

turns shake it again and give it to him, helping him to manipulate it.

2. Roll a ball, with a bell or bead inside, across the floor or table.

3. Push large cars from side to side, in front of the child and encourage him to push them.

4. Place rocking toys in front of him so he watches their to-and-fro movements.

5. Use large, wheeled toys on string that you can push away and pull back towards the child. Encourage him to push the toy away.

6. Encourage the child to watch his mother as she moves about.

7. *Roll-a-ball House*[6] is an exciting, colourful eye-tracking activity.

8. Blow bubbles or balloons over the child's head.

Activities to Promote Reaching

A child must gain first-hand sensory experience of an object in order to maintain his interest in it and learn about it. A child will usually reach spontaneously but may have to be taught. The best toys are those that the child can manipulate easily to produce a result. The following is a suggested procedure for encouraging reaching which must be modified for the individual child.*

1. Attract the child's attention with a rattle.

2. Place the rattle in his own hand and help him shake it.

3. Hold the rattle a very little way away and guide his hand to it. Make sure he grasps it and help him to shake it.

4. Start the reaching movement off for the child.

5. Prompt him by touching his arm.

6. Gradually move the rattle further away.

7. If he doesn't generalise spontaneously, repeat the procedure with a variety of toys, eg toys on strings, dangling toys etc.

Activities to Facilitate Attention Shift

It is important that the child can shift his attention from one object to another so that:

(a) he can explore all aspects of a large object or face in order to remember it

(b) he can make choices and comparisons between objects

(c) at a later level of attention he can shift from the speaker to the task and back again (Kiernan et al, 1978).

1. Having held the child's attention with stimulus (1) present stimulus (2) which must be of known interest to him and let the first toy drop out of sight. Capture his attention for a short time before re-producing the first toy (Kiernan et al).

2. Repeat the procedure but do not hide the first toy.

3. Repeat the procedure and relate the two objects, eg bang two bricks together.

* A child of six months has usually developed a good enough grasp to begin such activities (Sheridan, 1973).

4. Repeat but encourage the child to hold and relate the objects.

5. Use two toy cars in the same way; make them crash.

6. In the bath use two water toys.

7. Use a large doll, wearing a large hat. Remove the hat with a big show of surprise and put it on your head, then the child's head; redirect attention to the doll by putting its hat back, saying 'There!'.

8. Use a large toy that has an easily removable part, in a similar way. Encourage the child to take off the part and put it back.

Activities to Elicit Eye Contact and Response to Own Name

A child of 10 to 12 months should be able to respond to his own name.

1. You can encourage attention to your face by manipulating an interesting toy beside it, but this does not guarantee that the child will continue to attend to the face and not to the object when it is removed.

2. Put on a silly hat, false moustache or face make-up; anything to get the child looking at your face.

3. Call the child's name, wait for a response and call again, immediately turning his head gently by the chin. Smile and produce an object or toy as a reward. If he is taught to respond to his name for no purpose he will quickly learn to ignore it again (Kiernan et al). Gradually decrease the amount of help given but don't reward the child until he is looking at you.

Level 2 (1 to 2 Years)

Aim

To help the child tolerate the adult's presence and involvement in an activity of the child's own choosing.

Principles

1. Keep any verbal instructions intrinsic to the task.

2. Gradually move from simultaneously telling and showing the child what to do, to giving your instructions immediately ahead of your demonstration.

3. Make material rewards part of the task, eg put a sweet in a nest of beakers so that the child finds it on completion.

Suitable Materials

Very simple picture puzzles; take-apart toys; balls; bricks; shape-posting balls; nests of beakers; musical instruments; banging toys, large dolls and soft toys.

Activities

If the child cannot tolerate you sharing his toys at first, have a duplicate set handy.

1. Sit beside the child for brief periods but do not interfere! At strategic moments praise him for things well done.

2. Sit beside him and engage in parallel play. Begin to extend his play by demonstration without intervening in what *he* is doing; eg if he is playing with bricks, build a small tower with your bricks. He may respond in one of these ways:—

(a) he may appear not to notice but begin to imitate your action
(b) he may stop his play and watch you with interest
(c) he may knock over your tower!

In any case contact has occurred and you have caught his attention.

3. Generalise with plenty of games and activities, extending the child's exploration of the toy.

(i) Shape-posting box; take your shape and try it in several holes before finding the right one.
(ii) Nests of beakers; pile them on top of each other and use them as containers, as well as fitting them together.
(iii) Floor toys; show how cars and trailers can be linked up, raced and bumped together.
(iv) Water-play; demonstrate pouring from one container to another.
(v) Beads and bricks; sort all the red bricks from the yellow ones; build a blue train and a green one and see if the child can copy you.

4. When the child can tolerate the adult and begins to imitate, small modifications to his own play can be made.

(i) push the correct jigsaw piece in front of him
(ii) add a brick to his train or tower
(iii) encourage him to use different-coloured crayons when scribbling.

Accompany your actions with integral verbal instructions, eg 'The brick goes on top'; 'Let's turn it over'; 'Try a red pencil' etc. Gradually move towards giving simple verbal instructions immediately ahead of your actions.

Activities to Develop Listening Skills

1. Encourage attention to sounds, using activity-toys that also make noises, eg pull-along telephones and chiming carousels.

2. Experiment with musical instruments, emphasising the different sounds.

3. Sing nursery rhymes accompanied by mimes and actions, eg 'Ring-a-ring-a-roses'. The actions encourage attention to key words and changes in the rhythm.

4. Encourage the child to choose which of three toys he wants. Show him each toy as you ask, 'Do you want *dolly*, *teddy* or *train*?' etc. Emphasise these key words.

5. Ask the child to fetch familiar objects and large toys, eg 'I need a *cup*', 'Get me your *shoe*'. Remember that younger children need accompanying gestural clues.

Level 3 (2 to 3 Years)

Aim

To establish the child's own control over his focus of attention.

Principles

1. Keep tasks short and simple.

2. Help the child or prompt him, to ease frustration.

3. Rewards must be intrinsic to the task.

4. Clear instructions must precede the task when the child's full attention is on the speaker.

Suitable Materials

Simple jigsaws, nesting-boxes, Russian dolls, colour-graded abacus, dolls, wheeled toys, picture books, miniature toys.

Activities

1. Present the child with the task materials and allow him a few minutes exploratory play. Before giving any verbal directions make sure that he is sitting still and is not fiddling with the toys, then call his name, establish eye contact and deliver a short, simple instruction.

Suitable visual-manipulatory tasks include:—

   (i) 1-1 matching of shapes and primary colours.
   (ii) copying towers and trains with bricks, as an adult demonstrates.
   (iii) copying shapes on paper, eg

   (iv) playing gross motor imitation games with an adult.

2. Generalise with lots of similar tasks.

3. The next step is to gain the child's attention while he is actively engaged in the task. Call his name, say 'Look', 'Listen', but don't give him an instruction until you have established eye contact. Instructions must be related to the task.

4. Gradually decrease the number of alerting activities needed, until the child can look up and listen when just his name is called.

5. Generalise with lots of activities, eg:

   (i) parallel play with dolls, toy cars, etc; get the child to look up and copy what you are doing from time to time.
   (ii) follow-my-leader and other physical games.

Remember the child may be even more absorbed in these active games, and at first you may have to physically still him before you can get his attention. Again, gradually decrease the amount you have to do to gain eye contact. Keep instructions very short to begin with, eg 'Copy me', 'Do this', 'You dress dolly', 'Put her here', accompanied by appropriate gestures.

Activities to Develop Listening Skills

Some of these ideas are suitable for a small group.

1. Asking for objects: show the child three objects, regain his attention and ask clearly for one or two items, eg 'Give me teddy'. Miniature toys and pictures can also be used with children at a suitable level of symbolic recognition.

2. There are infinite variations on this theme:—

   (i) Post the objects, toys or pictures in a post-box, eg an old shoe-box with a large slit cut in it and painted red.
   (ii) Use the objects in a shopping game.
   (iii) Draw the animal's face on a large piece of cardboard and cut out a wide mouth. Ask the child to put the objects in the mouth, making it into an amusing game.

   (iv) Ask the child to hide one of the objects while you shut your eyes and then make a big show of looking for it.

3. Sing nursery rhymes and favourite songs and leave a pause for the child to supply the missing key word.

4. Tell well-known stories over and over again, pausing for the child to join in at key moments. Stories with repetitive lines, such as 'The Gingerbread Man' and 'The Three Little Piggies', are good for this.

5. Hide a loudly ticking clock or musical box and help the child to find it. Remember to use something with which the child is familiar.

6. Play 'Musical Statues'. The child dances around until the music stops and stands as still as possible, like a statue. It is important to play this individually as well as in a group, because in a group, a child may pick up visual clues from the other children.

7. Play *Mousie Mousie* (by Spears Games) in which children have to pull plastic mice away by their tails, before the adult catches them with a cup. The child must wait for the signal 'Go!'.

8. Ask the child to copy a number of beats on a drum. Another adult or child may model the required response.

9. In a group, ask each child to listen for his own name and perform a simple action, such as stand up.

Level 4 (3 to 4 Years)

Aim

To integrate auditory and visual channels. To begin to transfer attention skills to the group or classroom.

Principles

1. Give the child time to focus his attention before giving instructions.

2. Prompt him with difficult aspects of the task.

Suitable Materials

Jigsaws, colouring, cutting, plasticine and dough modelling, dolls, cars, trains, miniature 'real' items such as toy money and teasets, puppets, threading large beads.

Activities

1. Slowly teach the child to listen and take in what you say without stopping what he is doing, by following these steps:—

   (i) Alert the child to your presence while he is performing a visual-manipulatory task, by calling his name, waiting, and giving a brief, clear instruction.

(ii) Alert the child with a comment such as 'How are you doing?', 'That's good!' etc. Suggest a way he can modify the task.

(iii) Stand by the child without speaking until he is aware of you, and then give the instruction.

(iv) If the child continues to look up at you, encourage him to stick to what he is doing, with remarks such as, 'Don't look up, that's very good', etc. Repeat instructions as necessary.

(v) Stand behind the child occasionally, while commenting on his activity. He thus cannot look at you without turning right round.

2. Carry out a variety of activities in this way, including symbolic play with miniature dolls, construction games and sorting activities. Some children will stick at level 4 for some time and be unable to attend to instructions or questions without giving their whole attention to the speaker. Individually they will respond well but may find learning in class difficult.

Activities to Facilitate Transfer of Attention

Transfer to a child's classroom may be effected by:—

(i) Increasing the amount of environmental distraction, eg putting up interesting pictures and increasing background noise.

(ii) Increasing the number of people present in the situation.

1. The child is expected to attend in a one-to-one situation.

2. Another adult is introduced into the room, preferably a class teacher or aide who will be working with the child later on. At first she works quietly on something else and joins in after a while.

3. Another child at the same level of attention is included in therapy.

4. Attention-control work can be carried out in a small group. At first it may be necessary to increase the help given to the child as his attention will probably not be as good as it is in the one-to-one situation. The prompts can gradually be faded again.

Activities to Develop Listening Skills

Many of these can be adapted for small-group work.

1. Matching sounds to objects or pictures:

(i) Have three or four pictures of familiar animals. Make an animal noise and get the child to identify the correct picture of the animal which would make the noise.

(ii) Lay out several musical instruments and play one for the child to pick out. At first it may be necessary for the child to watch you; later he can rely on auditory skills alone.

(iii) Use familiar objects or toys that make a noise.

2. Make up a story with the child's name in it. Read it once and then repeat it explaining that he must put up his hand when he hears his name. If this is done as a group, call the names of the more able children first, to act as models.

3. As above but when the children hear one of the boys' names all the boys stand up, and when they hear one of

the girls' names all the girls stand up. Be sure to use the names of the children in the group. (This activity is only suitable for a small group.)

4. Asking for objects: similar to Level 3 activity but increase the number of objects displayed and requested.

(i) Shopping bag: use a real net bag and ask the child to put a series of objects inside.

(ii) Suitcase: have a real case and real clothes or doll-sized ones, and ask the child to pack the suitcase.

(iii) Draw a washing-line. Ask the child to 'hang up' a series of small pictures of clothes with Blu-Tack.

5. Following simple commands:

(i) Ask the child to touch two to three body parts.

(ii) Ask him to touch or hand you two related objects, eg table, chair.

(iii) Ask him to touch or give you two unrelated objects, eg shoe, book, which is slightly harder because he cannot guess the second object.

(iv) Give him simple actions to do to musical stimuli, eg when he hears the drum he must run to the door. This will need to be demonstrated.

6. In a group play 'Musical Chairs'. Each child sits down when the music stops. Real chairs are not necessary; the floor will do nicely!

Level 5 (4 to 5 Years)

Aim

To increase the child's concentration span. To continue transfer to the classroom environment.

Suitable Materials

Rhymes, riddles, construction, table-games, puppets, Punch and Judy, floor lay-outs, outdoor play and dressing-up clothes. Gradually increase the length of time the child spends on visual-manipulatory tasks. Also increase the complexity of the tasks and verbal instructions. See Chapter 6 for suitable activities.

Activities to Facilitate Transfer of Attention

1. The child should now be able to work alongside another child doing the same activity.

2. Increase his tolerance by either:

(i) including him in a small group of children at a similar level of attention.

(ii) working in a partitioned area of his own classroom; later remove the partition and have the child with his back to the class.

3. Include the child in normal classroom activities with the therapist or classroom aide present to prompt the child should his attention lapse.

4. Gradually fade your involvement in the classroom.

5. Find out what sort of tasks and games the child is expected to get on with by himself in class and practise these in individual sessions.

Activities to Develop Listening Skills

Use similar activities to Level 4 but increase the complexity of both the stimulus and the required response.

1. 'Simple Simon Says', with and then without gesture.

2. Asking for objects or pictures; as for Levels 3 and 4 but increase the number of items displayed and requested. Introduce a fantasy element, eg 'pretend you're going to a desert island and you must take a box of matches, a torch and a swimming costume'. The child collects these objects. (Further ideas include: holidays, space travel, mock battles, sports.)

3. Read a story to one or more children:

(i) about a dog or a cat, and whenever the animal is mentioned the child must make the appropriate noise or mime the particular animal.

(ii) about a child's birthday and all the different presents he gets; as the child hears the presents mentioned he collects the appropriate picture. Afterwards read the story again and help the child to check that he is right.

4. The children sit in a circle; they must call another child's name and throw a beanbag to him.

5. Auditory Discrimination activities:—

(i) Lay a number of everyday objects before the child, eg keys, bell, a spoon in a cup, a wind-up toy, and while he shuts his eyes, make the associated noise. He must correctly identify the object.

(ii) Use musical instruments in a similar way.

(iii) The child must copy a simple rhythm on a drum, eg two quick beats, pause, one quick beat.

(iv) The child pretends to be different things when he hears different musical instruments, eg a soldier when he hears a drum, a raindrop to the glockenspiel, a snake to a rattle, a car to a horn.

(v) Matching sounds to pictures, using tapes of everyday sounds, eg a running tap, frying bacon, the door-bell ringing; familiar classroom sounds, and familiar voices. In the last game the child points to the person whose voice he hears.

(vi) *Photo Sound Lotto* [5], using the taped sounds and corresponding pictures.

6. Two children sit on either side of a screen, each with a large sheet of paper and crayons. They take it in turns to tell each other what to draw, eg 'Draw a house. Put a red roof on it. Make three windows.' etc. At the end both drawings should look the same.

Level 6 (5 to 6 Years)

The child should not need attention training as such but the therapist should encourage the child's ability to concentrate on more and more complex stimuli and to complete his transfer to a normal learning situation.

CHAPTER 3
THE ROLE OF PLAY

continued

THE ROLE OF PLAY

Introduction

Children's play takes many different forms and serves many different functions. Its significance to the child's development is stated by Vygotsky: "Play is not the predominant form of activity, but in a certain sense, it is the leading source of development in pre-school years." It is through the medium of play that the child is able to develop new skills and practise those already acquired: skills that range from motor dexterity to social competence (Jeffree, McConkey and Hewson, 1977).

Play is a voluntary and usually a pleasurable behaviour. It enables the child to experiment with alternative skills and roles without the fear of failure. The child sets his own goals and makes his own rules. Play is an area of development that is of major importance in language teaching. It helps to develop the prerequisites that are essential to language development—listening, observation, imitation, concept formation and symbolic understanding. It is also used as a therapeutic tool. It is important to remember that the many types of play are inter-dependent; and progress relies on consolidation of these skills.

Functions of Play

1. Play allows the child to develop new skills through observation, exploration, discovery, conjecture and imitation.

2. A child is able to practise skills already acquired.

3. The child's symbolic understanding and concept formation develops through his play experience.

4. It is a pleasurable activity that relieves boredom and frustration.

5. It allows for a release of physical energy.

6. It provides an opportunity for expressing negative emotions of fear and anger in a harmless manner.

7. The child is able to learn about other people's roles and skills through make-believe and role-play.

8. Play forms a part in developing the child's sex-role identity.

Factors Affecting the Development of Play

1. Play may be delayed if a child is mentally handicapped.

2. A physical handicap may prevent the child exploring his environment and gaining experiences vital to the development of play.

3. Impaired vision or hearing can limit the kinds of play available to the child.

4. Perceptual problems may affect the child's ability to play.

5. Play may show abnormal patterns or be delayed in a child who has emotional or behavioural difficulties.

6. The child may lack the opportunities to play because of:
   (i) lack of toys
   (ii) lack of toys that are appropriate for his age and ability
   (iii) lack of playfellows, because parents and caregivers are unable to play with the child or the child has no companions of his own age and ability
   (iv) lack of space
   (v) lack of time.

7. Speech and language delay may restrict the development of certain areas of play.

Assessment

Spontaneous play is more likely to occur in a familiar environment for the child, with his toys and playmates close by. Therefore it is important to try to observe the child in his home, nursery or school playground. This can be supplemented by reports from parents and other caregivers, eg nursery nurse.

There are a number of developmental charts available, which provide a checklist of behaviours, including play. These can be used when determining the child's play level, eg *Children's Developmental Progress: from birth to five years*, Mary Sheridan, 1973.

There is also a standardised test procedure: *The Symbolic Play Test*, by Lowe and Costello, published by NFER. This is suitable for children of one to three years and assesses the child's symbolic understanding through play with miniature toys.

Types of Play

Although the following description classifies play into separate categories, in reality these types of play do not exist in isolation, but are closely inter-related and inter-dependent.

Exploratory Play

Most children have an innate curiosity about themselves and their world. They discover that objects and people exist apart from themselves. Exploration provides the means for the child to find out the properties and qualities of these other entities. It requires a combination of motor, perceptual and cognitive skills.

Physical Play

Play that involves the development and refinement of gross motor skills, eg sitting, running and balancing. It involves the ability to initiate, co-ordinate and pattern movements.

Constructive Play

This involves the integration of motor and sensory skills in an activity which results in an end product, eg building a tower with blocks. It also requires intellectual processes of memory, storage and retrieval; and the ability to translate stored material into practical form (Sheridan, 1977).

Imaginative Play

Fundamental to this type of play is the use of objects or gestures to represent other objects or events that are not present (Jeffree, McConkey and Hewson, 1977). It is characterised by make-believe and role-play activities. Imitation, motor, sensory and cognitive skills are central to its development.

Social Play

Play can be a solitary act, or a shared activity with an adult or other children. Inter-action is a key concept in social play, and refers to the two-way process of give and take between the players. The child needs to understand the ideas of sharing and turn-taking.

Games with Rules

To engage in this type of play a child needs to have the skills intrinsic to the game, and be able to follow the set rules. An understanding of sharing and turn-taking needs to be acquired, before children can play rule-based games.

Guidelines to Remediation

1. The activity must be developmentally appropriate, and may have to be adapted for the child who is handicapped in some way.

2. Toys and materials should be age-appropriate.

3. Find out the child's interests and make use of them.

4. Verbal instructions should be suitable for the child's level of comprehension.

5. Teaching should proceed in small stages and new skills should be introduced gradually (Kiernan et al, 1978).

6. At first it may be necessary to model the behaviour you are teaching. The following strategies can be used with a child who has difficulty in copying you.

   (i) Use physical prompts, eg holding his arm and moving it to help him imitate waving 'bye-bye'.
   (ii) Gradually reduce your physical involvement as the child becomes more competent.
   (iii) Finally, carry out the activity alongside him.

7. The duration of the activity is important. The child may become frustrated if the time allowed for the activity is too short; he may become bored with too long an activity.

8. A reluctant child will often join in if he sees that you are enjoying an activity. Do not coax or bribe him.

9. Reward the child with praise when he completes a task or game.

10. Showing your pleasure in the child's play is a high motivational factor.

11. If a child does not want to participate in an activity do not force him. Let him play as he wants to and gradually try to direct him to more purposeful activity. Play is meant to be enjoyable and should not be forced.

12. When a child gets bored with a toy, try presenting it in a different way, eg hiding it in a feelie bag or box.

13. As you play with the child, talk about what you are doing.

14. Encourage the child to talk about the toys and what he is doing.

15. Remember that a child needs time to play alone as well as with others.

16. Toys should be durable. Very young children like to explore objects by banging, throwing and biting etc.

17. If a child is aggressive towards material, remove it and make sure he knows it will only be returned when he plays properly. Take steps to find out why he is being aggressive. Remember that a developmentally delayed child may be at an earlier stage of play (Newson, 1979).

18. Re-evaluate your teaching regularly (Berry, 1980).

19. Share the child's progress with him in a meaningful way.

20. Always make sure the child has suitable play-clothes or arrange to provide overalls (men's old shirts will do).

21. Safety is obviously very important; this means ensuring there is adequate play space and supervision, and that equipment is safe, particularly any home-made items.

ACTIVITIES TO DEVELOP PLAY

Exploratory Play

Functions

1. To help the child discover objects and events through observation of the world around him.

2. To help the child discover the nature and workings of objects, through his observation and manipulation of them.

3. To acquire new skills, resulting from the child's discoveries.

4. To practise these skills in different situations.

5. To stimulate the child's curiosity, thus creating further need and desire to explore.

The Role of Exploratory Play

Exploratory play provides the child with the opportunity to observe and discover objects in his environment. He uses his sensory and motor abilities to find out their qualities and characteristics—by looking, listening, tasting, and also shaking, squeezing and dropping them. In this way the small child begins to build up concepts about his world.

These concepts are essential prerequisites to language development. Later, exploratory play helps to extend and expand the child's knowledge of his world.

Principles

1. A variety of objects and toys should be available to the child for exploration.

2. Materials should be related to the child's interests.

3. Activities and materials should be varied to maintain interest.

4. Activities may need to be adapted if the child is handicapped, either physically or perceptually.

5. Show the child how to explore an object, eg smell a bar of soap yourself and then hold it for the child to smell.

6. Let the child take the lead in activities. Your role should be to extend and guide his play.

The very young child needs the adult to bring experiences to him. Toys must provide experience of watching, listening, feeling, smell and taste.

Activities to Encourage the Child to Look

Toys need to look interesting, and preferably have movements and noises that the child will find exciting. For example: *Bubble Balls* [3]; *Jack-in-the-Ball* [1] (a rolling toy); when the button is pressed, out pops Jack.

1. Face Play: make lots of different expressions, varying your eye and mouth movements. Wear different hats, glasses and jewellery.

2. Mobiles can be hung near the child. These can easily be made at home with odd scraps, using wire coat-hangers as a support. Suitable materials can include: brightly coloured buttons, beads, cotton-reels, keys, pieces of fabric, silver paper, cut-out shapes, silver-foil bottle tops and so on.

HOME-MADE MOBILES

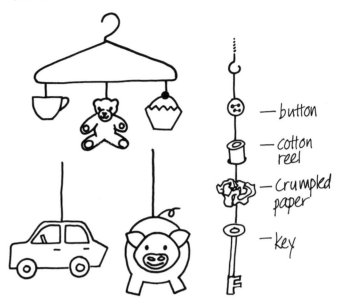

— button
— cotton reel
— crumpled paper
— key

3. Dangling toys, eg *Musical Mobile* [3], encourage the child to reach, touch and grasp as well as look. Thick elastic thread is preferable for hanging these toys, which should encompass a wide variety of shapes, colours and sizes. Materials could include plastic cartons, crumpled paper, silver streamers, tinsel, paper chains, rattles and bright, clear plastic; the display should be changed frequently.

4. Peek-a-Boo: start by hiding your face with your hands and peeking out at the child. Later try hiding behind things in the room, eg popping out from behind the curtain. Help the child to cover his own face and peek out.

5. Finger-play puppets attract the child's attention to your hands. Later you can try putting them on the child's fingers and encouraging him to play. Also paint faces on your finger tips with washable paints.

FINGER PUPPETS

6. Pop-up picture books and 'First Picture Books' are visually exciting.

Once you have gained the child's visual attention to an object, encourage him to track its movements.

7. Hold an object or toy in front of the child until you have his attention and then move it slightly, first to one side and then to the other. This gradually extends his field of vision. To begin with it may be necessary to move the child's head so that he looks in the right direction.

When the child is able to follow slow, simple, side-to-side movements, begin to vary the speed and direction. Moving objects that would be useful at this stage include: a puppet on a stick; balloons; bubbles; balls and extending toys such as Christmas paper-chains.

8. When the child is able to track a moving object he is ready to play with mobile toys, for example pull-along toys such as *Hippo Shape Sorter* [3], *Webster* [3], *Clatterpillar* [4] and *Pull-along Ladybird* [3]; and other moving toys, such as *Magic Man* [4], *Rolling Bells* [3], *Baby's First Car* [4] and *Clatterclowns* [4].

9. Skittles: the main idea is of things falling down, eg skittles, a tower of bricks, piled-up matchboxes, cartons, toilet roll tubes, toy people and boxes. The child can also watch the action of the ball rolling to knock them down (Jeffree, McConkey and Hewson). See Chapter 2 for more ideas for visual attention and tracking skills.

Activities to Encourage the Child to Listen

The young child needs to be introduced to lots of different sounds, but he should be given the opportunity to see what he can hear whenever possible. Sounds should be repeated often.

1. During the day there are lots of sounds the child can stop and listen to—running water, rustling paper, a spoon in a cup, plates rattling, etc. Show the child the source of the sounds and talk about them.

2. Voice play: vary the sound of your voice so that it is constantly changing. Contrast a loud and a soft voice; a deep and a high voice. Hum, sing and whistle to him. (It is best if the child sits on your lap for these games so that he is close to your face.)

3. Show the child different noise-making toys and let him listen. Examples are a ball with a bell inside; squeezy toys, etc.

4. Music box: let the child listen to the music as he holds the toy.

5. Encourage the child's participation in the above activities. If he cannot operate the toys by himself, eg roll the ball or open the music box, then prompt him by gently taking his hand and carrying out the action with him.

Activities to Encourage the Child to Feel

1. Let the child explore your hands and face.

2. Encourage him to explore the feel of his own body, which is very important to him.

3. Play finger games such as tickling the child's palm etc.

4. If the child cannot hold objects, then place them against the skin of his face, hands and body.

5. During the day draw the child's attention to the feel of different objects on different parts of his body, eg soft soap and scratchy nailbrush. Also let him handle toys that vary in texture, eg a hard building brick and a soft toy.

6. Use *Tactile Buttons* [4] and *Touch Cards* [4] which have different textured surfaces.

Activities to Encourage the Child to Smell and Taste

1. The child's attention should be drawn to the smell of objects in his environment. Place things close to his nose so that he can smell them. In the kitchen he can smell the different foods and the washing-up liquid; in the bathroom he can smell the soap, talcum powder, bubble bath, and so on.

2. Let the child have *small* pieces of food to taste.

Activities to Promote Reaching Skills

At six months the normal child is reaching out and seizing any play objects within reach of his extended arms (Sheridan, 1977).

1. Dangling mobiles: these can be made of materials similar to the mobiles described in the previous section. Hanging the objects on elastic allows the child to pull the objects towards him. When hanging the mobile, make sure it is within his reach!

2. Patchwork quilt: this can be made with several materials of different texture, eg velvet, denim, satin and nylon scraps (Jeffree, McConkey and Hewson). Objects can also be sewn on to the quilt; and ones which make a noise are particularly useful—small pet bell; crumpled toilet-paper (of the hard variety); rattle.

3. Reward the child for reaching out by using sound-making toys, eg *Animal Pram Toy* [3]; *Soft Cat Rattle* [3]; squeezy toys; balls with a bell inside and musical boxes. Home-made shakers are easy to make from tins, plastic bottles and small strong jars. They can be filled with water, sand, beads, buttons, pebbles, rice, lentils, cornflakes etc. There are endless combinations.

4. There are several commercial activity-boards on sale, eg *Activity Bear* [3] and *Activity-Centre* [4]; but it

ACTIVITY BOARDS

LOOKING BOARD

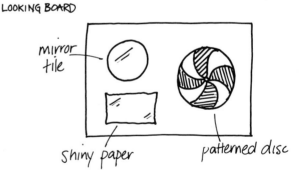

GRASPING BOARD

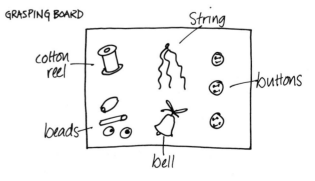

is easy to make your own. You will need a large board made from strong cardboard or similar material. Boards can have objects and materials attached with glue, thread or screws. Remember that the items must be secure and resistant to hard tugging and pulling. Boards can encourage looking—with mirror-tiles, shiny paper, patterned discs, holograms; feeling—use sandpaper, velvet, denim, carpet, sponge, grasping—use cottonreels, string, buttons, beads, ribbon, shoelaces, knobs; listening—use pet's bell, rattle, crumpled paper, miniature chimes.

Activities Involving Reaching and Grasping

1. Dangling toys, eg *Musical Bear* [3] and *Activity Bear Play Centre* [3], are useful to encourage the child to grasp. Different sizes and shapes require different grips so vary the material.

2. To help strengthen a child's grasp, place your finger in his palm and tickle it. The child's hand should close around your finger; now gently try to pull your finger away. Gradually increase the strength of your pull (Jeffree, McConkey and Hewson).

3. Let the child experience tearing, stretching and squeezing. Materials can be string, elastic bands, plasticine, cardboard boxes, moulded lining from food boxes, tissues. (Junk boxes can be kept containing lots of different items for the child to explore. Make sure everything is clean and safe.)

4. Pass the parcel: wrap toys up in newspaper or put toys inside each other, eg a pegman in a cup, inside a teapot.

5. Sand-pits encourage the child to explore the feel of sand and how it can be moved around.

6. Plasticine or dough can be pulled, stretched, squeezed by the child. Make your own dough with flour, water and salt.

7. At bathtime the child can be given lots of different toys, eg *Glug-glug Tug/Plane* [4] and *Elephount* [3]. Excellent bathtime toys can also be made out of household materials, eg corks, plastic bottles and cartons.

8. 'Feelie-bag': hide some objects in an opaque bag. Let the child take out one at a time.

Activities Involving the Understanding of Cause and Effect

Between 12 and 18 months the child is beginning to understand cause and effect (Sheridan, 1977).

1. Take advantage of the child's interest in banging objects. Give him a stick and provide lots of different objects to hit. A hard wooden brick will feel different from a soft cushion. An empty tin will sound different from a full one.

2. Give the child a variety of musical instruments and show him how to make sounds, guiding his hands if necessary. When he is able to make the sounds, let him explore on his own.

3. Fill some bottles with different amounts of water. Show the child how to blow into them, and let him listen to the different sounds; then encourage him to take a turn.

4. Use pop-up toys that the child releases by performing a certain action. They can include the following: *Jack-in-the-Ball* [4], *Trigger-Jigger* (obtainable from Mothercare), *Humpty Dumpty* [3].

5. Pop-up picture books: the child is able to make the illustrations move by pulling tabs and turning cardboard wheels, eg *The Haunted House* by Jan Pieńkowsky, published by William Heinemann Ltd, 1979.

6. Simple fitting-toys and puzzles.

7. Let the child have a selection of rolling toys to explore their different movements. Objects can be cylindrically-shaped rattles, toys with wheels, balls and balloons.

8. There are a number of commercial products that consist of a pegboard with pegs for the child to hammer into holes. These are all very useful.

9. *Tap 'n Turn Bench* [4]: a chunky bench with six little men that can be banged in with a hammer.

Activities Involving Manipulative Skills

Children begin to show increasing interest in the nature and detailed exploration and manipulation of small objects at around 18 to 24 months (Sheridan, 1977).

Provide the child with lots of experience of placing small toys in and out of containers, fitting and slotting toys together. This helps the child to build up concepts of size, weight and spatial relationships.

1. Putting *Pegmen* [4] into *Whirling Chairs, Seesaws, Merry-go-round, Fire-engine* and *Charabanc* (Galt). These are particularly popular with young children.

2. Lego produce a set of large nursery bricks for building.

3. Shape-posting boxes. Those with a large number of different-shaped holes are more difficult, so start with one that has only three or four holes.

4. Simple inset puzzles with lift-out pieces that consist of a picture of a real object.

Activities to Provide Experience of Following Sequences or Patterns

Between 2 and 3 years old the child begins to appreciate form-boards, nesting boxes, posting boxes, screw toys (Sheridan, 1977).

1. Nesting boxes or piling boxes help to establish the concept of size. First demonstrate the task to the child, starting with two boxes, and see if he can fit them together correctly. It may be necessary to use two that are very different in size. Gradually increase the number of boxes. If the child has problems, help him find the box that forms the base, and gently correct his errors. Give as many demonstrations as needed, and perhaps do the task simultaneously with a duplicate set. Other similar toys are: Russian dolls or eggs; nesting toys, stacking toys, *Billie and his Barrels* [1] ·

2. Size graded rings on a peg. (Some products form the shape of an animal when finished.) Demonstrate the task to the child and start with only two or three different sizes.

3. Size-graded puzzles.

4. Posting boxes that increase in size, eg *Postman Pat* [3] posting boxes.

5. Stacking toys, eg *Stacking Figures* [4]—stack clown/caterpillar; *Ring Figures* [4]—graded wooden pieces on a central pole, including a guardsman and policeman.

Activities for the Older Child

1. Hide various objects around the room.

2. Mirror games: pull faces, wave.

3. Take the child round the playground, or park. Collect objects. Talk about where you found them, what they look, feel and sound like.

4. Give the child lots of experience through visits to the zoo, farm or shops. Encourage the child to look around him on these visits and explore.

5. Gradually give the child increasingly complicated objects to explore. See if he can work out how to make mechanical toys go, take apart metal puzzles and make difficult models from kits.

6. Let the child experiment with colour, mixing up paints and creating new effects with chalks, crayons and so on.

Physical Play

Functions

1. To help the child to gain control over his body.

2. To help the child learn to co-ordinate his movements.

3. To help develop the child's mobility, and therefore his independence.

The Role of Physical Play

In order to be able to explore his environment, the child needs to be mobile. Through this exploration the child learns about the objects and events in his world—learning that is vital to the development of speech and language.

Principles

1. Physical play requires adequate space and careful supervision.

2. Ensure that all equipment is safe.

3. Make sure that the child has the need to move at home or in the nursery and does not have everything provided for him by the adult.

4. It may be necessary to physically support the child in some activities. Try to be relaxed and gentle in your movements.

5. Some activities may be too strenuous for children with health problems, eg a bad heart. Always check with medical staff, physiotherapists and parents before attempting any games.

Activities for the Very Young Child

1. Make sure the child can sit up and look at his environment. If necessary support him with cushions or sit him on your lap.

2. Swing, lift and rock the child in your arms. Bounce him on your knees.

3. Bathtime provides an opportunity to encourage splashing and kicking in the water.

4. See-saw: place the child on his back and kneel astride him. Take hold of him firmly by his hands, raise him gently to a sitting position, and then lower him down again (Jeffree, McConkey and Hewson).

5. Move the child's arms and legs about for him; up, down and round in circles.

6. When playing with him, put his toys out of immediate reach. Encourage the child to stretch forwards for them. Place the toys in various positions so the child has to stretch in different directions.

7. Use activities described in the exploratory-play section to encourage reaching.

Activities to Help Develop Walking

At 15 months the child can walk alone with uneven steps and feet wide apart. He often falls or bumps into furniture, and lets himself down from standing to sitting by collapsing backwards or forwards on to his hands and then back to sitting (Sheridan, 1973).

1. Give the child a purpose for walking. Make him walk to his food, drink or toys instead of taking them to him. Let him tidy his own toys; a toy box with a funny face will give him an incentive to put his toys away.

2. Stand in front of the child a small distance away. Call the child to you and stretch your arms out to him. When the child has managed a few steps on his own, catch him in your arms. Gradually increase the distance between you.

3. Place chairs in a circle with a different toy or sweet on each one so the child has to walk from chair to chair to get his reward. Start with a small circle and gradually make it wider (Jeffree, McConkey and Hewson).

4. Push-along toys, eg *Toddler Truck* [3], *Wooden Trike* [3]: these can be used to practise walking or to encourage its development.

5. Horsies: sit the child on your lap or back. Sitting on your back and staying on will help to develop his balance. Crawl around the floor or sway gently from side to side.

SEE-SAW

Activities to Encourage Walking, Climbing and Running

By 2½ years old the child's locomotor skills are rapidly improving. He can run well straightforwards and can climb easy nursery apparatus (Sheridan, 1973).

1. Obstacle courses are good fun. Tables, chairs, mats, play tunnels[4], steps[4], fun barrels[4], hoops and benches are some of the equipment you can use. Get the child to crawl under or step over items and walk round or between objects. Help the child to walk along a bench or between two chalk lines or follow a pathway made with *Tac Tracks*[2] (see 5) or *Stepping Stones*[1].

PLAY TUNNEL

2. Any form of chase game can be used.

3. The staircase can be used for practising climbing, but this must always be supervised.

4. Playgrounds have slides and climbing frames. Again this needs supervision.

5. *Tac Tracks*[2] : plastic footprints for the child to place his feet on. Children with more advanced skills can follow footprints put into odd positions, so that they have to twist and turn as they move.

6. The *Dyna-Balance Walking Board*[2] encourages correct foot position for walking.

7. O'Grady: the adult carries out various actions which the child has to copy. These can be accompanied by commands using the name O'Grady, eg 'O'Grady says put your hands in the air'. If a command is given without the name and the child still does the action, he is out.

8. Movement to music: children walk or run while music is played, then stand still or sit on the floor when it stops.

9. Various actions can be associated with different sounds. When a drum is beaten, the child walks forward, but when a bell is rung he sits down.

10. Interpreting music with dance, mimes, action songs and nursery rhymes.

Activities for Catching, Throwing and Kicking

Around 2½ years old the child is able to kick a large ball, although not very accurately. By 3 years he is able to kick a ball with force, and catch a large ball on or between extended arms. When the child is 4, skills in throwing, catching, bouncing and kicking are greatly improved (Sheridan, 1973).

1. When trying to get the child to kick, give him some support to help his balance. At first it may be necessary to get the child to kick a ball while walking. Place a large ball in front of the child and he will then naturally kick the ball while taking a step. Be ready to catch him if he falls.

2. When the child can kick a ball without falling over, give him some targets, eg skittles, a goal or a playmate.

Grasping is an early form of catching, so activities for developing this skill will help his catching ability (*see page 31*).

1. Hold a toy above the child's extended arms and let it fall into his hands. Gradually increase the distance. Another person may be needed to prompt the child by manipulating his arms into the right position.

2. When the child first tries to throw he may just drop the ball. Get a box and catch it. Gradually move further away until the child is actually throwing (Jeffree, McConkey and Hewson).

3. When the child is able to throw, provide him with some targets. Get him to throw at skittles, to a friend, into a hoop on the floor etc.

4. Traditional throwing games: use a beanbag or sponge-ball etc as these are safer and easier to catch.

Activities for the Older Child

1. Supervised play on trampolines. This gives children plenty of practice in balancing and gross motor skills.

2. *Space hopper*[4]: this is a tough, inflatable, bouncing toy with built-on ears for the child to grip as he sits on it.

3. Children love the sensation of rocking so let them try out the *Space Horse*[4] and *Rocking Boat*[4].

4. Children can hold races, using stilts and pogo-sticks.

5. Place upside-down flowerpots on the floor. The children have to walk on them without touching the floor. A fantasy situation can be invented, eg the child has to cross a dangerous river full of child-eating crocodiles.

Constructive Play

Functions

1. To help develop hand-eye co-ordination.

2. To aid learning. As the child manipulates different materials, he learns about their characteristics and qualities.

3. To develop and improve memory.

4. To help the child become more independent through the acquisition of new skills.

5. To promote feelings of self esteem and achievement through the completion of a concrete task.

The Role of Constructional Play

By manipulating objects, the child learns about their shape, size, colour, weight and texture. This learning is important in helping to establish concept formation. It also helps the child to understand what effect he can have on these objects; and what effect they have on each other.

The ability to store visual information and then later retrieve it from memory is intrinsic to constructional abilities. The child then uses this information to carry out a visuo-motor task. Concept formation and memory skills are important to the development of verbal language (Reynell, 1977).

Principles

1. Take each task and break it down into its component skills. Find out at which level the child is failing and start intervention to develop the necessary skills.

2. First model the task.

3. Practise the task with the child, keeping the completed model in view.

4. Demonstrate the task and then remove the model from sight.

5. Get the child to do the task from memory without demonstration immediately beforehand.

6. Encourage the child with praise.

Skills needed for the development of constructional play are an ability to:

  (i)   look at an object
  (ii) track a moving object
  (iii) reach for and grasp an object
  (iv) make a pincer grip
  (v)   co-ordinate hand-eye movements
  (vi) perceive and store sequences of movements and patterns
  (vii) store auditory information related to the task
  (viii) retrieve stored information and translate it into a visuo-motor activity.

(For activities to encourage looking, visual tracking, reaching and grasping, see Chapter 2 and the section on exploratory play in this chapter.)

Activities to Encourage a Pincer Grip

By 1 year of age the child is able to pick up small objects with a neat pincer grip between thumb and tip of index finger (Sheridan, 1973).

1. Fitting things together: ordinary household articles, or specially made toys can be used, eg screw-top jars, Russian dolls, *Billie and his Barrels*[1], nuts and bolts. At first make sure lids or nuts are fairly loose and only require a little pressure to open. If the child is having great difficulty, then unscrew the item until it is almost off, and then let the child move it the last fraction. This way he has achieved something.

RUSSIAN DOLLS

2. Give the child lots of different containers and small objects or toys, eg *Pegmen*[4] and the various *Pegmen*[4] sets; *Animal Allsorts*[4], etc. The child will enjoy putting things inside boxes and will also practise his pincer grip.

3. Make the child an activity book from material or thick card. Appliqué pictures can be sewn or glued on to each page. Use odd scraps of material and zips, buttons or poppers that the child can undo and do up.

ACTIVITY BOOK

buttons sewn on a pocket

zip opening a tent

balloon poppers

apple poppers

threading a shoe

presents hooked on a tree with hook-and-eyes

4. *Penny Felt Puzzle Pictures*[4] can be taken apart and put back together, practising various fastening skills. *Educat*[1] is a felt cat with pieces joined together with laces, buttons and press-studs.

5. Picture Wheel: around the outside of a circular piece of card draw or stick small pictures. On another similar piece of card cut out a little square window near the edge. Join the two together with a pronged pin through the middle. Flatten out the prongs to secure it. As the child turns the top card a different picture appears through the window.

PICTURE-WHEEL

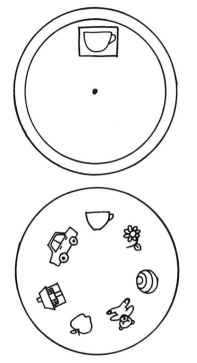

6. Give the child some stacking toys. These come in lots of different shapes, eg *Stack clown/caterpillar* [4]; *Ring Figures* [4].

7. Kiddicraft make a toy called a *Floot-a-Tooter*, which consists of ten tubes that can be put together in a variety of ways. The child can blow through the tubes which make different sounds with each combination.

8. Let the child do lots of colouring, drawing and painting.

9. Jigsaws: early puzzles have pieces consisting of one figure in an inlay-type construction. These usually have small pegs to help the child remove the pieces.

Activities for Threading

It is not till 3 years of age that the child is able to thread large beads on a shoe-lace (Sheridan, 1973).

1. Start with large items and a thick thread. Materials used could follow this hierarchy: large rings, cotton reels, wooden beads, small beads, used with thick dowelling, string, shoe-lace, thread. Encourage the child to name the item he is making. It could be a necklace, snake or a train.

At first show the child how to thread. Thread one cotton reel and then give the string to the child to hold. If the child has difficulty in threading another one, thread it yourself and let him pull it down the string. Gradually move on to getting the child to hold the cotton reel and string at the same time. Help him put the string through the cotton reel by moving his hands for him. Keep practising till he is able to get the reel on by himself. He may need help in co-ordinating this with pulling the bead along the thread. Gradually move on until the child does not need an immediate demonstration.

2. Threading toys: there are numerous commercial products available which make use of a variety of shapes and objects.

3. Sewing: simple sewing-kits have squares of material with large holes in to make threading easier. Some also have printed patterns. The child can make a tapestry picture, a purse, a table mat and so on.

Simple Constructional Activities

By 3 years the child is able to build a tower of nine cubes; by 3½, he can build one or more bridges of three cubes from a model (Sheridan, 1973).

1. Most children like to build towers, especially when they can knock them down again. Use cotton reels, egg-boxes, milk cartons, egg-cups, matchboxes or even building blocks!

2. *Lego* and interlocking plastic cubes can be used to make interesting buildings and vehicles.

3. Get the child to make specific constructions, such as a train, a bridge, a house, a car, a spaceship, but always show the child what to do. These constructions can vary from the very simple—a three-brick train or bridge, to the quite complex. Later encourage the child to invent his own.

Activities for Older Children

The older child should be able to make complex structures from memory. Between 3 and 4 years the child starts to plan ahead and name what he is going to build (Sheridan, 1973).

1. *Rotello* [1]: a set of interlocking plates, pins and pegs, wheels and gears, used to create a variety of vehicles and pull-along toys.

2. There are many jigsaws on the market, eg *Friends Jigsaw* [4].

3. *Construct-o-Straws* [4]: these are flexible straws, spindles and wheels that can be fitted together in a variety of ways.

4. Build a *Super Helta Skelta* [3]: tubes and channels can be connected to form a helter-skelter for marbles, etc.

5. *Slot-o-build* [1]: coloured squares of plastic that slot together.

6. *Disco-shapes* [1]: interlocking plastic discs.

7. *Reo-click* [1]: coloured plastic tubes, wheels, rings and plates.

8. *Basic Builder System* [4]: contain wheels, baseplates, spacers, nuts and bolts.

Imaginative Play

Functions

1. To develop new skills and practise old ones.

2. To help develop thought and language (Jeffree, McConkey and Hewson). Verbal comprehension can not develop without symbolic understanding (Cooper, Moodley and Reynell, 1974).

3. To allow for emotional release through the acting out of fear and anger.

4. To provide the child with the opportunity to try out other roles, which leads to a greater understanding of others.

5. To encourage creativity.

The Role of Imaginative Play

Imaginative play is probably the most important type of play in encouraging children's language development, as it deals with the child's ability to recognise and use symbols. Dr J.K. Reynell has emphasised the symbolic nature of language. True verbal language consists of verbal symbols and cannot develop until the child has developed symbolic recognition. (The development of symbolic understanding is dealt with more fully in Chapter 1.)

Principles

1. Rather than expensive, detailed shop-bought items, use simple home-made toys as these encourage the child to be more imaginative.

2. It is essential that the child has playfellows.

3. Encourage the child to talk about his games.

4. Imaginative play should be fun; so do not give commands but join in and have fun.

5. Provide lots of models of behaviour for the child; and extend his play. Even imaginative children can get stuck in a play routine—your role is to provide stimulating materials and suggestions to help move children on.

6. Children need lots of different experiences in order to act them out.

7. Use spontaneous incidents throughout the day to suggest new play situations, eg if somebody cuts himself, you can turn it into a hospital game.

Activities to Encourage Early Pretend-Play

At 12 months the child is demonstrating 'definition-by-use' of everyday objects, eg drinking from an empty cup (Sheridan, 1973).

1. Imaginative play begins through imitation (Jeffree, McConkey and Hewson). At first the child will need to observe lots of modelled behaviour, before he will begin to copy pretend-play. Using everyday objects, demonstrate make-believe play, eg pretend to feed yourself from a spoon during a make-believe tea party.

2. Hand the child some everyday items, eg cup, comb, flannel. If the child makes no attempt at play, but just bangs or mouths them, demonstrate the required behaviour on the child, eg comb his hair. Again give him the objects and repeat the model if necessary. When the child carries out the action reward him with lots of praise, and reinforce his action by imitating him.

3. Next encourage the child to use a toy cup, comb, etc in the same way.

Activities to Promote Large-Doll Play

By 18 months the child will briefly imitate simple everyday activities, eg feeding baby; brushing the floor (Sheridan, 1973).

1. Using a large doll, eg *Large Baby Dolls* [4], carry out various actions with toy objects, eg cuddling, washing, feeding and walking. Keep them simple at first. Give the doll to the child and encourage him to carry out the actions. If he uses the items on himself, then take, for example, a cup—feed yourself and then the doll, saying 'Now, it's dolly's turn'. Hand the cup to the child and encourage him to feed the doll. Give him lots of praise when he does.

2. Provide the child with toys that allow him to copy everyday activities in the home. At first he may need to use them alongside real activities, eg when mum bathes baby, the child bathes the doll.

Activities for Early Make-Believe Play

The child will spontaneously carry out simple role or situational make-believe activities at 2 years (Sheridan, 1973).

1. Let the child act out his recent experiences using dolls, eg a visit to the hairdressers; an outing to the park.

2. Puppets can be used in a similar way to dolls. They can wave goodbye, eat dinner, wash, etc. Galt produce Asian Puppet Family and Black Puppet Family, including grandparents.

3. Use hand, glove or finger puppets to play peek-a-boo and hiding games.

HAND, GLOVE AND STRING PUPPETS

4. Finger-play: paint faces on your fingers and use them as puppets. Make them run, jump, dance, etc.

FINGER PUPPETS

5. Toy telephones provide children with endless fun.

6. Using toys on wheels: push them along the floor and make car noises. Encourage the child to join in.

7. Toy cars: children can pretend to drive the car and learn to stop and go at a signal.

8. 'Let's pretend': play at being a giant or an animal. Strike appropriate poses and make suitable grunts or growls (Jeffree, McConkey and Hewson).

Activities for Imaginative Play

By 3 years old the child engages in make-believe play involving invented people and objects (Sheridan, 1973).

1. Use old refuse to build models with the help of the child, eg cotton reels joined together and painted can be a snake (Jeffree, McConkey and Hewson); an empty cereal packet can be a house; an empty egg-box can be a boat. These can be used in make-believe stories.

COTTON REEL SNAKE

2. Children can act out different social situations, eg a party, a disco, McDonalds!; visiting relatives.

3. Provide the child with miniature toys such as animals; *Duplo World People* [1]; dolls' houses; garages; farms. Show the child how to use the toys to act out a story with different characters.

4. *Play mobile* [4] have a fascinating range of miniature people and accessories, including an Ethnic Playpeople and Children Pack. Children can pretend to land on the moon in their spaceship; fight fires with a fire-engine and its crew, or drive in a rally. These are just a few examples.

5.(i) *Cellograph* (produced by Philip and Tacey): this provides a base on which self-sticking vinyl pictures of people and objects can be arranged to form a picture. When the child has finished, they can be peeled off and stored for later re-use.

(ii) *Fuzzy-felt* [4]: a similar product except felt cut-outs are used on a special board (includes farm, circus and playschool scenes).

(iii) A home-made picture-board can be made from stiff backing card. The child can make up his own picture using junk materials. A 3D effect can be achieved using empty boxes, cartons, crumpled paper, foil etc.

PICTURE BOARD

cotton wool

yellow felt

cardboard box cut in half

crumpled silver foil

(iv) *Uniset boards* [1]: these are base boards printed with familiar scenes. They each have a set of self-sticking vinyl cut-outs of objects to place on the backgrounds, and include a house, playground and a space scene. Encourage the child to make up a story around the picture.

6. Layouts: large cardboard pieces can be painted and laid on the floor to represent various backgrounds, eg a park. Miniatures and models can be used in conjunction with layouts to form a make-believe village or farm. The children can help to make their own. Ideas for layouts are: seaside, zoo, street, garden, town etc. Materials can include: packaging, felt, gummed paper, sponge, corrugated paper, silver foil and scraps of material. Much of the refuse in your home you would usually throw out can be used in some way, so start saving! For example: Park–trees can be cardboard cut-outs covered with green gummed paper, a pond can be silver foil stuck on to the layout, seats can be corrugated paper, and roundabouts made from cheese boxes.

7. *Inset Puzzles: Playground* [4] and *People at Work* [4] are puzzles that depict children and adults doing familiar things. Encourage children to talk about them and make up stories.

Activities for Role Play

Dramatic make-believe and dressing-up are favourite activities for the 4-year-old (Sheridan, 1973).

1. Dressing-up: build up a collection of commercially produced dressing-up clothes or gather some old clothes, especially accessories like hats, scarves, bags, jewellery etc. Here are a few suggestions to spark off your imagination: cowboy hats, toy guns, belts, waistcoats, Indian headband, police helmet, notebook, purse, basket, handbag, gloves, watch, glasses, shawls, old tights or stockings stuffed with paper or material for animal tails, shoes, wellington boots.

Children can be doctors, nurses, teachers, bus drivers, policemen, spacemen, cowboys and indians etc.

2. *Ethnic Dressing-up Clothes* [4]: Japanese, North African, Arabs and Pakistani clothes.

3. Playhouse: this can be a corner of the room where materials, dressing-up and make-believe games are kept. Toy furniture and kitchenware can be used to set the scene. Some suggestions are: saucepans, stove, sink, washing bowl, plates, cups and saucers, *Ethnic Serving Utensils* [4], *Asian Cooking Sets* [1] and *Chapati Pan* [1].

4. Shop: collect empty tins and packets of food. Be careful to choose tins without jagged edges and clean all items first. A toy till is very useful; also pretend money, purses, shopping bags. Food can be made from plasticine, *Soft Stuff* [3] and papier mâché. (Galt produce a play shop with shelves and a serving counter which can also serve as a puppet theatre.)

5. Other pretend places can be: police station, bus, hospital, school, post office etc.

6. Puppets: these are great fun and often very useful for the shy child. All puppets should be given a character with a voice to match. Children can act out stories.

7. Animal puppets are useful for children with limited language as they can be encouraged to make animal noises.

8. 'Who am I?' or 'What am I?': the child acts out a mime. The other children have to guess who they are, eg a policeman, or what they are, eg a tree. Giving the children pictures of people or objects may help to fire their imagination, eg Winslow Press object cards and *Photocue Occupation Cards* [5].

9. Action stories: the child carries out actions described in a story or nursery rhyme. At first use only those requiring simple actions, starting off with the child's favourites; but later perhaps you can include the child as one of the characters.

10. Drama or mime: the child acts out an event he has seen or heard. This can be something from a recent outing, eg a visit to the zoo.

11. Play: the children can be taught a simple sequence of mime to which the teacher provides the story-line. Perhaps later the children can join in on simple dialogue. They may enjoy performing for their parents and other children.

12. Acting-out, not acting up. Children can be helped to act out a forthcoming event that they may find worrying, eg a visit to the dentist or hospital; starting school; performing in front of the class. Adult, child and doll can all take turns at taking different roles. Such role-play may help children to understand difficult situations and lessen their fear.

Social Play

Functions

1. To allow the child to develop new skills from observing and imitating his playfellows.

2. To allow the child to practise old skills in different situations.

3. To provide an opportunity for the child to develop and expand his communication skills.

4. To encourage the child, through shared play, to become more sociable and make friendships, thus increasing his communicative confidence.

The Role of Social Play

The primary concern here is the development and remediation of the child's communication skills. Social play offers a natural situation in which these abilities can be practised and extended (Jeffree, McConkey and Hewson, 1977). Social play provides the child with an opportunity to observe and imitate others, which are basic prerequisites for language learning (Bloom and Lahey, 1978).

Principles

1. Model the required behaviour first, eg making pretend tea for another person. Give the child time to respond; it may take several demonstrations before the child attempts to imitate.

2. Talk about what you or the child are doing during the activity. Keep language at a level appropriate for the child's comprehension.

3. Some games can be taught and practised initially between the teacher and the child, and later on played with other children at a similar developmental level.

4. In group activities, ensure that all the children take their turn. Do not allow one child to dominate the group.

5. Early group activities need to keep all the children involved. As the children learn to share and take turns, they will be able to wait during the game.

6. Make sure activities require more than one player!

Activities for Social Play Between Parent and Child

The child's first playmates are its parents. At 9 months he needs to be playing near them for security (Sheridan, 1977). Parents can be encouraged to try the following activities with their children.

1. Sit the child on your lap so he is close to your face and voice. At first the child will probably be just an observer in the activities, but gradually he will become more active and copying can be encouraged. As he participates more, let him take the lead and respond to his actions and verbalisations by imitating him. Some of the following games can be used:

   (i) cuddles
   (ii) tickling
   (iii) voice play: hum, sing, talk to your child. Vary the pitch and volume.
   (iv) make lots of different faces with exaggerated eye and mouth movement.
   (v) wear funny hats or unusual jewellery; keep changing them round. Let the child look at them, feel them etc.

2. Rough-and-tumble play: lift, swing or roll the child. Sit him on your knee and bounce him. Encourage the child to join in by suddenly stopping and not moving till the child makes some response.

3. Peek-a-boo: cover your face with your hands and peek over the top of your fingers. You can extend this to peeking from behind chairs and curtains etc but make sure the child is close by. Let the child be the leader—cover his face and then let him peek out. If you use a scarf or flannel, he can push the cloth down when he peeks out.

4. Hide and seek: hide from the child somewhere in the room and keep popping out until he comes to find you. Also let the child hide with you while another person seeks you out, and then you and the child can look for a third person. This will help the child to understand hiding.

5. Imitation games:

   (i) Sit with the child and as he makes some action or sound, copy him. Repeat this activity several times.
   (ii) Copy his action and add another that you know he can already do. At first the child may need help in making the movement; another adult can help by prompting. When the child imitates the action, reward him with lots of praise. Repeat the activity frequently, gradually reducing the number of prompts (Jeffree, McConkey and Hewson). Mirrors can make copying games a lot more fun, but must be used with sensitivity.

6. Teach the child some nursery rhymes. Start with one with a simple action, eg ring-a-ring-a-roses-child falls down.

7. Look at a picture book together. First picture books with simple, clear pictures of very familiar objects or favourite toys are best for the young child. The pages need to be fairly thick so that the child can turn them.

8. Balls or toys on wheels can be pushed to and fro between you and the child. Reward the child with lots of praise when he pushes the toy back.

9. When changing to a new activity, hold up the new toy, but don't let the child have it till he has given you the one he has. Hold out your hand to help him understand (Jeffree, McConkey and Hewson).

Activities to Encourage Children to Play Together

At 2½ years old the child will sometimes play with other children nearby, but in solo play. By 3 years he will join in make-believe play with his peers (Sheridan, 1977).

1. Many activities can be played by two children alongside each other at the same table, including the following: drawing; threading; puzzles; constructional activities (*see also Chapter 6 for more ideas*).

2. See-saw, swing, go-kart and pedal-cars, where the children must take turns to push each other.

3. Tug-of-war.

4. Ball games, kicking, throwing or rolling the ball back to each other. Give praise for throwing the ball to the other child.

5. Cars and toys on wheels can also be used to pass between two children.

6. Hide and seek; 'He' and chase games.

7. Imitation games. Children take it in turns to be leader, eg 'O'Grady Says', 'Follow my leader', 'Simple Simon Says'.

Activities to Promote Play Between Groups of Children

By 4 years old, the child needs the friendship of other children and can understand sharing and turn-taking (Sheridan, 1973).

1. Tea party: use a commercial product or collect durable items, such as plastic cups, spoons, and teapot. Let each child take it in turn to be responsible for setting out the plates and cups; and making tea (pretend, of course). Encourage the children to accompany their play with appropriate language. Join in and model behaviour for the children.

2. Shopping: collect empty food containers that are clean and do not have sharp edges. The children can take it in turns to be the shopkeeper and the shopper. An old shopping bag and a purse with pretend money are very useful. Get the children to talk about what they have bought and give each other shopping lists.

3. Pass-the-Parcel: this can be made more interesting by wrapping a small toy inside each layer. This way the child has something to keep and something to pass on.

4. Ball games: there are lots of varieties of games. Here are just a few suggestions:

   (i) Children stand in a circle. One calls another child's name and throws him the ball. This child does the same and so on.

   (ii) Pig-in-the-Middle: one child stands between two players, and tries to catch the ball as they throw it to each other.

   (iii) Children stand in a circle and throw a ball to each other. If the ball is dropped that child is out. Winner is the last one in.

5. A group of children join hands. The aim is to tie a giant human knot. The children twist and duck under each others arms and legs, but keep holding hands. Other children can be enlisted to break the knot by picking out people to free their hands and move away.

6. Team games, races and relays: 'Oranges and Lemons' etc.

7. Children form a large circle and begin to move in one direction holding hands. At a given signal they change direction and place their hands on each other's shoulders. The game continues with the children holding different parts of the body!

8. 'Whispers': children sit in a circle, including the teacher. They take turns to send a whispered word or phrase round the circle.

9. Children stand in a circle, holding hands. The teacher or a child squeezes his neighbour's hand. Everyone has to pass the 'squeeze' round the circle and back to the beginning.

10. 'Caterpillars': children sit on the floor, one behind the other with their legs outstretched. Each child sits between another child's legs, grasping the left ankle of the child behind and waving his other hand in the air. The caterpillar then shuffles along the floor most effectively. Two caterpillars can have a race.

CATERPILLAR

each child sits between the legs of the person behind

each child grasps the ankle of the child behind.

11. 'Twisters': this is a commercial game, in which two children get into a fine muddle-up as they twist between each other's legs and arms.

12. Charades: children divide into two teams and act out the names of television programmes, films and books, without speaking.

13. 'Fizz-Buzz: the children sit in a circle and number round. Every time a number contains a '4' the child must say 'Fizz' and if it has a '7' he must say 'Buzz'. If the number is '47' of course, he must say 'Fizz-Buzz'. If a child forgets, he is 'out'.

Games with Rules

Functions

1. To provide an opportunity to practise acquired skills such as turn-taking, waiting, and sociable play.

2. To enable the child to learn new skills, eg learning to win and lose.

3. To develop the child's ability to follow instructions.

4. To improve memory.

Importance of Games with Rules

This type of play requires a high level of communication involving discussion and planning. It also demands that the child understands sharing, turn-taking, and how to follow verbal and non-verbal instructions. It is not until a child is 4 that he learns to share his play and to take turns (Sheridan, 1973).

Discussion, planning, sharing and turn-taking are all essential skills in social and language development.

Hierarchy for Teaching the Rules of a Game

(adapted from Jeffree, McConkey and Hewson, 1977)

1. Play alone with the child and introduce the rules gradually. Let the child learn to lose.

2. Some games have lots of rules so you will need to introduce a few at a time:

  (a) List all the rules.

  (b) Choose a few basic rules and build a simpler version of the game around them.

  (c) Increase complexity by applying the rules to different versions of the game.

  (d) Gradually introduce new rules until you have a full set.

Example: A board game involving dice in which players move around a track. If they land on a coloured square, they move back a specified number of spaces.

  Simplifications:

  (i) Teach the child the idea of start to finish by using paper strips divided into squares. Give one to the child and one to yourself. Use a coloured dice, or stick coloured paper over the numbers on an ordinary die, starting with two colours. Make a simple rule: if red is thrown, move forward one square; if blue is thrown, do not move. When the child is finished, give him a reward if necessary. Some children need to be taught that completing a game, or even winning, is rewarding.

START–FINISH

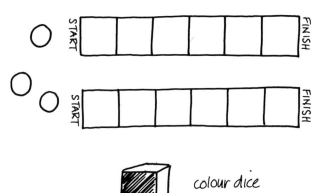

colour dice

(ii) When the child is used to the idea of throwing the dice and moving from start to finish, make the course longer and a different shape, eg circular or S-shaped.

BOARD GAMES

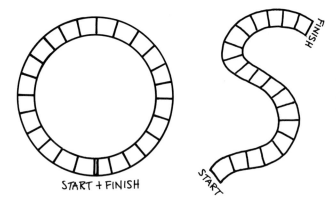

START + FINISH

(iii) Gradually introduce more rules. Some children may be able to cope with the introduction of more than one rule at a time.

3. Once the child has mastered the rules he can play with another child at a similar level. At first you must join in with them to remind them of rules and to keep fair play but later you can just supervise them.

4. Move on to letting the child play in a group.

5-year-olds and 6-year-olds enjoy indoor games involving complex rules (Sheridan, 1973).

Indoor Games

1. Dominoes.

2. Card games, eg: *Snap, Happy Families.*

3. Board games, traditional, modern and home-made.

4. Bingo and Lotto.

Outdoor Games

1. Ball games, eg rounders; French cricket; pig-in-the-middle.

2. Chase games, eg tag; stick-in-the-mud.

3. Race games, eg three-legged; sack; pogo-stick; stilts; egg-and-spoon.

4. Jumping: high jump, long jump and hurdles.

5. Charades: children act out a sequence of actions.

6. Relay races.

7. Obstacle courses.

8. Target games, eg skittles, bowls, 'hoop-la'.

_____CHAPTER 4_____
THE DEVELOPMENT OF COMPREHENSION

_____
ACTIVITIES FOR DEVELOPING COMPREHENSION OF SPOKEN LANGUAGE/46
_____

CHAPTER 4
THE DEVELOPMENT OF COMPREHENSION

Introduction

Verbal comprehension and expressive language have been divided, for the sake of convenience, into separate chapters; however, in real life there is obviously no such division. This chapter deals with the understanding of spoken language, which begins with the child relating a verbal label to an object.

Traditionally, it has been thought that verbal comprehension precedes expressive language (Reynell, 1980; Mittler, 1972). Bloom and Lahey, however, feel that "knowing a word, knowing a grammar, and understanding structured speech apparently represent different mental capacities: it may be misleading to consider such capacities develop in linear temporal relationships, with comprehension simply preceding production".

The child's level of understanding cannot always be inferred from his expressive language and needs to be thoroughly assessed by formal and informal methods. It is essential that everybody involved with the child is aware of the child's comprehension ability so that they can modify their language accordingly.

Factors Affecting the Development of Comprehension

1. **The child's intellectual abilities:** a child who is mentally handicapped may have delayed language.

2. **Attention levels:** a child needs to attend to stimuli in order to extract its meaning.

3. **The child's cognitive abilities:** some children have difficulty in conceptualising and therefore language development is delayed.

4. **Type of language input:** the child learns his first words from his caregivers, who provide him with an environment which stimulates and facilitates language learning (H. McDade, 1981). The child's early vocabulary reflects the categories found in the parent's language input, ie food, body parts, clothes, people and everyday objects in the child's daily routines (E.V. Clarke, 1979).

There have been many studies of parental language which have shown that parents modify their language when talking to the child. The parents simplify their language and use shorter sentences (Snow, 1972; Broen, 1972; Moerk, 1976). This reduction in complexity does not affect the meaning or reduce the information the parent wants to convey. They use repetition, paraphrasing and redundancy in their language to the child; and offer expansions and comments on the child's language to the parent (H. McDade, 1981). The parent restricts his or her language to the here and now when interacting with the child and thus facilitates language learning. Throughout the child's pre-school years the parents' language input remains slightly above the level of the child's (Baldwin and Baldwin, 1973). This slight discrepancy stimulates the child's interest and motivation to learn new language. However, if the discrepancy is too great the child will lose interest and be distracted from the new information (Hunt, 1961).

5. **Amount of language input:** the child not only needs the right type of language input, but also the right amount.

6. **The child's experiences:** the type of words a child learns reflect his daily experiences. Culture, social class and position in the family all play a part in determining which words are learnt first.

7. **Sensory impairment:** the child who hears little or no speech will obviously have difficulty acquiring spoken language. Similarly, the visually-impaired child will have problems relating spoken language to the objects or events that he cannot see.

8. **Physical impairment:** a physical handicap may prevent the child from exploring his world, and thus impair his conceptual and language development.

9. **Motivation:** many language-impaired children lack the motivation and curiosity to learn about their world (Berry, 1980).

Assessment

In order to determine the appropriate language input for an individual child, his understanding of verbal language needs to be ascertained.

There are a number of standardised assessments of verbal comprehension, including the following:

1. The Reynell Developmental Language Scales by Dr Joan Reynell (published by NFER-Nelson).

2. The Sentence Comprehension Test by Peter Mittler (published by NFER-Nelson).

3. Northwestern Syntax Screening Test by Laura L. Lee (published by NFER-Nelson).

4. The Receptive-Expressive Emergent Language Scale (REEL) by K.R. Bzoch and R. League, 1970.

These tests have the advantage that they reduce cueing to a minimum, enabling the assessor to establish exactly what verbal language the child is understanding. However, they do not provide a full assessment of the child's comprehension levels. It is still important to find out how much and what sort of cues the child needs in order to understand the verbal language that he failed to recognise in the formal situation. Also many children may be inhibited in an unfamiliar situation or by an unfamiliar tester.

The child should be observed while playing at home or in other familiar situations. He will respond better to an assessor that he knows well. Supplementary reports can be obtained from caregivers, and compared with test results.

What is Verbal Comprehension?

In early development the child may only understand a word or phrase when spoken in a particular context and accompanied by gesture. True verbal comprehension begins when a child can relate a verbal concept to a meaningful object in any form it may occur (Reynell, 1977) and in any context (Bloom and Lahey, 1972). (*See Chapter 1, page 5.*)

A single verbal label has several different meanings which vary with context. Bloom and Lahey (1972) have detailed the different levels of perceptual and linguistic knowledge required by the child in the reception and understanding of spoken language.

1. Recognition of a word's sound pattern /k-a-t/.

2. Ability to recall the pattern from memory for the production of a word.

3. Knowing the word's specific referent, ie what object, action or event the word refers to, eg 'cat'. This is called 'referential meaning'.

4. Knowing its full range of referents, ie knowing the word in relation to that object, action or event in any context, eg all cats. This is called 'extended meaning'.

5. Knowing the relations it encodes, ie its meaning in regard to other words (eg object of an action or the agent of an action). This is called 'relational meaning'.

6. Knowing the word's semantic category, eg cat = animal. This is called 'categorical meaning'.

7. Recognising that the sound pattern is a word, and that a word can consist of sounds, spoken and written. This is called 'metalinguistic sense'.

Until the child is able to show he understands all these meanings in all contexts, without cues, he does not really 'know' a word (Bloom and Lahey, 1972). This knowledge is acquired over a period of time.

The Development of Comprehension

First Verbal Labels

Words first begin to have some meaning for the child at around 6 to 10 months (Weiss and Lillywhite, 1981); but this understanding is limited to certain contexts. The child relies on contextual and non-verbal cues, such as the direction of the adult's gaze, gesture and pointing, to extract meaning from the word. He may, for example, respond correctly to a request to fetch his cup as his mother brings out the orange juice, but fail to select the cup from a number of objects during play. He is merely responding to the situation and has not learnt the word 'cup' as a symbol for that object.

It is not until 15 to 18 months that the child begins to demonstrate true verbal comprehension (Reynell, 1977) and is able to recognise familiar objects by name even when these objects are not in their familiar surroundings.

The child first learns the names of those objects that he has experienced in his everyday environment; and therefore children will differ in which words they learn first. However, shorter, less abstract words are easier for the child to learn than longer multi-syllabic words and those more specific in their reference (Berry, 1980).

At this stage the child is able to understand several verbal concepts (Reynell, 1977), but is unable to assimilate these same concepts when they are contained within a complex sentence (Mittler, 1972). Although the child may respond appropriately to phrases such as 'Where's the ball?', he can only understand the word 'ball'.

Noun-Noun Combinations

Between the ages of 2 and 2¼ years the child begins to relate two verbal concepts, eg 'Put the *biscuit* in the *tin*'. These concepts are nouns, as the child does not yet understand verbs, prepositions, adjectives etc.

Verbs

The child first learns to understand action verbs at 2½ years (Reynell, 1977; Berry, 1980). These early verbs reflect actions the child can carry out himself, eg run, sleep, walk; actions upon objects, eg hit, ride, push; and actions that produce changes in the child's environment, eg break, cut (Cole, 1982).

Verbs are perceptually more abstract than nouns, and therefore are more difficult for the child to learn. A noun represents an object that can be seen and manipulated, whereas verbs are without meaning unless there is a subject present to demonstrate its action.

The understanding of noun-verb combinations requires a greater degree of conceptualisation, and therefore occurs after the child is able to relate two noun concepts (Reynell, 1977).

Attribute and Spatial Relationships

Between the years 2½ and 4 the child's understanding rapidly expands to include a variety of adjectives and prepositions.

Attribute

The child needs to appreciate that attribute represents something that is not bound to any particular object or context (Clark, 1973). He needs to be able to recognise and distinguish different dimensions as a separate concept from that of the object. This conceptual development is helped by tasks that involve matching and sorting of objects by different dimensions, eg colour, shape, size. When he is able to perceive these differences, he is ready to learn the word. Language-impaired children may not learn attribute from everyday living and play, but need to be taught the relevant language alongside sorting and matching tasks, so that the association is made clear (Reynell, 1977).

As each child's experience is different, it is not possible to give a precise age by which different attribute terms are acquired. However, general terms, eg big/little, are learnt before more specific terms such as tall/short, wide/narrow and thick/thin. By 3 years old the child should know several colours, and by 4 years nearly all of them (Weiss and Lillywhite, 1981). More abstract terms such as hard, soft, rough, smooth are not learnt until 4½ years (Weiss and Lillywhite, 1981).

At 2 and 3 years the child perceives attributes as absolutes relative to himself, eg a big elephant and a small mouse. It is not until 4 years that he can appreciate that the attributes are not fixed but are determined by context, ie a mouse can be big as well as small.

There is some disagreement about how adjectives are learnt, some saying the child learns the 'positive pole' of the pair first, eg long, big, wide (Clark, 1973), and others that the more unusual term is learnt first (Greenfield and Smith, 1976). However, it seems that the child is not likely to learn both adjectives together (Cole, 1982).

Prepositions

The spatial terms of 'in', 'on' and 'under' are usually acquired before those of 'in front of', 'between' and 'below'. Again, it is important that children learn the concept of position before being taught the word. This way the child's understanding of the verbal concept does not become attached to a particular situation.

Pronouns

The understanding of pronouns develops at about 2½ years. By 3 years they are used appropriately in expressive language. 'I' (me, my, mine), 'you' (yours, your) and 'we' are learnt more easily as they relate directly to the speaker or the listener; whereas 'he', 'she' and 'they' are less fixed and are learnt later.

Tense

It is generally agreed that the past tense is understood before the future (Cromer, 1974) (*see also Chapter 5*). As the immediate past forms part of the child's experience, it is more easily learnt.

Guidelines to Remediation

1. Activities should be appropriate for the child's age and stage of development. Before attempting to teach verbal concepts, check that the child has the necessary prerequisite skills for that level (Reynell, 1980; Rieke et al, 1977). (*See 'Early Language Skills', Chapter 1.*)

2. Tasks should be adapted to suit the child's level of attention.

3. Activities should be modified to accommodate any sensory or physical problems. For instance, a physically handicapped child may have difficulty in pointing; a visually handicapped child may find scanning a problem.

4. Materials should reflect objects and events in the child's environment.

5. The child's interest can be maintained by varying materials and activities.

6. Assessment should establish where the breakdown of language is occurring. Goals and strategies can then be carefully planned, although it is necessary to be flexible and adjust to the day-to-day changes in the child's needs and responsiveness.

7. Language activities should take place in a natural communication situation.

8. Language goals should aim to fulfil the child's immediate needs in the environment.

9. Encourage different types of communicative interaction, eg question and answer, descriptive monologue.

10. Give the child lots of examples of the language structure you are teaching.

11. Speech should be clear with varied intonation. Key words should be emphasised, but speech should always follow a normal intonation pattern.

12. Language input should be adjusted to suit the child's verbal and cognitive abilities.

13. Model the task first for the child.

14. Decide how the child's errors will be dealt with (*see Introduction*).

15. Inappropriate behaviour should not be reinforced. The child should be taught that this is not acceptable by stopping the activity or withdrawing the child from the situation.

16. Record the child's progress (Gillham, 1979).

17. Help the child to evaluate his own progress (Berry, 1980).

Planning a Teaching Programme

1. When choosing materials for an activity it is important to consider the child's level of symbolic understanding. For example, miniature toys require a greater degree of symbolisation than real objects and therefore increase the complexity of the task for the child.

2. Materials should be within the child's field of vision so that language is taught in association with its referent.

3. The arrangement and number of items presented will be affected by the child's ability to scan. Start with two or three items and gradually increase them until you find the child's limit. It will be easier for him to locate smaller items in a large group if they are placed in the centre (Reynell, 1977).

4. The number of items presented at any one time will also be determined to a large extent by the child's memory skills. The child should first be allowed to play with new objects in order to familiarise himself with them. New objects should be introduced among familiar items, one at a time.

5. It is very important to monitor your language input to the child. The level of complexity is affected by:

  (i) introducing new vocabulary or abstract concepts.
  (ii) increasing the length of the command.
  (iii) increasing the amount of information contained within the sentence (Derbyshire Language Programme).
  (iv) the type of utterance, eg embedded sentences require a greater level of understanding.
  (v) the position of the key word or words, ie words at the end of a phrase are understood more easily.
  (vi) the novelty of the request—the child will be unable to use his own pragmatic knowledge to work out meanings, eg 'Put the doll on the chair' may be easier to understand than 'Put the doll under the carpet'.

6. When teaching a new language skill the following strategies may be used:

  (i) Before teaching a word make sure that the child understands the relevant concept. Show him how to match and sort items according to the concept.
  (ii) Accompany verbal commands with appropriate facial expression, gesture and eye gaze.

(iii) Place the key word or words near the end of the phrase, eg 'Where's the *biscuit*?'; 'Put the milk *in* the *cup*'.

(iv) Emphasise the key words with stress, but still retain the normal intonation patterns.

(v) Gain the child's attention before giving him a command, or making a request or statement.

(vi) When teaching a new verbal concept do not expect the child to understand it within a complex command. Activities can be modified so that the other words in the command become redundant. For example, when teaching 'under', give the child a toy bed and a small doll and ask him to 'Put the doll *under* the bed'. The child is not being asked to understand or remember the objects, but only the word 'under'.

(vii) Gradually reduce the number of cues until the child has to rely on verbal comprehension.

(viii) Give the child time to consolidate his new skill through practice and reinforcement. This means ensuring that the people in his daily environment encourage him to practise his new skills and also provide the necessary feedback and repetition of language; eg saying 'Yes, that's a *ball*', when the child fetches it on request.

(ix) In the normal communication situation, support through rewards and reinforcement does not occur systematically, so these should gradually be made more realistic.

(x) When the child is able to understand the verbal concept in isolation, it should be gradually introduced into longer and more complex commands, eg prepositions.

    (a) Give the child a toy bed, a toy table and a small doll. Ask him to 'Put the doll *under* the *table*'. He now has to assimilate the noun (representing location), ie 'the table', as well as the preposition, in order to carry out the command correctly.

    (b) Gradually increase the number of locations, eg 'bed', 'table', 'chair', 'bath'.

    (c) Next, introduce another subject by using a boy doll and a girl doll. At first keep the choice of locations to two or three. A command may be 'Put the *boy under* the *bed*'.

    (d) Gradually extend the number of subject choices, eg 'man', 'lady', 'boy', 'girl', and 'baby'. The child now has to assimilate several verbal concepts in order to carry out the command successfully.

    (e) Commands can be further extended and complexity increased by using attribute terms with the subject, eg 'the *big cat*', or place noun, eg 'in the *big, red* box'.

Generalisation of Comprehension Skills

It often happens that the skills taught do not transfer into the child's everyday communication. The child may have learnt a certain concept as specific to that situation and teacher. Therefore, it is essential to make sure that teaching is designed to facilitate transfer of the child's new skills to his everyday life.

1. Some children need to have a structured teaching situation in a one-to-one session with the teacher or with a small group of children. Thus distractions are reduced to a minimum and learning can take place in an optimum environment.

2. Materials should be varied so that the child does not learn to relate a word to only one particular object or event (Gillham, 1979), eg the word 'cup' can represent two or three non-identical cups, a toy cup, a miniature cup and a picture of a cup.

3. Language should be taught in a variety of contexts (Gillham, 1979), eg demonstrated as the item is used at mealtimes, during a pretend tea-party or while looking through a picture book.

4. Present the vocabulary you want to teach in a variety of sentence structures, eg a command, 'Give me the *ball*'; a request, '*Ball*, please', or a statement, 'This is a *ball*'. Be careful not to increase sentence complexity, however.

5. When a child first acquires a new skill, he needs time to consolidate his learning with lots of practice in games and play situations.

6. The home or classroom environment has many distractions and the child may find it difficult to maintain his new skills. Carry-over can be assisted in the following ways:

    (i) Involve the parent or classteacher where possible.

    (ii) Carry out activities in varied environments.

    (iii) Cues and strategies are used when the new skills are introduced into the home or classroom, even if these have been faded out in more structured teaching.

    (iv) The child will need praise and reinforcement for correct responses in the new setting, even though these may have been reduced in structured teaching.

    (v) The environment may have to be modified in order to provide the child with opportunities to practise his new skills.

    (vi) Cues, prompts, and rewards should be gradually faded out as the skill becomes established (Rieke, Lynch and Soltman, 1977).

ACTIVITIES FOR DEVELOPING THE COMPREHENSION OF SPOKEN LANGUAGE

First Verbal Labels

The first words taught to the child should reflect the objects and events that are familiar to him in his everyday environment. A vocabulary can be chosen by looking at each individual child's daily routines, favourite toys, food and pets and so on. Early words should have few syllables and be general in their reference, rather than specific, eg dog rather than spaniel, as these are usually understood and remembered more easily.

The child needs to hear the verbal label in association with its referent many times and in a variety of contexts (Gillham, 1979). At first accompany commands with lots of visual and contextual cues, gradually reducing these till the child is relying on verbal comprehension alone. The verbal label should be at the end of the phrase and emphasised, eg 'Where's the *dog*?'. The rest of the information in the phrase should be redundant as the child can only assimilate one verbal concept at this stage.

1. Food

  (i) During mealtimes talk about the food the child is eating, drawing his attention to each item as you name it clearly. When offering him a choice of things to eat, hold them up and name them, eg 'Do you want milk?'—showing him the milk, or 'Do you want orange?'—showing him the orange. Let the child experience hearing the food names in different situations.

 (ii) Take the child shopping with you and talk about what you are going to buy. Let him watch and perhaps help if he can, while you prepare his meal.

(iii) Make pretend food with the child out of plasticine, papier mâché etc. Choose his favourite foods as a model.

(iv) Use the child's models in a shopping game. A good make-believe shop has shelves and a table for a counter, or use a commercial toy shop, eg *Superstore*[4]. The child and teacher or a group of children can take it in turns to be the shopper and the shopkeeper. Give the child a bag to collect his purchases in, and tell him what to buy, eg 'Get me some cake'.

 (v) Give the child a pretend tea-party with his friends or some of his favourite toys. Use toy food, naming it as you play.

(vi) Keep a daily diary with the child by recording the events of the day in pictures. Meals can be photographed, drawn by the teacher or the child can look through magazines for pictures. However, there should not be too long a gap between the event and recording it.

2. Clothes

  (i) Name pieces of clothing as you dress and undress the child. Also name your own clothing, eg 'Look, I'm putting on my *hat*'.

 (ii) Let the child help you to tidy up by putting clothes in the drawers or the washing basket. Give him one article of clothing and name it, eg 'Now, the *coat*'. Later give him a choice of two or three articles and ask him to put one away.

(iii) Play dressing-up games using silly hats and colourful clothes. Take one item and put it on saying, 'Look, I'm wearing a *hat*'. Then give it to the child, again naming it—'Sammy's got a *hat*'. Use a mirror and have lots of fun posing. Move on to giving him a choice of articles and ask him to choose one.

(iv) The child can dress large or miniature dolls, or put paper clothes on cardboard cut-out figures. Authentic outfits for African and Indian dolls are contained in *Ethnic Dolls' Clothes*[4]. Show the child what to do with the clothes and name them as you dress the doll. Let the child join and talk about what he is doing (Derbyshire Language Programme).

 (v) A washing line can be hung in the play corner and washing-day can be acted out by the teacher. As she pegs up the clothes she names them for the child. They can be real clothes, dolls' clothes, or cut-outs made from stiff card. The child can join in and perhaps be given instructions by a doll or puppet, eg 'Hang up my sock'.

3. Toys

  (i) As you play with the child at bath-time, in the sandpit or in the play corner, name the toys you are playing with. Let the child have different variations of the same toy, eg three different dollies, so he learns that the word 'dolly' is not just for his favourite doll. Show him that the dolls can be used for the same things, eg cuddling, dressing and feeding, and that they look, feel and move in the same way.

 (ii) As you tidy toys away or get them out for play, hand them to the child and name each one. Ask the child to fetch toys from his play box. If he doesn't understand find the toy for him and show it to him.

Make his toy box into a giant posting box by cutting a hole in the side. You can make the hole into the mouth of a funny face. Let him tidy his toys by posting them through the hole, eg 'Put away *Teddy*'.

(iii) Make a picture book of the child's favourite toys out of real photographs, drawings or cuttings from magazines. Look through the book naming each picture for the child; then ask him to find the one you name.

(iv) Hide a few of the child's toys around the room; as he finds each one, name it. Next, hide two or three toys and ask him to find one, eg 'Where's *Teddy*?'.

4. Everyday Objects

  (i) During the day talk about the objects you or the child are using. Choose those objects that are very familiar to the child, eg spoon, cup, brush, soap.

(ii) Play pretend games that involve these real objects or toy replicas. Spoons, cups and plates can be used in make-believe tea parties, and brushes, combs, soap and flannel can be used to give dolly and teddy a 'wash-'n'-brush-up'. Talk about the objects as you play with them and ask the child to give you different ones.

(iii) Put a few familiar items in an opaque bag and say 'I'm going to find *my* cup'. Put your hand into the bag, draw out the cup and exclaim with great surprise, 'Look, a cup'. Hand the bag to the child and ask him to find a named object. If he finds it difficult then go through all the objects in the bag, naming them as you pull them out. When you've finished, put them back into the bag and let the child try again. (Start with two or three objects and gradually increase the number.)

(iv) Early pegboard puzzles have pieces showing different objects, eg *First Lift-Out Puzzle* [3]. Name them as the child takes the pieces out. You can ask for specific pieces and either let the child put them in or do it yourself.

OBJECT PELMANISM

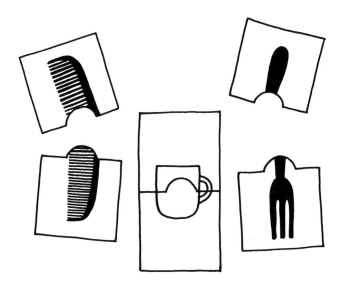

(v) Play a simpler version of pelmanism with two-piece puzzles of everyday objects. Place two or three of the puzzles face up on the table and show the child each picture, naming it for him. Then break up the pieces and mix them up keeping the pictures in view. Ask the child to find the 'comb' etc. If he doesn't respond then match up the pieces for him, and when you find the right combination exclaim, 'Look, a comb'. Ask the child to find another object.

5. Animals

(i) Point out different animals to the child when out walking, repeating their names for him.

(ii) Arrange lots of outings to see animals in the zoo or at a farm. There are many 'city farms' now, so even the urban child is able to see country animals. He can help feed some of the tame animals and perhaps stroke or even ride on them!

(iii) Once the child has met the real animals, help him find pictures of them in books, eg *Old MacDonald had a Farm*.

(iv) Animals are a favourite theme for early puzzles. Use them as in 4 (iv) above.

(v) Draw the child pictures of animals you have seen on outings and then ask him to draw one for you. He can choose an animal shape from *Galt Creative Templates* [4] to draw round or to trace over, and then you choose one for him.

6. Transport

(i) There are lots of opportunities during the day to point out different vehicles to the child. Use simple names, like bus, car or train. The excitement of a ride in a bus or a train will help him to remember these words.

(ii) Play with toy cars, buses, etc in pretend garages or along paper roadways. Push the toys along, naming them and making the appropriate noises, eg 'Look at my train—ch-ch-ch-ch'.

(iii) Use puzzles in the same way as in 4 (iv), but make sure the vehicles depicted are familiar to the child.

7. Generalisation

The child's learning can be reinforced and practised through the following games. Suitable pictures can be obtained from *All-purpose Photo Library* [2] and Winslow Press *ColorCards* and *ColorLibraries* [6].

(i) Give the child a picture cube of *Soft Blocks* [4] and ask him to find a specific picture.

(ii) Place object pictures around the outside of a circular board which has a spinning arrow. Ask the child to point the arrow to a picture.

(iii) Make a toy fish-pond by folding a long strip of card three times to form a box. A fishing rod can be made from a short stick and a piece of string with a magnet attached. Fish can be cut from cardboard, with object pictures pasted on, or just use picture cards. Slip a paper clip on each one to attract the magnet. Ask the child to 'catch' different objects.

FISH POND

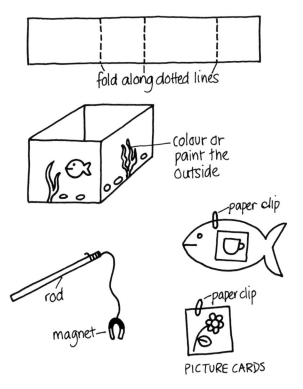

fold along dotted lines

colour or paint the outside

paper clip

rod

magnet

paper clip

PICTURE CARDS

(iv) *Lotto Games*: give the child a lotto card and keep the pack of matching individual cards. Name the pictures, eg 'Have your got a *dog*?' If the child has the picture and recognises its name he gets the card. (This game is more exciting in a group, as the children can see who is first to complete their card.)

(v) *Happy Families*: each child is given a card from one category, eg fruit. This is the master card which depicts all the members of the family, eg pear, apple, banana, orange. The teacher has matching individual cards from which she takes one and asks, 'Who's got an *orange*?' The winner is the first to complete his family.

HAPPY FAMILIES

See also activities for body parts (*page 53*).

Relating Two Verbal Concepts (Noun-Noun)

A child may be able to respond appropriately to the command 'Sit dolly on the chair' at this stage, but he does not understand the words 'sit' and 'on'. He is merely relating the two objects in the most usual way, and would probably make the same response to the command, 'Stand dolly under the chair'.

When deciding on an activity make sure the child is familiar with the vocabulary, and that phrases only contain two information-carrying words, ie two verbal labels. Show the child how you want him to relate the objects by modelling the activity or allowing him to use his own pragmatic knowledge, as in the above example.

1. (i) Roll a ball gently to teddy, telling the child what you are doing, eg 'Look, I'm rolling the *ball* to *teddy*'. Draw his attention to the objects as you name them.
   (ii) Replace teddy with a second toy, eg a dolly, and repeat the activity.
   (iii) Using both toys, roll the ball to one or the other, again commenting on what you are doing.
   (iv) Give the ball to the child and ask him to roll it to either teddy or dolly. Point to the right toy if he needs help.
   (v) Replace the ball with a car and repeat steps (iii) and (iv).

(vi) Give both the toys to the child and ask him to roll one of them to either dolly or teddy. Again, help him if necessary. At this point the child needs to understand both nouns in order to follow the command.

(vii) As the child becomes more confident, gradually increase the choice of toys.

Follow the above teaching hierarchy in the following activities.

2. Make several posting-boxes with different painted faces, eg clown, dog, cat, and give the child an assortment of objects to post, eg 'Put the *ball* in the *clown*!'

POSTING BOX

child posts toy into mouth

3. Put some toys, eg *Ready Teddy Go-Boat* [3], *Glug-Glug Tug/Plane* [4], in a water-tray and ask the children to push them to each other, eg 'Push the *boat* to *John*'.

4. Set out the child's favourite toys and dollies for a tea party, and give the child instructions about handing out crockery or pretend food, eg 'Give *dolly* some *cake*'.

5. A group of children can play hide and seek. One child leaves the room while another is told where to hide an object, eg 'Hide the *ball* in the *box*'.

6. Collect some old clothes for the children to play a dressing-up game. The teacher gives instructions, eg 'Mary, give *Paul* the *scarf*'.

7. Children love playing with miniature people and animals, *Pegmen* [4], dolls' houses, miniature parks, farms and zoos. Pegmen can be put into a *Charabanc*, *Fire-engine*, *Round-about*, *Merry-go-round*, *Whirling chairs* or *seesaw*, all made by Galt Toys.

8. During daily routines, eg tidying up toys and clothes, at mealtimes or bath-time, children can be given the opportunity to hear phrases containing two verbal concepts, eg 'Put the *soap* in the *bath*'.

Verbs

Verbs are more difficult to learn than object-labels (Reynell, 1977) so the child needs lots of repetition of the relevant language. Talk about actions as they occur, so that the association between action and word is made clear.

Action Verbs

Start with action-verbs that do not involve an object, as these are easier for the child to understand. They describe movements, such as running, sleeping and jumping, which the child can carry out himself.

1. (i) During PE or physical play, talk about what you or the child is doing, eg 'Look, I'm *jumping*'.
   (ii) Carry out an action and ask the child to join in, saying 'Let's *jump*. We're *jumping*' emphasising the action word.
   (iii) Ask the child to do the action. If he hesitates or makes a wrong response, repeat the action and the word again.

2. Sing nursery rhymes or action songs while carrying out the actions with the child. Later, let the child do the actions alone, while you sing the song.

3. 'O'Grady' or 'Simple Simon Says': at first do the actions with the child and later just give him the commands.

4. Set up an obstacle course and talk about what the child is doing, as he makes his way through the course. Next time, ask him to carry out specific commands as he comes to each obstacle, eg '*Climb* over the boxes'; '*Run* round the table'.

5. Describe the child's actions as he plays with dolls, and say, 'Look, dolly's *running*' etc. Ask the child to show you different actions with the doll.

6. In a group, give each child several 'Action-Pictures'. Ask each child to mime one of the actions and see if the other children can identify the right picture. Hold up the correct picture and say, 'Yes, Mary is *jumping*'.

7. *Logic People* [4]: these are brightly-coloured plastic figures that are standing, running, walking and sitting, which can be used for teaching action verbs in the same way as the above activities.

8. Collect together puzzles that have lift-out pieces, showing people carrying out actions. Show the child the different pictures, describing each one, eg 'The boy's running'. Ask the child to take out the pieces.

9. Look through picture books and talk about the different actions of the characters. Ask the child to find the different pictures.

Action-upon-object Verbs

These are verbs that describe an action on an object, eg hitting (a ball) and pushing (the door).

1. During play activities, show the child how different toys can be moved, talking about what is happening. Give the toy to the child and describe his play. There are a number of toys that are good for teaching specific verbs.
   (i) *Humpty Dumpty* [3]: when the lever is touched, the coloured cones jump off the rod. This is useful for teaching 'push', 'go' and 'press'.
   (ii) *Jack-in-the-Ball* [4]: this toy can be rolled along the ground, and when a button is pressed Jack pops out ('push', 'roll').
   (iii) Dolls can be 'wiped', 'brushed', 'combed' and 'dried' etc.

2. Place several different toys and objects in front of the child, eg rattle, ball, balloon, wheeled toy, car. Choose one action and carry it out on all the suitable toys, describing what you are doing, eg 'I'm rolling the balloon; now I'm rolling the *ball*'. This teaches the child that an action is not specific to any one object.

   After lots of similar examples, use the toys in a game. A group of children could play at passing toys to each other, using the method chosen by the teacher, eg. '*Roll* the ball to *Tim*'.

3. Playground and park equipment provides a medium for such actions, eg the child can be pushed on the swing, lifted on to the seesaw and caught off the slide. Tell the child what you are doing, eg 'I'm *pushing* you'; 'I'll *catch* you!'.

4. Ball games are useful for teaching verbs such as 'throw', 'catch', 'kick', 'roll', 'bounce', 'chase' etc (but use sponge balls, beanbags or soft toys for safety's sake).

5. Talk about the child's actions on food in cookery, eg 'stirring', 'beating', 'cutting'; or on clay and plasticine in craftwork, eg 'squeezing', 'rolling', 'stretching', 'cutting'.

6. Gather together lots of junk materials, eg string, elastic, plasticine, cardboard boxes. Explore the different actions you can perform on one object, eg plasticine can be rolled into a sausage, pulled into a long snake, squeezed into a round ball, cut into shapes. Discuss what you are doing. Choose another item upon which the child can perform the same activities.

7. Make up several picture books of separate actions in the following way. On each page draw a picture of a person carrying out an action, eg kicking a ball, varying the drawing slightly so that as the pages are flicked through the figure appears to move. (Note: the pages should be flicked from back to front.)

SEQUENCE OF ACTIONS

Front page   Last page

Attribute Verbs

These verbs describe a change in physical state, eg 'break', 'clean', 'cook', 'melt'. The child needs to have first-hand experience of these concepts and plenty of repetition of the related language.

Example: 'Melting'

1. In cooking, show the child how different foods melt when heated, eg butter, chocolate, sugar.

2. During winter bring in a cup of snow and let the children watch as it melts.

3. Place an ice cube on top of a radiator, on a table and outside on the window sill. Let the children compare how long each one takes to melt.

4. In winter help the children build a snowman. Each day they can check to see how much it has melted.

5. Read the children a story about a snowman who melted in the sunshine.

Understanding Object Functions

Give the child lots of experience of seeing how different objects are used and help him to use them himself. Talk about what you are doing with objects during play and everyday activities, eg 'Look, the *scissors* are *cutting* the paper'.

1. (i) Put a selection of objects on the table. Pick up one of them, eg soap and mime its use. Say, 'Look, some *soap*. You *wash* with soap'. Then choose another object and this time encourage the child to do the mime with you, saying, 'Yes, that's right, you *eat* with a *fork*', etc.

(ii) When you have done this with all the objects, see if the child can mime their functions on his own.

(iii) Ask him for one of the objects, eg 'Find me something you *drink* with', emphasising the word and miming the function. If he has difficulty, show him the correct item, again miming and naming its function.

(iv) When he is able to do this, ask him the same things without using gestures.

Once the child can identify objects by use, generalise with the following activities.

2. *Lotto Games:* each child in a small group is given a lotto card and the teacher has the matching individual cards. She takes one card at a time and names the functions of the object, eg 'something you *cut* with'. The winner is the first to complete his card.

3. Place object pictures around a circular board that has a spinning arrow in its centre. Ask the child to point the arrow at different objects that you have identified by use.

4. Hide object-picture cards around the room. Ask the child to find them, eg 'Find me something you *cook* with'.

5. Make a scrapbook with the child and ask him to find pictures in magazines or catalogues, identifying them only by use, eg 'something you *draw* with'.

6. Puzzles that have clear lift-out pieces of objects can be used in a similar way to the above.

7. The same basic activity can be carried out during play sequences and the child's daily routines.

Prepositions

Not all prepositions are learnt at the same age so the child's general comprehension abilities should be established before deciding on which ones to teach first.

The expressive chapter has some activities for eliciting specific prepositions, eg on, off, and in, and these can be adapted for aiding their understanding.

1. Start with activities that involve gross motor movements, eg PE, active play or an obstacle course. The following equipment provides lots of opportunities for practising prepositions:

climbing frames: up/down/off/on top of
slide: up/down
seesaw: up/down/on
chairs and tables: on/under/over/next to
large boxes: in/behind/in front of/beside
Play tunnels [4]: through/in
benches: along/over/on/off
ladders: up/down/along
hoops: in/over

(i) Demonstrate the meaning of two contrasting prepositions. Talk about what you are doing and emphasise the key word, eg 'Look, I'm *under* the table'.

(ii) Help the child to carry out actions that demonstrate the same two prepositions and describe what he does.

(iii) Ask the child to carry out actions for you, at first using gesture to help the child understand. Keep the location constant so he has to understand only the preposition.

(iv) Gradually reduce the cues until the child is relying on his verbal comprehension.

Practise the two prepositions in the following activities.

2. Sing nursery rhymes or songs that involve prepositions, eg Ring-a-ring-a-roses—'we all fall *down*'. Do the actions with the child at first but later see if he can do them by himself at the right verbal cue.

3. During the day try to incorporate prepositions into what you say to the child, eg while tidying up, ask the child to put toys in specified places, eg '*under* the bed', '*in* the cupboard'. If he doesn't understand, take the toy and the child to the right place and say 'Look, *under* the bed'.

4. Stories can be modified to give lots of practice of one preposition, eg 'Snow White hid *under* the table'; '*under* the bed'; '*under* the chair'.

5. Play hide-and-seek with a group of children. One is sent out of the room while another is told to hide a toy, eg '*under* the flowerpot'.

6. Give instructions to put out items for a pretend shop, eg 'Put the coffee *under* the counter'.

7. Using miniature dolls and objects, arrange a scene out of sight of the child, eg a man in a bed, or a cat on a chair, or a boy behind a wardrobe. The child is given a duplicate set and instructed how to set it up. When he has finished he can compare it with the teacher's model. (Suitable equipment includes *Playmobile* [4], *Pegmen* [4], toy farms, zoos, garages and plastic animals.)

Later you can set up a complete room with several dolls, but continue to give the child one doll and one piece of furniture at a time, so that only the preposition needs to be understood. By the time he has finished, the child should have a complete copy of the teacher's model.

8. Describe a picture to a child who has to recreate it using *Fuzzy felt* [4], *Cellograph* (produced by Philip and Tacey) or *Uniset Boards* [1].

9. Tell a story around a picture scene, eg a small mouse hiding from a big, bad cat. The child has a cardboard mouse which he moves around the board as the story is told, eg 'The little mouse hid *under* the table'. It will help the child if you perhaps tell the story first, moving the mouse for him, before asking him to join in (Derbyshire Language Programme).

10. Draw pictures of a chair, table and bed. Ask the child to draw a ball under the table, on the bed etc.

Attribute Terms

At first children can only understand attributes by comparing them to themselves, eg an elephant is big and a mouse is small. It is not until later that they can understand gradations in size, eg you can have a big mouse and a small mouse. Children learn the more general terms, big and little, before specific ones such as thick and thin (Cole, 1982).

There is some disagreement among researchers about how children learn attributes (*see page 43*). In the following activities, attributes have been presented in pairs, but the reader can adapt the activities to his own teaching preference. At first give the child materials that have very obvious perceptual differences along the dimension you are teaching.

Size

Big/Little

1. Make two boxes, one big and one small. When tidying up toys with the child, say 'Look, I'm putting teddy in the *big* box', as you drop it in. Give a toy to the child and say 'Put it in the *big* box', pointing to the appropriate one. Later, see if the child can put it in the right box without cues.

2. Use two different-sized dollies or teddies in a pretend tea party. Take a cup and say to the child 'I'm giving the cup to *big* teddy', putting the cup in front of the big teddy. After lots of examples, give an item to the child and ask *him* to give it to the 'big teddy', etc.

3. Play a dressing-up game with different-sized articles of clothing. Name the items as you put them on, then try them on the child, 'Look at my *big* hat'. Ask the child to put on different-sized clothing, helping him if he still doesn't understand. When the child is able to follow verbal commands he can compete with another child in a dressing-race, with the teacher giving instructions, eg 'Put on a *big* hat'.

4. Give the child two dolls of different sizes and ask him to dress them, eg 'Put the *big* doll's hat on'.

5. Put out some big and small hoops for PE and ask the child to stand in 'the *big* hoop' or 'the *small* hoop'.

6. Construct an obstacle course so that the child has a choice of different-sized obstacles, eg a big table and a small table. Direct the child through the course, eg 'Next, the *big* cushion'.

7. Using puzzles that depict different-sized objects, ask the child to take out the pieces.

8. Place different-sized pairs of objects in an opaque bag; ask the child to 'Find the *big* brush', etc.

9. Make up funny faces using pieces of coloured felt for the nose, eyes, ears and mouth. Give the child directions about making a face, eg 'a *big* nose'; 'a *small* ear'. (Derbyshire Language Programme.)

10. Ask the child to draw or colour big or small objects.

11. Cut out different-sized animals and a cage from stiff card. Stick the border of the cage on to a backing card, leaving one side unstuck to form a pocket. Ask the child to slip one of the animals into the cage, eg 'Put the *big* lion in the cage'.

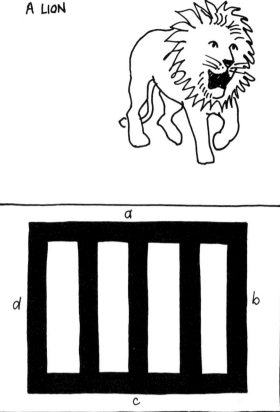

CARDBOARD CUT-OUT OF A LION

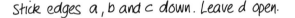

Stick edges a, b and c down. Leave d open.

Other ideas are: dogs and kennel; fish and pond; cars and garage; cakes and oven; children and bed. (Adapted from an idea in the Derbyshire Language Programme).

Length

Long/Short

1. Collect together pairs of everyday objects that vary in length. Show the child each object, describing it to him, eg 'Look, a *long* pencil', and putting it with the other long or short objects as appropriate. Ask the child to put away each object, saying 'Now, the *short* ribbon', pointing to it if necessary.

2. During constructional or creative play, talk about what the child has made, eg 'Well done, that's a *long* snake'. Copy the child's snake, making it shorter. Compare your model with his, eg 'I've made a *short* snake; yours is a *long* snake', drawing his attention to the difference in length with your finger.

3. Form a large group of children into two lines. Arrange them so that one line is long and the other is short and point this out to the children. Ask each line to carry out instructions, eg 'The *long* line, hop!' and join in with them (Dowling, 1980).

4. During doll-play, talk about articles of clothing that are different lengths, eg 'Look at dolly's *long* ribbon', holding it up for the child to see. Tell the child to dress dolly in different clothing, eg 'Put on her *long* scarf'. (Make sure there are paired items of clothing that differ in length, so that the child needs to make a choice.)

5. Ask the child to draw a long train, a short snake, etc, or to colour in your drawings, eg 'Colour the *long* snake'.

6. In a group, talk about the different lengths of children's hair, arms, legs, hands and feet. Compare and talk about the differences between two children, eg 'Look, Jane has *long* hair, and John has *short* hair' (Dowling, 1980).

7. Using musical instruments that can maintain a note, eg recorders and whistles, play a long note, and then a short note. Say to the child 'Listen. This is a *long* note', etc. After lots of examples, ask the child to play a long or a short note. (*Fun with Sounds*[1] set illustrates the concepts of long and short.)

Height

Tall/Short

1. Compare the different heights of children in a group. Talk about the differences in height of two children, eg 'Paul is *tall*, and David is *short*'. Ask the children to point out somebody who is tall, etc.

2. Take the children into the playground or the park and point out the different heights of objects, eg 'Look, a *tall* tree', or 'a *tall* house'.

3. Look through picture books and talk about the different heights of the characters. Ask the child to find you different pictures.

4. Ask the child to draw or colour pictures of tall and short people, trees, etc.

Weight

Heavy/Light

1. Collect together objects of different weights; for instance, let the child hold a piece of paper and a very heavy book. Say 'This paper is *light*. This book is *heavy*'. Repeat this with lots of different objects. Then ask him to find something heavy. Help him if he hesitates or makes the wrong response.

2. During cooking activities, let the child compare different foods by weighing them in his hands. Talk about their different weights as he holds them.

3. Play games where different people and toys sit on the child's lap. Ask him if they are light or heavy. Make a joke of it and bounce up and down.

Texture

Hard/Soft; Rough/Smooth

1. Gather together a group of objects and let the children feel their different surfaces. Taking an object, let one child at a time feel it and say 'It's *hard*', etc.
    Suitable items are:

    fruit or vegetables: plum, banana, raspberry
    different materials: silk, net, denim
    different toys: building bricks, teddy, ball
    everyday objects: spoon, brush, cup
    cooking ingredients: dough, flour, sugar, lentils, cereals

2. Ask the children to collect items of a certain texture, eg 'Find me things that feel *soft*'. Talk about the things with the children, letting them feel them. Put the items on a touch table.

3. Get the children to draw the objects they have collected and put them in a picture book. Look through the book with the children, talking about the different pictures.

4. Take the children on a 'touch walk'. As they feel different things, talk about their texture, eg 'Yes the leaf is *smooth*' (Dowling, 1980).

5. Place different textured items in a feelie bag and ask the child to find something, soft, hard, etc.

6. Collect many different kinds of material and ask the children to group them by texture. Stick them into a scrap book or make a collage.

7. Bake sweets, cakes and biscuits, etc and let the child compare them before and after cooking. (If you are lucky enough to have access to a kiln, you can do the same with clay.)

Sounds

Loud/Soft; Loud/Quiet; High/Low

1. Put out a selection of musical instruments and let the children hear and play each one. Take an instrument and play a loud sound, saying 'It's *loud*'. Then make a soft sound, and say 'It's *soft*'. Do the same with the other instruments. After lots of examples, ask the child to make different noises. If necessary make the sound first for him. (Use the same method for other pairs of adjectives.)

2. Fill bottles with different amounts of water and talk about the different sounds they make as the child blows into each one. Take two bottles that are distinctive in sound and ask the child to make 'a *loud* sound' etc.

3. Take the children on a 'listening walk'. Talk about the different sounds you can hear, eg 'Can you hear the car? It's *loud*'. Ask the children to tell you something that makes a loud noise, etc.

4. Ask the children to collect items that make a loud sound. In a group make a noise with each one, saying 'Yes, that's a *loud* noise', etc. Get the children to draw the objects and put them in a book. Do the same for soft sounds, etc.

5. Use the objects the children have collected to make a sound table.

6. *Fun with Sounds*[1] set: includes the concepts of high and low, loud and soft, long and short. (*See also Chapter 6.*)

Colour Labels

Start off with a few primary colours.
    During matching and sorting tasks colours should be named clearly so that words are taught as the concept is learned (Reynell, 1977).

1. During the day talk about the colour of different items that the child is using or is in contact with, eg clothes, food, pencils, toys, pictures, furniture, soap.

2. Tidying up: ask the child to put away articles by colour, eg 'the red pencil', or use different-coloured 'tidy boxes'.

3. In PE place different coloured hoops on the floor. Ask the child to 'jump into the *blue* hoop', etc.

4. Set up an obstacle course with mats, chairs, tables, benches, etc and put large coloured paper on each of the obstacles. Give the child directions that involve understanding colour, eg 'Run round the *blue* table', 'Run round the *red* table'.

5. Ask the child to go round the room collecting objects of one colour, and help him make a collage table.

6. Hide-and-seek: one child leaves the room while another is told to hide an object, eg the red brick.

7. Dressing-up: put a pile of clothes on the floor. Two children can compete to put on clothes that the teacher has described, eg 'a blue glove'.

8. *Logic People*[4]: give instructions to the child about setting out the figures.

9. Drawing: ask the child to draw a red picture, etc.

10. Using gummed paper shapes, ask the child to sort them into colours; then help him to make a picture collage.

11. *Lotto Games*: use cards that show different coloured items. Each child has a lotto card and the teacher has a pack of individual cards. She asks, 'Has anyone got a *blue* bag' etc.

12. Use constructional toys that have different coloured pieces that can slot together, eg *Slot-o-build*[1]; *Reo-click*; *Disco Shapes*[1]. Give the child instructions about which pieces to fit together.

13. There are lots of board games that require an understanding of colour.

Body Parts

1. When you are dressing or bathing the child, name the different parts of the body. He will learn the names of larger parts of the body first, eg arm, leg, hand.

2. Look in the mirror together, point out different parts of his body and name them. Then point to the same parts of your body, eg 'There's your nose, and here's my nose'.

3. Draw his attention to different parts of his body at bath-time by dabbing it with soap or blowing bubbles on to it (though not in the eyes or mouth!). Name them at the same time.

4. During PE or at playtime, name the parts of the body. Play chase games that involve just one part of the body, eg 'I'm going to get your *arm*' (Derbyshire Language Programme).

5. Play a silly dressing-up game by putting articles of clothing on the wrong parts of the body, eg a sock on your hand. Make comments about what you are doing and ask the child if it is right. See if he can point to the correct body part. If he can put the article on the appropriate part, name it for him.
   Give the child a piece of clothing, eg a sock, and ask him to put it on his head or hand, etc.

6. Paint the child's hands, feet, knees and elbows so he can make prints on paper. As you paint each part, name it.

7. Play 'O'Grady' or 'Simple Simon Says'. At first point to each part of the body as you name it; but later just give the command and see if the child is correct.

8. Sing rhymes and songs about body parts to the child, pointing to the different parts as you sing them. See if the child can carry out the actions alone as you sing to him.

9. During play with dolls, name the different body parts, eg 'Wash dolly's face'; 'Wash dolly's ears', etc (Derbyshire Language Programme).

10. There are a number of commercially produced puzzles for learning about parts of the body. Help the child put the puzzles together, naming the pieces for him and relating them to his own body. Ask the child to show you different body parts on the puzzle.

11. Tell the child to carry out actions involving different parts of the body, eg getting up from the floor without using the hands (Dowling, 1980).

12. Draw a picture of a boy or a girl and ask the child to colour in the different parts.

13. Give the child an outline of a boy or girl and ask him to fill in the missing parts.

14. Draw a set of pictures of a boy or girl, omitting different parts. Ask the child to find you the picture 'with no *arm*', etc. Let him finish the drawing as a reward.

15. Look in a mirror so that the children can compare parts of their bodies that are the same, eg the same-coloured eyes, and the same length of hair.

16. Talk about what you can do with different parts of the body.

17. Older children can make up a matrix which compares the similarities between members of the group. One axis could be hair length and the other eye colour.

eg

	long	medium	short
brown	Mary		Sam
blue		John Peter	
green	Tim	Pat	David

18. Look at pictures of animals and discuss which body parts are common to both animals and humans, and which are not. Compare the different vocabulary, eg 'hand' and 'paw'; 'nose' and 'beak' (Dowling, 1980).

Emotions

1. Tell stories about children who are happy, sad or excited, etc. As you talk about how they feel, show the children their faces in the pictures, eg 'Look, this boy is *happy*, he's *smiling*'.

2. Encourage the children to talk about special events that have happened at home or at school, eg a party. Ask the children how they felt and why they felt that way. A special time can be put aside for this.

3. Make a picture-story book to illustrate the event that made him feel particularly sad or happy. Get him to draw his own face.

4. Collect together lots of pictures of faces from magazines, etc. Try to pick those that express a clear emotion, eg a clown laughing; a baby crying. Show them to the children and discuss what makes the face look happy or sad. Ask them why they think the people feel that way.

5. Put some of the pictures on the table and ask one of the children to find a certain expression, eg 'the *angry* face'. Ask him to mime the feeling.

6. Play lots of acting and miming games. Using props, such as masks, stage make-up or face paints, will help the children to express themselves. Children can pretend to be characters from stories.

7. Lay out several pictures of different facial expressions and play a tape of laughing, crying, shouting, etc. Can the children match the sounds to the pictures?

8. Make cards showing different scenes and a set of smaller cards depicting different facial expressions. See if the children can match the faces to the scenes, eg a happy face to a birthday party; a sad face to a car accident.

9. Ask the children to draw different faces or to make masks that are happy, angry or sad.

10. Help the child to make a scrapbook of different emotions. Weave stories around the pictures.

11. *Photographic Language Lotto* [4]: shows different facial expressions and body postures.

Pronouns

Before introducing pronouns, use the children's proper names and lots of gestures, eg '*Paul*, put the book away', pointing to Paul as you name him. Then include the pronouns, still using proper names to help the child understand, eg 'Paul, *you* put the book away', pointing to Paul as you emphasise the word 'you'. Gradually reduce the cues, but continue to give plenty of models and to emphasise the pronouns in your own speech (Cole, 1982).

Personal Pronouns

1. Ask questions and give commands that emphasise pronouns during everyday routines.

2. Read the child a story about a girl or a boy, or both, stressing the pronouns, eg 'Mary went to the shops, and Paul—*he* went to the park'. Then ask questions, eg 'Where did *he* go?', using pictures to help the child remember.

3. Daily diary: the events of the day at school, or in the evening at home, can be recorded in a diary in pictures, or a few words written by the teacher or parent. A special time can be set aside to hear different children talking about their diary. The teacher can reiterate the child's news using pronoun forms, and then ask the children questions about it, again using pronouns, eg 'What did Kelly do at the weekend? She went to the . . . . [park]. Where else did she go?'

  Make your own diary too, so that you can model the pronouns, 'I', 'we', 'my', 'our', etc.

Possessive Pronouns

1. During the day model the structures for the child using proper nouns and gestural cues, as above, eg 'Put it in *his* drawer, *Paul's* drawer'—pointing to Paul as you emphasise the pronoun.

2. Ask the children to bring in their favourite toys and books, and photographs of their family and pets, to talk about. Afterwards, the teacher talks about the different contributions, providing lots of examples of possessive pronouns, eg 'Peter's brought some photos of his family—this is *his* Dad, this is *his* Mum', etc. Lift up a photo of somebody else's Mum and ask, 'Is this *his* Mum?', pointing to Peter.

3. Show the children a composite picture with either a boy or girl character. Ask the children to show you 'his nose', 'his shoes', 'his dog' or 'her hair', 'her ball', etc. Then make a picture showing both the boy and the girl with similar possessions. Now, when you ask the questions the child must understand the possessives in order to make the correct responses.

4. Set up a pretend tea party and give directions about putting out the crockery and food, eg 'Put the cake on *my* plate'; 'Put the tea in *your* cup'.

5. Give the children commands involving possessive pronouns when tidying up or putting out an activity, eg 'Put the pencils on *my* desk'; 'Put the paint on *your* desk'.

6. Using a doll's house and some furniture, give the child commands, eg 'Put the bed in *my* room'. Make sure the child is clear that one room is yours, and one room is his (adapted from a Derbyshire Language Programme idea).

Tense

The child first needs to understand that actions and events occur in a sequential order, before he can begin to understand the concept of time (Cole, 1982). Give the child routines and help him recreate them with sequenced pictures, eg washing, having breakfast.

1. Sequencing pictures (Winslow Press *Basic Sequences; Sequencing Treasure Chest* [6]): as an alternative you can make your own. Start off with a simple sequence of two cards, eg tree upright/tree cut down; whole biscuit/half-eaten biscuit. Introduce sequences with three pictures, showing the child the first picture if he has difficulty.

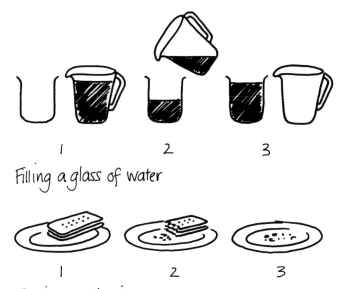

Filling a glass of water

Eating a biscuit

  When the child can understand that actions or events can be linked in time, he is ready to learn tense. Studies have found that understanding of the past tense appears before that of the future tense (Cromer, 1974). The following activities can be used to teach all tense forms.

2. Provide the child with set routines and talk about what the child is doing, what he has done and what he is going to do.

3. During play, talk about the child's actions, eg tell the child to stand on a box and ask him 'Are you going to jump?' As he jumps off, say 'You're jumping'. Then ask him 'What did you do—you jumped' (Berry, 1980).

4. Keep a daily diary with the child. Each day talk about what the child did yesterday and what he will do tomorrow.

5. Read the child a story that involves time. Ask the child questions, eg 'What did the boy do?', 'What happened yesterday?'

Extending the Older Child's Language Experience

Many children with language handicaps still have a limited vocabulary in later years, and need to be given the opportunity to expand their language experience. Some of these activities are based on ideas in *Early Projects* by Marion Dowling.

The Family

1. Ask the children to bring in photographs of their family. Talk about the different jobs their parents have. Compare the ages, heights, hair colour, etc between different families and discuss how members of the same family look similar. Show them your own family photographs.
2. Make a picture book with the children containing drawings of their family.
3. Show the children how to make a family tree.

Occupations

1. Talk about different occupations, perhaps relating them to the children's own parents. Find out what the children would like to be when they grow up. Ask them what jobs they think would be interesting, exciting, boring, etc and discuss why they made those choices. *Equal Opportunities Jigsaws* [1]; *Occupation Inset Trays* [1] and *Single Figure Jig-saws* [4] can be used to stimulate discussion.
2. Choose one occupation at a time to look at in depth, eg a postman.

   (i) Arrange a visit to a post office and if possible a sorting office, to find out what a postman does.
   (ii) Talk about a postman's uniform. The children can draw and colour-in pictures of the clothes.
   (iii) Get the children to role-play situations. A postal service with letter boxes, deliveries and collections can be set up in a school. The children can design their own stamps.
   (iv) Visit museums to look at the history of the postal service. Discuss how it has changed over the years.

Food

Take a type of food and talk about it in depth, eg vegetables:

1. Collect together some vegetables. Talk about their colour, the feel of their skin, their smell and what they taste like.
2. Get the children to draw the whole vegetable, its inside and its peel.
3. Take the children to shop for some vegetables.
4. Try growing some, preferably one that has a fast rate of growth, so the child's interest is maintained. Let the children see the vegetables in different stages of growth. They can draw them and make a pictorial record of their life-cycle.
5. Cook the vegetables for a meal. Children can write out recipes that tell you how to prepare them.
6. Make a matrix, with colour, size, taste or texture for the axes.
7. Make pretend vegetables for a toy shop.
8. Use photographs to stimulate discussion, eg *Photo Resource Pack – Food* [4] illustrates the cultural diversity of food preparation, shops and restaurants.

(Many manufacturers are very willing to provide information about their food-making processes and to arrange visits to see food being manufactured.)

Clothes

1. In a group talk about what people are wearing. Ask children to say what clothes would be suitable for different seasons.
2. Talk about the different clothes that children from other countries wear. Collect together pictures and dolls in national costume to help discussion.
3. Look at different materials. Talk about how they are made and their various uses. Use the materials in collages of colour and texture.
4. Ask the children to design their own fantasy clothing.
5. Discuss the different fashions throughout history, and perhaps show the children photos of the fashions in your own youth! This should generate some interest and amusement.
6. Finish up with a fashion show!

Animals

1. Ask the children to bring in photographs of their pets and to tell the other children how they look after them.
2. Visit farms and zoos. The children can draw pictures of the animals they have seen. Talk about the different countries the animals come from.
3. Talk about the foods animals eat, and the differences in appearance.
4. Help the children to group animals according to their similarity, eg which ones eat meat, which ones have stripes, which ones live in Africa.

Other topics can include the weather; the seasons; festivities; foreign countries; hobbies; sports or topical events. Discover how one topic can generate another, eg a discussion on clothes can lead to talking about different materials, such as wool and leather, and from there to animals and their relationship to man. Although it is important that children should learn to focus on the current topic and explore it in depth, it is equally important to be flexible and show how events are linked. If children bring up related issues, acknowledge them but save detailed discussion for another day. If you promise to return to a topic, make sure that you do.

CHAPTER 5
THE ACQUISITION OF EXPRESSIVE LANGUAGE

Introduction

This chapter sets out to describe the normal development of expressive language. It is not a review of the abundant literature that is available, nor is it a comprehensive account of the current state of knowledge; rather, it serves as a basic guide to the ways in which children's talk develops over time.

It is generally believed that comprehension precedes production of verbal language, and as a rule of thumb this may be so, but the situation may be more complex than we yet realise. Some researchers believe that comprehension is only a little advanced, while others believe that production helps to confirm or refute children's hypotheses about language and therefore influences the process of understanding. Whatever the answer, it is clear that comprehension and expression develop together and must be considered together, and so, although we have split the two chapters for the sake of convenience, this division is not a true reflection of normal communication.

The majority of the activities listed in this chapter presume an existing comprehension of the language involved. The reader should therefore refer to the previous chapter for ideas on the presentation of comprehension activities.

Assessment

There are several formal tests of children's expressive language, which provide a standardised score and usually an equivalent language age, so that children's language can be measured against an appropriate standard. Most of these tests tend to concentrate upon vocabulary and syntax.

Some examples of formal language tests are:—

1. Berry and Mittler Language Imitation Test. Age range 3+ years.

2. Carrow Elicited Language Inventory. Age range 3 to 5½ years.

3. Reynell Developmental Language Scales (Expressive Scale). Age range 1 to 7 years.

4. Receptive-Expressive Emergent Language Scale (REEL), by K.R. Bzoch and R. League (1970). Age Range 0 to 3 years.

5. *Northwestern Syntax Screening Test.* Age range 3 to 6 years.

The relative merits of these and other tests cannot be discussed here. Suffice to say that although formal tests have a part in the assessment of children's language, they are limited and must be backed up by good, informal observation and assessment. There are also informal check-lists and language charts available, such as the Derbyshire Language Scheme, which can be used to assess early language.

A language sample may also be taken and analysed, using a linguistic tree-analysis or one of the published procedures. These include the *Language Analysis Remediation Screening Procedure* (LARSP), devised by Crystal, which looks at syntactic structures and the *Bloom and Lahey Language Analysis*, which looks at content, form and use of language.

Detailed observation of the child in his own environments, backed up by reports from his family and school, is an essential part of a good assessment of a child's expressive ability and communicative competence.

The Functions of Language

Language serves many functions which the child learns to express in various ways in the first few years of life. Even the newborn baby soon realises that he can influence his environment by making sounds, smiles and movements. Later he develops more effective skills through the use of gestures, actions and language.

Halliday distinguishes between the pragmatic function, which refers to the use of language for communication, and the mathetic function, which refers to the use of language to explore and learn about the world. For the very young child these functions are served by the same utterances, but as language becomes more sophisticated, he learns new ways of expressing them.

Bloom and Lahey suggest that for any utterance, four elements can be described:

(i) the propositional meaning, ie the content of the utterance.
(ii) the locutionary act, ie the act of uttering.
(iii) the illocutionary act, ie the speaker's intentions.
(iv) the perlocutionary act, ie the effect on the listener.

(i) and (ii) are described elsewhere in this chapter; (iii) has to do with the functions of language and (iv) concerns how the speaker adapts his language according to the listener, the context and the situation.

Types of Speech Act

There are many kinds of speech act serving many different functions. They include the following:

1. to ask questions
2. to make statements
3. to give information
4. to request and refuse objects and actions
5. to give orders and make suggestions
6. to solve problems
7. to describe events

8. to form concepts
9. to make threats and promises
10. to maintain conversation.

There are no exact correlations between kinds of speech act and types of syntactic structure; for instance, the same basic request can be made in the form of a question, 'Can I have a biscuit?'; a declarative, 'I'm hungry'; or an imperative, 'Make me some tea'.

It is important that language-delayed children have the opportunity to practise all the types of speech act appropriate to their stage of development.

Communication

The child must learn rules for initiating and maintaining conversation as well as how to modify what he says according to the listener and the situation.

Initiating Conversation

Before the age of 2 to 2½ years, children tend to address themselves to the listener without first attempting to engage his attention. Two and a half to 3-year-olds will say the person's name before starting to speak (Bloom, 1978), but they often do not wait for him to respond with his full attention.

Maintaining Conversation

One of the basic rules of maintaining a conversation is 'turn-taking'. The child is already fairly skilled at this before he begins to talk, as he has engaged in reciprocal smiling and smiliar games since he was tiny (*see also Chapter 1*).

Another foundation stone of satisfactory conversation is the 'shared topic'. The 2-year-old has a short memory and concentration span and tends to switch topics of conversation frequently. Between 2 and 3 years his ability to keep to the subject improves although he can rarely sustain it for more than two consecutive responses (Cole, 1982). The child's response is usually related to a preceding adult utterance by containing either alternative or additional information, although there may be a phase when echoing is normal.

At 3 years the child's responses begin to reflect the syntax as well as the content of the adult's preceding utterance, which helps to make the conversation flow and misunderstandings less likely (Bloom and Lahey, 1978). However, although the 3-year-old is a reasonably competent conversationalist, a study of conversational patterns by Umiker-Sebeok (1979) showed that the 3-year-old often fails to attract a listener's attention, and indulges in monologues which require no response, whereas the 4 to 5-year-old tends to converse more and to allow the listener an opportunity to respond to and discuss the message.

Appreciation of the Listener

De Villiers and de Villiers (1978) propose four skills that are needed in order to modify one's speech according to the demands of the listener and the situation. These are:

(i) enough grammar and vocabulary to be able to choose amongst different language forms.
(ii) recognition that different listeners need different amounts of information.
(iii) knowledge of polite forms.
(iv) recognition of which listeners require polite forms.

At 2 to 3 years old the child is deficient in these skills and so he tends to talk about what is already apparent to his listener (Bloom, 1978), and to address all listeners similarly. Sometimes small children, and those with poor communication skills, are considered 'rude' by adults who do not realise that an appreciation of other people is an acquired skill. However, although young children tend to be egocentric (Piaget, 1929), there is sufficient evidence to suggest that they can adopt another person's point of view to a limited extent. For example, 2-year-olds with deaf parents modify their speech according to whether their listener is deaf or hearing (Schiff, 1976); 3 to 4-year-olds provide more verbal description to blind than to sighted listeners, and 4-year-olds adopt aspects of 'Motherese' when talking to 2-year-olds, but not to peers and adults (Shatz and Gelman, 1973). (*See Chapter 4 for a description of parental input*).

The Intellectual Use of Language

One of the major functions of language is its intellectual use. We use language to martial our thoughts. The relationship between language and thought is very intricate and fascinating, and the subject of much research and literature; therefore we will not tackle the subject here.

The very young child cannot integrate language with his own activities, eg he cannot simultaneously build a tower of bricks and listen to an adult's instructions (Reynell, 1980).

Between 2 and 2½ years the child begins to relate language to his actions and can follow instructions; at 3½ he can direct himself out loud, saying such things as, 'That goes there!'.

At 4½ to 5 years, he can begin to think silently as language becomes internalised. The language-performance link is forged and the child can now start to plan ahead and to think through a sequence of events to its outcome, rather than proceed, as hitherto, on a trial-and-error basis. (*See also 'Levels of Attention', Chapter 2*).

The Meanings of Language

For convenience we have divided semantics into 'word meanings' and 'sentence meanings'.

Word Meanings

Words stand for objects, people, actions, events, ideas and so on. The child must learn which words stand for which things in order to use language effectively. Through their sensori-motor experience children may have quite a lot of knowledge sorted into categories before spoken language develops (Clark, 1974). For instance, they know that some things move by themselves and others must be moved; that some things make sounds and others do not. The child does not at first understand and produce words as an adult would. He makes a hypothesis about the new word based on the context in which he hears it used, and this may or may not coincide with its full meaning. The hypotheses are:

(i) that the word has a greater meaning than it does for an adult, eg the child hears 'dog' and thinks it refers to all four-legged, furry animals. He thus 'overextends' the word 'dog' to sheep, cats and cows etc.
(ii) that the word has a narrower meaning than it does for an adult, eg he uses 'dog' only to refer to his neighbour's dog; thus he 'underextends' the word.

(iii) that the word has a different meaning than it does for an adult, eg the child hears 'dog' whilst looking at a dog's bowl and uses 'dog' to refer to bowls and dishes.

(iv) that the word has the same meaning as it does for an adult.

Overextensions are very common up to 2½ years. Clark states that the child gradually narrows down the range of objects covered by one word as he learns both new vocabulary and the essential differences between objects. He needs feedback from adults to confirm or refute his hypotheses (Brown, 1973). It is probable that for a while the child may use 'dog' for other animals, although he *understands* that they are different, because he has to stretch a limited vocabulary (Thompson and Chapman, 1975).

Two to three-year-olds learn words first at an intermediate level, eg 'dog'. At the age of 4 to 5 they acquire the superordinate terms, eg 'animal', and specific terms, such as 'Alsatian'. The awareness of size follows a similar pattern, ie children use the general terms 'big' and 'little' at first, and as they develop both cognitively and linguistically, they learn more and more specific terms, generally in the order 'tall/short', 'wide/narrow' and 'thick/thin' (de Villiers and de Villiers, 1978).

Sentence Meanings

Children talk mostly about what they are doing, what they are about to do or what they are trying to do, and what they want other people to do (Bloom and Lahey, 1978). In other words, their talk revolves around actions and how objects affect actions or are affected by them.

Children's early rules for sentence construction appear to be based on words functioning in semantic roles such as agent, action and object, and not as syntactic constituents such as subject, verb and predicate, which are learnt much later. Young children express a limited set of semantic relations based on concepts that they acquire in the sensori-motor period (Brown, 1973). These relations develop in a relatively consistent order according to Bloom, Lightbown and Hood (1975) who describe them thus:

(i) Existence—'there ball'; non-existence—'all gone'; recurrence—'more milk'.
(ii) Action—'Run Mummy'.
(iii) Locative Action—'Put dolly there'.
(iv) Locative State—'Box', in reply to 'Where's teddy?'
(v) Possession—'Daddy sock'; attribute—'Dirty'.
(vi) Other categories, which occur only rarely before MLU*2.5 are: Instrument—'bang (with) hammer'; Intention—'want go park'; Dative—'Give Mummy soap'; Place of Action—'swim bath'.

Although action relations appear after existence, its relative frequency soon surpasses the other categories. Early verbs are usually very general ones which can be used in a variety of ways, eg 'make', 'do', 'put' and 'go' (Bloom, 1978).

Locative Action refers to an object that is moving to a place and is usually expressed before Locative State, which refers to objects that are stationary.

These semantic categories have very narrow definitions for the child early on, for instance, an agent of an action is nearly always animate while the object of an action tends to be inanimate, so the 3-year-old might

* MLU = Mean Length of Utterance.

say, 'Man hit bus', but rarely 'bus hit man' (Cole, 1982). When expressing possession, the young child refers to alienable possessions, eg 'Mummy bag', before inalienable ones such as 'Mummy nose'. Possession and attribution are rarely used contrastively by small children, ie they say 'red sock' and 'baby bottle' as part of naming, and not to distinguish them from 'blue sock' and 'Mummy bottle' (Bloom, 1978).

The Development of Language Structure

First Words (9 to 18 months)

The child says his first consistent and recognisable words at about 12 months, although the normal range varies from 9 to 18 months. At this stage, clear words may be embedded in long, jargon-like patterns. The first meaningful word or two may be followed by a gap and then a gradual increase in word acquisition, accelerating at about 18 months (Rutter and Martin, 1972). By the age of 2, the child may use about 200 words and understand several hundred, again with wide normal variation.

First words may have a unique, idiosyncratic significance for the child, for example before he becomes aware that 'Mummy' stands for a particular person, he may understand it as a means of getting someone to smile and play with him (Grieve and Hoogenraad). Early words are predominantly a way of initiating and maintaining interaction, rather than a symbolic representation of objects and people. Such words include social expressions like 'hi' and 'bye-bye', as well as object names.

This early use of words is distinguishable from the first verbal labels which appear at about 18 to 21 months, usually coinciding with the later stages of symbolic development. The earliest verbal labels usually stand for familiar objects in the child's environment; people, food and drinks, toys and household items that are involved in his daily routines (Reynell, 1980). These are words with a clear referent. Words such as 'yesterday' without a tangible referent are learnt much later (de Villiers and de Villiers, 1978).

First words are usually very context bound, ie the child uses 'cup' only for his own cup at meal-times, and not for other cups or for his own cup in other situations. Later the word becomes more flexible and overextensions are common. (*See also Chapter 1*.)

Although many of the early verbal labels are nouns, this does not always mean the child is simply naming an object; he may be referring to its role as agent or object of an action, or to an action associated with it (Greenfield and Smith, 1976). Verbs are less common but their use increases sharply at the two-word stage.

Single-Word Utterances

There is general agreement that many single-word utterances have propositional meaning and the child is not just naming objects. The term 'holophrase' was formerly used to describe this, but it is now outdated because of its implied suggestion that the child has syntactic knowledge, which many researchers agree has not yet developed. The single-word utterance may stand for one of many different functions, eg 'coat' might mean 'Please take my coat off', 'Where is my coat?' or 'I want to go outside'. The child uses context, gesture and intonation to specify the content and intention of his utterance, eg he says 'Mummy' and points to a toy that he wants (Dore, 1974). The adult must do likewise in order to infer the message.

The two major functions of the single-word utterance are:

(i) request: including requests for objects, actions, attention and interaction.
(ii) reference: calling attention to things in the environment, by naming them, using gestures and words such as 'look' and 'there' (Griffiths, 1979).

Although these functions have been sub-divided by other researchers, Griffiths believes that almost all a child's single-word utterances fall into these two categories, and further sub-divisions are unnecessary.

From Single Words to Two-Word Phrases

During the first half of the single-word stage each communication act entails just one word. In the latter half, several different single-word utterances may be used in succession. They are still single-word utterances because they have equal stress, and are separated by intonation and pause, but they refer to one event and comprise a single communication act, eg 'Tommy. Milk. Dirty' (meaning that Tommy has spilt his milk).

Children often combine two words in a fixed expression, such as 'geddown' or 'all gone' and treat them as if they were single words. The individual words are not used flexibly in other expressions such as 'get coat' or 'all bricks'. This use continues into the two-word stage in such utterances as 'all gone soap'.

Before true two-word phrases occur the child may combine a real word with a meaningless phonetic string, eg 'derder doggy', which creates a syntax-like structure without the child having to process two meaningful items.

Two-Word Phrases (18 to 30 months)

True two-word phrases appear at about 18 months, distinguishable from successive single-word utterances because they are bound by a single intonation contour. They have the same functions, ie mostly request and reference, with a slight increase in statements and possessives.

Early two-word combinations consist of a relational word, eg 'more', and a verbal label, eg 'biscuit', related through word order. Braine (1963) called this 'Pivot Grammar'. He postulated that the child has two classes of word: a small number of 'pivots', eg 'all gone', which occur in a fixed position with any of a larger class of 'open' words, eg 'teddy' and 'milk'. This is now seen as an over-simplification of the way children generate new utterances. Bloom calls this type of sentence, which does not create any new meaning, a pivotal combination. Later combinations, which Bloom calls hierarchical combinations, do create new meaning, eg 'Mummy baby' expresses a relationship between Mummy and baby that is not inherent in either of the two words separately.

Reynell states that at 2 to 2¼ years old, the child can assimilate and combine two operative words, usually nouns representing objects and actions, such as 'Daddy car'. At 2½ his two-word phrases also include noun-verb combinations, eg 'Daddy wash', which are more complex, as verbs involve both an action, an agent to perform the action, and in some cases, an object to be acted upon (Reynell, 1980).

The child shows a good grasp of word order. Errors are rare, eg if a 2½-year-old is shown a picture of a man

carrying a lady he might say 'man carry', 'carry lady' or 'man lady', but not 'carry man' or 'lady man' (de Villiers and de Villiers).

Bloom suggests that if a child uses the relations agent-action, eg 'Mummy wash', action-object, eg 'wash baby' and agent-object, eg 'Mummy baby', he must be able to understand the superordinate structure, agent-action-object, 'Mummy wash baby'. Therefore if a child is producing these two-word relations consistently, he should be ready to progress to three-word phrases.

Three-Word Phrases

Brown (1973) and de Villiers and de Villiers (1978) have proposed two ways of moving from two- to three-word phrases.

(a) by combining two previously learned constituents:

eg	Agent	+	Action	+	Action	+	Object
	(Jack		throw)		(throw		ball)
	=		Agent		Action		Object
			(Jack		throw		ball)

(b) by expanding one previously learned constituent:

eg	Action	+	Object
	(throw		ball)

Child is taught attribute (big)

	Attribute	+	Object
	(big		ball)
=	Action	Attribute	Object
	(throw	big	ball)

The first type tends to expand clause structure and the second type, phrase structure. The level of difficulty seems about the same, and both types of expansion may co-occur.

Syntax at this stage is often called 'telegraphic' because the child's utterance contains only the most informative words, especially nouns and verbs, and omits grammatical words such as 'the', 'of', 'to' etc. The adult uses context, questioning and inference to interpret the full message.

Children still produce two-word phrases at this stage. Bloom found that the following factors influence the length of utterance:

(i) grammatical complexity (eg noun and verb inflections, adverbs)
(ii) new vocabulary
(iii) whether nouns or pronouns are used
(iv) the conversational context.

She discovered that complex and novel language produced a constraint on the length of utterance, whereas using pronouns such as 'he' and 'it', rather than noun-phrases such as 'the man' or 'the dog', made it easier for the child. It is also easier for the child to produce a three-word utterance if two of the constituents have already appeared in the conversational context. For instance, if an adult asks a child 'Can you see the doggy eating?' this facilitates an answer such as 'Doggy eating bone'. The child's own preceding two-word phrase may likewise prompt a three-word sentence, eg 'get car', 'Mummy get car'.

Beyond the Three-Word Phrase

Children can achieve goals and satisfy needs by using simple sentences in context but they cannot divorce language from context or convey shades of meaning until they use more complex syntax, inflections and words.

Between 2½ and 4-years-old there is very rapid language development. The 3-year-old understands directions involving three or more operative words, including nouns, verbs, adjectives and prepositions, and produces short simple phrases (Reynell, 1980). Pronouns appear relatively late; before 2½ the child refers to himself by his own name, and at 2½ he begins to grasp the meanings of 'I', 'me' and 'you'. At 3 years he starts to use other pronouns consistently, although there may be frequent errors such as 'me do it', which have generally disappeared by about the age of 4½ (Crystal, 1976). Gender errors are common amongst 3 to 4 year olds.

The length and complexity of utterance is increased by:

(i)   combining and expanding constituents as described above.
(ii) adding morphological inflections, eg 'ing', 'ed' and auxiliary verbs.
(iii) introducing new vocabulary.

Increasing the Complexity of Utterances

1. Grammatical Morphemes

Grammatical morphemes emerge between MLU 2 and 2.5 (Brown, 1973), at about 2 to 3 years of age. The rate of development varies but the order is relatively consistent.

The order of acquisition according to Brown is:

(i)   progressive [-ing] as in 'running'
(ii)   the prepositions 'in' and 'on'
(iii)   the regular plural [-s] as in 'balls'
(iv)   the irregular past tense, eg 'sang'
(v)   possessive [-s] as in 'Mummy's coat'
(vi)   the uncontracted copula [-is] as in 'Daddy is tired'
(vii)   determiners 'a' and 'the'
(viii) the regular past tense [-ed] as in 'walked'
(ix)   3rd person singular, regular [-s] as in 'he walks'
(x)   3rd person singular irregular, eg 'he catches'
(xi)   the uncontracted auxiliary '-has' as in 'she has finished'
(xii)   the contracted copula [-s] as in 'Daddy's tired'
(xiii) the contracted auxiliary [-s] as in 'she's finished'
(xiv)   superlatives, eg 'biggest', 'best'
(xv)   comparatives, eg 'bigger', 'better'
(xvi)   adverbials [-ly] as in 'quickly'

This order was confirmed by de Villiers and de Villiers (1973). Morphemes modulate basic meanings, ie the child expresses old knowledge in new forms, which makes the message clearer to the listener.

Children often produce common irregular forms correctly at first, but when they learn grammatical rules they tend to apply them to everything, producing words such as 'sheeps', 'runned' and even 'ranned', which may persist for some time. It is rare, however, to find errors across categories; the child does not inflect nouns with verb endings, or precede verbs with articles.

The child may not distinguish between mass and count nouns for some time, and even a 7-year-old may produce forms such as 'a snow' and 'some spaghettis', but other noun-inflection errors usually disappear between the ages of 3½ and 4½.

Confusions between determiners are still common at 3½ to 4 years, especially between terms such as 'this' and 'that', which change their referent relative to the speaker (Crystal, 1976).

2. Auxiliary Verbs

The stereotypes 'gonna', 'hafta' and 'wanna' are the first to appear, followed by the negative auxiliaries, 'don't', 'can't' and 'won't'. Their positive counterparts appear much later as they are semantically redundant elements, whereas the negative auxiliaries convey negation.

Children rarely use auxiliaries with the wrong verbs, eg 'I am liking you'; or in the wrong constructions, 'Have get me book'. Occasionally they do use other words as if they were auxiliaries, eg 'you better'd do it!', but this kind of error is usually gone by 4½ to 5 years.

At about 3 years, children may begin to use two auxiliaries, although they continue to make errors, eg 'He have been crying' (Crystal, 1976). By MLU 3.5 at around 4 years of age, most of the auxiliaries have appeared except complex ones involving subtle mood or tense.

3. Tense

Researchers are unanimous that very young children talk exclusively about the here and now, but they do not agree whether children learn to express past or future events next. One school of thought believes that the 2 to 3-year-old first makes occasional reference to future events without marking tense. From 3 years future-tense markers are common, with the past tense following shortly after. Bloom comments that children typically talk about what they are about to do, using the form, 'I'm gonna', rather than what they have done, but many comprehension studies have found that understanding of the past is better than the future. Reynell, and others, however, say that reference to the past precedes the future, in both comprehension and expression, as the immediate past is part of the child's actual experience and therefore more easily understood than the future, which has yet to happen.

Appropriate and consistent use of the future tense is not expected until the child is 4 to 4½, as it involves pre-planning, a higher language function. The form 'I'm going to' or 'I'm gonna' is both simpler and more frequently used in everyday conversation, even between adults, than the more complex 'I will' and 'I shall', which appear later.

Children initially refer to past events using the present tense, eg 'Look at the picture I do'. Subsequently they mark the past time with an adverb, eg 'Last night I see it', before using the appropriate inflections.

While children are acquiring the auxiliary system, inflections, and rules for marking tense certain types of errors are common. They frequently double-mark tenses and leave out essential words, eg 'I did painted that picture' and 'I running very fast'.

Increasing the Length of Utterances

An early way of increasing the length of a sentence without increasing complexity is to copy a part of somebody else's utterance, eg an adult might say, 'We're all very mucky', and the child responds, 'I all very mucky too' (Clark, 1974).

Children continue to expand their utterances by combining and expanding constituents, as previously described. Object-noun phrases are usually elaborated earlier than subject-noun phrases as children tend to expand the ends of sentences first. In other words, a sentence such as 'I painted birds and flowers', would be produced earlier than one such as 'The boys and girls went to the seaside'.

Complex sentences begin at about 3 years of age (MLU 3). The child begins to express two or more thoughts in a single utterance by first using co-ordination, and later, embedding.

Co-ordination* is the joining together of two separate utterances that are related by context, with a conjunction such as 'and' or 'because'. 'And' appears earliest and is used in a variety of constructions whether or not it is appropriate or necessary, eg the 3-year-old may say, 'I got tummy ache and I goed to bed'; 'I sit here and you sit here'. The order of appearance of the main conjunctions was found by Bloom (1978) and Clark (1970) to be: 'and', 'because', 'what', 'when', 'but', 'that', 'if', and 'so', with the use of 'and' decreasing as the other words are learned.

Embedding* refers to the joining of two interdependent clauses within one utterance, which results in a new meaning. There are two types of embedding:

(i) The first type uses a preposition or adverb to connect two separate events, eg '*I can come out* when *I finish my dinner*'.

(ii) The second type refers to two or more factors within a single event, eg '*I make/my doll walk*' (Bloom, 1978).

Types of Sentence

There is general agreement about the order of appearance of sentence types:

(i) Simple active affirmative declaratives (SAAD)
(ii) Negative statements
(iii) Yes/no questions
(iv) Wh- questions
(v) Truncated negatives and questions (Brown and Scanlon, 1970) or Imperatives (Cole, 1982)
(vi) Tag questions (Brown and Scanlon, 1970)

1. Negatives

The child expresses various forms of negation usually emerging in the following order:

(i) Non-existence
(ii) Disappearance
(iii) Non-occurrence
(iv) Cessation
(v) Rejection
(vi) Denial
(vii) Prohibition

Initially these are all expressed by 'no' or 'not' preceding the utterance, eg 'no juice', 'no tickle', 'not play now'. The negative auxiliaries 'can't' and 'don't' emerge next but they do not reflect knowledge of the auxiliary system as they are used interchangeably with 'no' and 'not' and the positive auxiliaries do not occur. Initially the child omits the subject when using negatives, which reduces the length and complexity of the utterance, eg 'can't see me', 'don't want book!'. Finally, the child uses negative auxiliaries consistently as he masters the auxiliary system at about MLU 3.4 to 3.9 (de Villiers and de Villiers, 1978).

2. Questions

From 1½ to 2 years children can discriminate between Yes-No type questions and Wh- type questions, but are unable to respond appropriately to the latter (Cole, 1982).

At about 2 years the child asks many stereotyped questions, eg 'What's that?', 'What's it called?', without any real understanding, which is evident from their inability to respond to similar questioning by adults. From 2 years the child can ask Yes-No questions with rising intonation but no subject-auxiliary inversion, and often omits the auxiliary altogether, eg 'That my juice?'. Subject-auxiliary inversion occurs in these questions at around MLU 3.

The child cannot use Wh- questions appropriately until he can understand them (Soderburgh, 1974). He can only do this after he has learned to express the appropriate concepts in a simpler form in his own speech. For instance, he can only understand why-questions once he is able to express causal relations (Hood, 1977).

It seems that children learn specific questions individually and not the question form as a single concept. At 2½ the most common Wh- question is 'What?'. At 3 it is 'Where?' and 'Who?' and by 4 years, 'Why?' predominates. The child may repeat the same questions over and over again to begin with, suggesting that he is practising and confirming the linguistic forms as well as seeking factual information (Rutter and Martin, 1972).

Until MLU 3 the child typically puts the Wh- word at the beginning of the sentence and uses appropriate intonation, but does not invert the subject and auxiliary, eg 'Where you go?'; 'What you are doing?'. Subject-auxiliary inversion usually occurs with some Wh-questions before others.

At about 4 years, tag-questions appear. These are questions that are literally tagged on to the end of a sentence, as in, 'You did the washing-up, *didn't you*?'. These are often preceded by the easier forms 'right?' and 'OK?'.

Introduction to Teaching

Expressive activities are normally best carried out in small groups, because language functions primarily as a medium for communication.

Groups

(i) Provide an opportunity for communicating and interacting with peers.
(ii) Are more flexible and allow a greater range of games, play situations, projects, outings and discussions, etc.
(iii) Provide more opportunity for using language to request, command, suggest, ask and answer questions, and so on.
(iv) Allow a mixture of abilities so that children who are good at certain aspects of language act as models; children often find it easier to model themselves on older children, whose language behaviour does not seem too remote from their own (Berry, 1980; Holt, 1967).

Individual Work

(i) May be more suitable for shy, disruptive or highly-distractible children.

---

*These words are defined here very much in Bloom's terms. For a more linguistic interpretation the reader must consult a linguistics textbook.

(ii) May be more suitable for teaching the comprehension of difficult concepts.

(iii) Provides a good back-up to group work.

Whenever possible, language teaching should be an integral part of the activities that the child is engaged in, for example vocabulary such as 'run', 'jump' and 'quickly' would be introduced during a physical activity. There may be times when face-to-face teaching is necessary however and the older child can certainly tolerate periods of working on specific aspects of syntax or content, as long as these are presented in an interesting manner.

The uses and functions of language should be paramount, both in planning and carrying out activities. Both general theories of function and the individual child's particular needs in his own environment are to be considered. Language should not be something that happens for a specific half an hour period; it is a tool for the child to use throughout the day. Therefore, although we have suggested specific ways of eliciting language, these are supplementary to the kinds of language stimulation that should be taking place during the child's everyday activities.

The child will be motivated to speak if:

(i) he needs to speak.
(ii) he wants to speak.

He will need to speak if his needs are not always anticipated and satisfied before he has to express them, so sometimes see that his favourite toys are out of reach, that his orange juice is not provided at a predictable time every day, and that he has to make choices between drinks, foods, toys, and so on.

He will want to speak if he is having fun or has created something he is proud of and wants to tell other people about it. He will not want to speak if he is cajoled, bullied, ignored or pushed too far too soon.

Guidelines to Remediation

1. Materials used should be at an appropriate developmental level and of interest to the child.

2. Language input should be at the child's level of comprehension.

3. The child should understand the concepts you intend him to use in his expressive speech (Gillham, 1979). If he has not reached the necessary cognitive level, he may learn linguistic forms parrot-fashion but be unable to use them meaningfully and creatively.

4. The adult should be a good model for the child.

5. Be flexible and take the child's lead as far as possible. If the child is showing no interest in your choice of materials, adapt your planned activity to whatever he is interested in. This does not mean the child should 'rule the roost', but he will learn more quickly if he is learning willingly.

6. Most activities can be adapted for different purposes, eg sand and water play can be used to facilitate exploratory play (by stimulating visual, tactile and auditory senses), imaginative play (by building castles and creating fantasy situations), comprehension and expression of related language.

7. Allow enough time for the child to explore new equipment before expecting him to use it in a specified way.

8. If a child is absorbed in a task do not change it as this usually indicates that he is still learning from it, but if his actions should become stereotyped, demonstrate a new aspect of the materials (Holt, 1967).

9. Don't persist with a game that the child has lost interest in.

10. Ensure that the child gets all the repetition and practice he needs to consolidate his learning.

11. Be prepared for periods when children's use of linguistic forms and words fluctuates; they must test out and practise language before it becomes firmly established.

12. Give the child time to spot and rectify his own mistakes. This is good for self-monitoring and self-esteem.

13. Generalisation is all important. The child should practise new skills in as many and varied situations as possible, and with people other than the teacher (L. Rieke, et al). This can be achieved by:

(i) involving other adults, eg parents and classroom-aides.
(ii) taking the child out, for example to the shops or café, to use the language that has been taught.

14. Always try to understand the child and encourage him to point, show you or give other clues to the content of his message.

15. Be interested in *what* the child is saying, over and above *how* he is saying it.

16. Encourage other people to respond to the child whenever he tries to communicate in an appropriate manner. Let them know what to expect from the child.

17. Monitor your own speech to prevent yourself becoming an inquisitor, asking endless questions. This could not only put the child off talking but provide him with a poor communication model.

18. Remember that in a group children do not all progress at the same pace.

19. Last, but not least, do not forget that parents, care staff, nursery nurses and so on have a very important part to play in the child's language development.

Specific Techniques

Some useful procedures are imitation, modelled imitation (Gillham, 1979), role reversal and forced alternatives, which are themselves forms of modelling. It is not within the bounds of this book to describe these procedures in full; it is suggested that the reader refers to a standard textbook.

Briefly, imitation-procedures usually involve the child directly imitating the adult's utterance, either immediately or with a calculated delay. Modelling is less overt and relies on the child actively analysing the model and reproducing it, or aspects of it, in his own speech. The adult has to model the desired behaviour many times.

Role reversal is a very useful technique; usually the adult models the behaviour first, eg giving the child a two-part command and then they swap roles, and the child gives the same, or similar, command. Reducing the amount of equipment to choose from may be helpful as the child can then concentrate more upon what he is saying (Derbyshire Language Programme).

Forced alternatives is another way of covertly modelling the required vocabulary or linguistic form, eg the adult asks the child if he would like an apple or an orange; the child then has only to imitate one or other of the words.

Speaking in unison may also be put to minor use. The whole class can speak together or an adult can help the child to imitate the teacher's model.

Sentence-closure can be used to elicit specific structures, eg if you want the child to produce a verb, say 'Mummy is cooking; Daddy is eating; baby is . . . . . (sleeping)' (Derbyshire Language Programme).

General Stimulation Activities for the Younger Child

Children are motivated by curiosity, a competitive instinct, success, being given responsibility, intrinsic and extrinsic rewards and penalties (Berry, 1980).

1. lucky dips, mystery-bags and boxes; unusual containers for toys, such as miniature chests of drawers.
2. collect a selection of interesting objects and miniature toys, the more curious the better, and keep them in a portable expanding tool-box (of the type you can buy at *Halfords* or any similar shop).
3. treasure hunt and hiding games.
4. toys, games and play activities of all kinds, but especially glove puppets, which rarely fail to break the ice with small children.
5. physical activities where children can let off steam.
6. pass-the-parcel.
7. rough-and-tumble; being swung and given piggy-backs etc.
8. acting 'silly' by the teacher, including talking 'gobbledegook' and saying ridiculous things, and getting things wrong.
9. surprises; the unexpected.
10. outings, eg going to the park.
11. sand and water play.
12. toy telephones, especially ones that really work (although very young children may be too surprised to talk).

Rewards and Motivators for all Ages

1. use chance games, eg spinners and dice, to choose an activity (from 3 to 6 years).
2. wind-up toys, jumping beans, sparklers and bubbles.
3. kaleidoscopes, slide-shows.
4. music-boxes, chimes, dangling toys.
5. watching television, playing records.
6. badges to pin on the clothes; stars to stick in books etc.
7. colouring and drawing.
8. any toy or game the child is currently interested in.
9. counters, points and other visual and scoring systems, eg a cat climbing up a tree that has been marked off into divisions.
10. being allowed outside to play.
11. verbal praise.
12. material rewards, eg crisps, sweets, orange juice etc.
13. affection and attention, including smiles, cuddles, playing with and talking to the child.

ACTIVITIES TO FACILITATE EXPRESSIVE LANGUAGE

First Words

Bloom suggests some useful early words to teach children.

(i) 'no'; 'more': these express the early sentence meanings of non-existence and recurrence
(ii) 'all gone'; 'gone'; 'away': useful words which combine well with names of objects and actions
(iii) 'this'; 'that': useful for calling attention to objects and as early forms of reference
(iv) 'give'; 'make'; 'go': flexible all-purpose verbs
(v) 'up'; 'down': early action markers
(vi) names of family and toys, etc.

None of these words have a clear referent and might seem difficult to teach, but in fact they are among the earliest words used by the normally developing child. If they are consistently and regularly used by adults in the appropriate context then the child should soon begin to associate them with their underlying meanings (Gillham, 1979).

Activities to Elicit 'More' and 'Again'

1. If the child shows that he wants more of something, eg he finishes his orange juice and holds out his mug, say 'more?' with exaggerated intonation and pour some out. Gradually encourage him to say the word.

Do not worry that the child will think 'more' stands for 'orange juice'; he may do so for a while, but if the word is used with a variety of objects in a variety of situations he will soon generalise. Also, saying 'more' *before* producing the orange juice would lessen the likelihood of such an error being made.

2. Give the child a simple lift-out puzzle to do but pass him one piece at a time. Once he is absorbed only give him the next piece when he asks 'more' or ''nuther one'.

3. Blow a few bubbles. When they have all burst, say 'more?' and blow some more. Next time wait until the child asks.

4. Any activity that the child enjoys can be used to elicit 'more' and 'again', eg rough and tumble, being tickled and chased, being pushed on a swing or roundabout, playing Ring-a-ring-a-roses, singing a song.

5. Use a wind-up toy, musical-box, spinning top, anything that the child has to ask an adult to do for him.

6. At mealtimes give the child a small amount of food and drink so that he needs to ask for more (Derbyshire Language Programme).

Activities to Elicit 'Gone'; 'All Gone; 'Bye Bye'

1. Wave and say 'bye bye' when a person leaves the child's presence, or a toy goes out of sight. Encourage

the child to join in and when the person has gone, say 'Gone!'

2. The child puts his toys away and says, 'all gone'.

3. The child posts objects into a post-box, saying 'bye bye' and 'gone' (Jeffree and McConkey, 1976).

4. Blow bubbles and as he bursts each one the child says, 'all gone' etc.

5. Use various object-permanence activities to elicit the words, eg when playing with a train or truck, push it into a tunnel or garage for a moment (*see Chapter 1*).

6. Make a picture book with clear colourful pictures. Make every other page a blank and as the child turns to the blank page he can say 'Oh, gone'. When he can name objects, get the child to name the picture, turn the page and say 'gone', and this will soon lead to two-word phrases such as 'Ball gone' (Jeffree and McConkey, 1976).

PICTURE-BOOK

Activities to Elicit the Word 'Go'

1. The child gives the signal 'Go!' to the teacher and other children to start a whole range of activities, including races, drawings, drinking milk, etc.

2. The child gives the signal 'Go' in the game 'Mousie-Mousie' (*see Chapter 2*).

3. The child is encouraged to say 'Go' in situations where he wants to go somewhere, eg to the toilet, to the shops etc. This has two uses: firstly, the adult can ask the child 'Go where?' and elicit single-word utterances expressing action and place, and secondly, 'go' can be paired with many kinds of word to produce two-word phrases, eg 'go bye byes', 'go toilet', 'go fast', 'go there', 'go 'way!'.

Activities to Elicit 'Here', 'Here y'are'

1. The child is encouraged to attract a person's attention by saying 'here' or 'here y'are' while pointing to an object. He can be shown that this is more useful than silently pointing or making noises which may be misunderstood or go unnoticed.

2. The child says 'here' while handing objects to the teacher to put away or set out.

3. The child says 'here y'are' or 'here it is' when an object reappears, eg from a tunnel, a posting-box, a helter-skelter, a money-box, etc.

Activities to Elicit 'Up' and 'Down'

1. The child uses these words during physical games:

  (i) as he is picked up and swung, and put down again

 (ii) as he climbs up and down from chairs and climbing-frames

(iii) as he goes up and down a slide

(iv) as he goes up and down on a see-saw, firstly with an adult, and later with another child, taking it in turns to say 'up' and 'down'

 (v) as he goes up and down on a swing.

2. There are lots of curious little toys in the shops and on market stalls that illustrate these actions, eg little clowns on sticks that the child can push up and down; a 'slinky' that climbs down stairs on its own; little people and monkeys that climb up and down ladders, and so on.

3. *Playmobile Swing* [4] – make the figures go up and down on the swing.

4. *See-saw* [4]: the repetitive movement of this toy gives ample opportunity for the child to practise the words.

5. Build a tower of bricks and knock it down again.

6. Draw a large ladder and stick it on the wall. Cut out a little person or climbing animal and stick it to the bottom of the ladder with Blu-Tack. The child makes him climb up and down.

7. Snakes and Ladders: make your own uncluttered board. The child pushes his counter 'up' the ladders and 'down' the snakes.

8. Other simple board games can be devised that require the child to move up and down, eg

SIMPLE BOARD GAMES

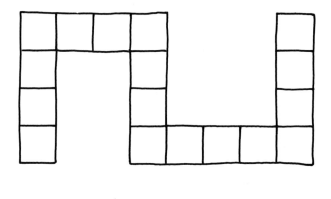

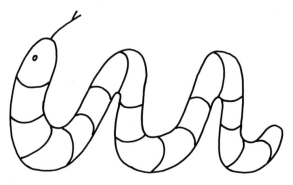

Remember that even simple board games require a fairly good level of comprehension and memory. See Chapter 3 on 'Games with Rules'.

Activities to Elicit 'On' and 'Off'

1. These expressions can be used as the child switches on and off a torch or flashing light, the television, radio and tape-recorder, the electric light, domestic appliances, a music-box or electric organ, and so on.

2. The child says 'on' as he puts on his shoes, socks, coat, etc.

3. He says 'off' as he takes them off again.

4. The adult puts a rubber ring or beanbag on her head, nods and lets it slide off. She then places it on the child's head and encourages him to copy her. After a few turns she puts the ring on her head but waits for him to signal 'off'. Likewise she waits for the child to say 'on' before putting the ring on his head (Holt, 1967).

5. Repeat the activity with a funny hat or wig.

6. Do a similar activity with a false moustache or beard, or plastic glasses.

Activities to Elicit People's Names

When considering what to teach first it is best to look at the demands made by the child's environment. Names of family, care-staff and pets are usually very important.

1. Teach the child to get somebody's attention by calling their name. Make sure the person responds.

2. Help the child to take a toy or object to somebody and direct their attention to it either by saying the person's name or a word such as 'Look!', 'Here!'. Accompany this with appropriate gestures such as touching the person's arm.

3. Play various team-games (*see Chapters 2 and 3*).

  (i) Throwing games: everybody stands in a circle and the child names the person he is going to throw the beanbag to.
  (ii) Tag: the child names the person he is going to chase.
  (iii) Piggy in the Middle: the child names the person who is Piggy.
  (iv) The child is 'Captain' and chooses his crew by naming the children. If there are two Captains, a tug-of-war or game of tag can then ensue.

4. Pass the Parcel: the child names the person to whom he passes the parcel.

5. Show the child photographs of his family and ask him to name them.

6. The child gives real names to his toys and dolls (which will probably be the names of his family and friends).

Activities to Elicit Object Names

The child must learn how to use words to draw attention to, comment on and request objects.

Attention

1. Teach the child to attract an adult's attention to an object by holding it up, pointing or carrying it to the person, and saying its name.

2. Encourage the child to point to things in the environment, eg while he is out shopping or looking out of the window, and to say their names.

Request

1. When the child shows by his gestures and intonation that he wants something, eg a biscuit, then show him the object and model the word, before you give it to him. Gradually expect him to say the word or an approximation of it before he gets his reward.

2. Choosing activities: the younger child needs to be shown the objects but the older child at the appropriate cognitive level may not need these visual clues.

  (i) The child is given a choice of toys to play with and to get his choice he must correctly name the toy. If he doesn't get the name right this will still teach him something, ie he has made an error!
  (ii) The child is shown a picture book with large clear line-drawings. He chooses one to colour in by naming the picture.
  (iii) The child can choose what he has to eat or drink by naming it.

3. The child may also request an action involving an object by naming the object. Help him to carry the object, eg a ball, over to another child or adult, and say 'ball'. Encourage the other child to respond by playing ball.

4. One child acts as shopkeeper and the other children buy certain articles from him. The level of difficulty can be varied; either the teacher tells the child what to buy so he has only to imitate, or the child has to make a free choice.

5. Fold a piece of thin cardboard in half and draw an outline of an animal. Cut it out so that you have two shapes. Cut one into large jigsaw pieces and use them as stencils to make the same outlines on the other animal-shape. Then draw or paste small pictures on to each piece. The end result should look like this:

JIGSAW ANIMALS

The child matches the pieces to his copy by correctly asking for the picture. This can be turned into a game for older children, eg when a six is thrown the child can ask for a jigsaw piece.

Suggestion and Command

1. Play a hiding game, taking turns to tell each other what to hide.

2. Shops: the children take it in turns to tell each other what to buy. For children who enjoy role-play they can act 'Mummy telling Daddy what to buy at the shops'. Afterwards Daddy tells Mummy what he's bought.

3. Setting up a construction, floor lay-out or play situation: the child has to tell the adult or other children what he needs, eg if he wants to do some painting, he asks for 'paper', 'paint', 'apron'; and if he is making cakes, he asks for 'eggs' etc. (Make sure that the items are in view as a visual reminder for the child.)

4. The child tells the adult what to draw, prompted and encouraged by another adult when necessary.

5. Children tell each other what to draw or paint, while sitting either side of an easel. Afterwards they compare their drawings, which should be the same. The adult is on hand to prompt. (If a child is very delayed in drawing this may not be a suitable activity.)

6. Beanbag Toss: the child names the picture for another child to aim at (Holt, 1967).

Naming

1. In response to the adult's questions 'What's that?', 'What's its name?', 'What have you got/found?':

   (i) Puppets: the adult addresses the questions to a puppet and the child answers on his behalf.
   (ii) The child names objects as he posts them into a box.
   (iii) The child names objects as he hands them to the adult.
   (iv) The child names objects as he or the adult pulls them out of a mystery bag or box.
   (v) The child names objects as he tidies up and puts toys away.
   (vi) The child names 'presents' as he takes them out of Father Christmas' sack or a Christmas stocking.
   (vii) The adult hides toys around the room and as the child finds them he names them.
   (viii) The child names pictures in a book.
   (ix) The child names pictures as he posts them in a box (Jeffree and McConkey, 1976).
   (x) The child names pictures as he puts them on to a cellograph. The adult can then tell a simple story about the pictures.
   (xi) The child is given jigsaw-puzzle pieces as he names them correctly and completes a simple puzzle.

PICTURE-CUBE

   (xii) The child names pictures on a picture-cube. This can be bought from a photographic suppliers or made at home by pasting pictures on to a large play-brick. A more elaborate cube can be made by covering a large block with clear plastic, folded so that each surface has a plastic envelope which will hold a picture or photo (Jeffree and McConkey, 1976).

   (xiii) Beanbag Toss: The child throws his beanbag and names the picture on which it lands (Holt, 1967).

2. As part of a game:

   (i) Make a sturdy board and mark off large squares. In each square paste a picture-card. The child has to flip a tiddly-wink or 'shove ha'penny' on to the board and name the picture it lands on.
   (ii) Fishing-game: a large empty container or washing-up bowl can serve as the fish pond. The fish are made out of robust card and have paper-clips attached to them. The fishing-rod has a small magnet attached which attracts the 'fish'. The game can be played either as a reward, eg if the child names a picture correctly he has thirty seconds to hook as many fish as he can; or it can incorporate the naming activity, by pasting pictures on to the fish themselves. If the child names the picture he keeps the fish.
   (iii) Spinning-Wheel: a spinner is attached to a board. Around the outside of the board are placed miniature objects or pictures. To make this more natural the children try and guess which picture the arrow will point to.
   (iv) Croquet; Golf: very large cardboard pictures are made that will stand up on the floor. A hole is made in them large enough for a small ball to pass through. Child-sized croquet or golf sticks are used to knock the balls through the holes. If the child can name or describe the picture he doubles his score.
   (v) Returnable Posting-box: a special posting-box is made so that any object the child puts in at the top can come back of its own accord at the bottom. A delaying device can be employed so that the object will not return until the child has named it (Jeffree and McConkey, 1976—see *Let Me Speak* for instructions on how to make this.)
   (vi) The child names pictures as he plays various games, such as dominoes, Snap, Happy Families and Lotto. The naming should be woven into the game as far as possible so that it does not detract from the fun.
   (vii) Pass the Parcel: inside each wrapper is a small toy which the child can keep if he names it correctly.

3. In guessing games:

Guessing games have an intrinsic purpose. It also gives more purpose to the act of naming if the adult cannot see what the object or picture is; the child is then giving worthwhile information.

   (i) Feelie-box: a selection of objects is placed in a box with a hole cut out, large enough to place one hand through. The child manipulates the object and tries to guess what it is.
   (ii) Feelie-bag: used in the same way as the feelie-box. An older child may attempt to guess the objects by feeling them through the bag.
   (iii) Blindman: the adult blindfolds herself. She then chooses an object from a tray and names it. She asks the children, 'Am I right?' and they either agree or tell her what it really is.
   (iv) Kim's Game: the children have to memorise the objects on a tray, and then name the ones that the adult has taken away.
   (v) Presents: wrap up some distinctively shaped objects and see if the child can guess what they are. This is only suitable for children with fairly good shape-recognition.

(vi) Lotto: the caller shuts her eyes, holds up a card and asks the children what she is holding.

(vii) The child looks at pictures through a toy viewer or a real slide-viewer and tells the adult what he sees.

(viii) The adult begins a drawing from the least obvious angle and the children guess what it is.

(ix) Show the child photos of objects taken from unusual angles. He must guess what they are (Derbyshire Language Programme).

(x) Halves-to-Wholes: this is a set of pictures of halves of objects which have to be matched up. At a simple level the child is given the halves of very dissimilar objects, eg car, apple, cup and he has to guess what they are. At a higher level the pictures are perceptually more similar.

(xi) As a variation of the above you can make your own halves-to-wholes dominoes. As each piece is laid, the player guesses what the object is. Children love correcting adults so occasionally give a wrong guess, but do not use this ruse if the child is likely to be confused or intimidated.

(xii) Christmas Crackers: the children name the objects that fall out. You can doctor the crackers beforehand by unwrapping them and putting miniature toys inside.

Activities to Elicit Action Names

1. The adult asks, 'What are you doing?' while the child is engaged in a range of activities, eg during mealtimes when he is 'eating' and 'drinking'; during PE when he is 'jumping' and 'climbing'; during play-time when he is 'playing' and 'reading', and at bath-times, when he is 'washing' and 'splashing', etc.

2. The adult makes a doll carry out actions and asks the child 'What is (s)he doing?'

3. The children give each other, and the adult, commands, eg 'Skip', 'Smile', 'Hop', 'Crawl', 'Cry', etc.

4. 'Bossing Teddy or Dolly': the adult gives Teddy a command and helps the child to manipulate him. Then she asks the child to tell Teddy to 'dance', 'walk', 'run', 'wave', etc. Later she can say, 'Now you tell Teddy what to do' and expect the child to generate his own ideas.

5. The child tells the adult what actions to make dolly do.

6. The child completes a simple action-oriented jigsaw and names the action.

7. The child names the actions depicted in pictures and action cards, which can be both home-made or purchased.

8. Make pictures of children with moving parts that the child can manipulate, eg a leg can be moved so that it

seems to kick a ball. The concept of action then comes alive for the child (Jeffree and McConkey, 1976).

9. Flip-book: this is a small book with a series of pictures illustrating a particular action. Each page has a picture slightly different from the last so that as the child flips through, the pictures appear to move (Jeffree and McConkey, 1976). (*See also Chapter 4*).

10. A series of action cards are placed face down. The children take turns to pick a card and mime the action, eg 'digging', 'cutting', 'swimming', 'throwing'. The others try to guess and name the action. The adult helps by giving clues and close guesses.

11. The adult mimes actions which the children try to guess.

Activities to Elicit Two-Word Phrases

Many of the activities listed above can be used for eliciting two-word utterances and therefore we will not repeat them all.

Early Pivotal Combinations

The early two-word utterances to teach are combinations of either a relational word plus the name of a person, object or action, eg 'look, car'; 'more Mummy'; 'all gone milk'; 'again tickle', or a name of a person plus an object or action, eg 'Daddy coat'; 'Sammy push'. Each of the 'pivotal' words should be used with many different objects and actions to facilitate generalisation (*see page 67*).

1. Graded-size inset puzzles are useful as the child can repeat the same expression many times, eg 'more dog'.

2. Posting-boxes: the object only returns if the child produces a two-word utterance, eg 'Bye bye ball' or 'Where dolly?' (Jeffree and McConkey, 1976) (*see opposite page, 2v*).

3. Picture-book with every other page blank (*see page 66*).

4. Other activities listed under one-word utterances.

Later Hierarchical Combinations

It is quite usual for the child at this stage to express relations by combining two object names, eg 'dolly cake'. This need not be discouraged in favour of the noun-verb combinations, 'dolly eat' and 'eat cake', although the adult should model these for the child (*see page 61*).

When introducing new object names keep the verb constant, and vice versa, eg 'give ball, give brick, give apple'; 'show cup, get cup, hide cup' etc.

Commentary and Description

1. The child is asked what he is doing while engaged in play, physical activities, 'doing the housework' and so on. He must answer in a two-word phrase, eg 'sweeping floor'; 'dressing dolly'.

2. The adult and child act out symbolic play sequences with large toys and the child describes what is happening.

3. Show the child various objects and ask 'What do we do with this?' The child answers 'brush hair', 'clean teeth' etc.

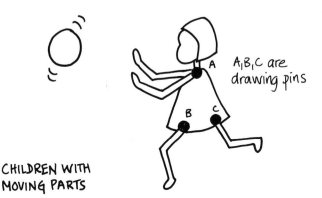

A₁B₁C are drawing pins

CHILDREN WITH MOVING PARTS

4. The child is shown a picture of a person and then another picture of him performing an action. The child progresses from naming the pictures separately, 'man', 'digging', to definite two-word phrases, 'man digging'.

ACTION PICTURES

man   man digging

5. Split picture books: the book is divided into upper and lower halves; the upper halves depict persons and animals, while the lower halves show actions. The child flicks through naming the agent-action relation, as above. He is encouraged to discuss which combinations can and cannot go together, eg 'doggy read' (adapted from Jeffree and McConkey, 1976).

6. Picture books of the Bremark and Marks & Spencer series are very useful. On one page is a picture of an object, eg a bib, and on the opposing page a picture of somebody using the object, eg a baby wearing the bib. The child produces 'baby bib', etc.

7. Make two packs of picture-cards, one showing objects or people, and the other actions. Shuffle the separate packs and lay them face down. The child turns over the top cards in each pack, 'reads' the sentence and judges whether it is 'silly' or 'proper'.

Some amusing sentences can be created, eg 'eating teddy'. The cards can be placed in different orders to create either agent-action relations, or action-object/location relations.

8. Word-order games: draw pictures to illustrate the importance of word order, eg 'fish eating' and 'eating fish' (*see below*) have quite different meanings. The child must name them correctly (Derbyshire Language Programme).

9. *Logic People* [4]: these can be used to elicit such phrases as 'Man running'; 'Boy sitting'; 'Girl standing' and 'Lady walking'.

Commands and Suggestions

1. Each child has a chance to be 'boss', telling the others what to get out for the day's activity, eg 'get scissors' (with the adult's help!)

2. The children take turns to give each other commands:

(i) involving parts of the body, eg 'touch nose', 'find ear'.
(ii) involving actions, eg 'stand up', 'touch wall', 'sit down'.
(iii) involving objects, eg 'cut paper', 'throw ball', 'open box'.
(iv) involving musical instruments, eg 'bang the drum', 'blow whistle'.

3. Follow-My-Leader: one child acts as leader and performs lots of actions, the sillier the better, as he leads the others around the room, in and out of the furniture. He accompanies his actions with verbal directions and the other children copy him.

4. O'Grady Says: similar to the above but the children stand in a line facing the leader. Initially the child gives just the commands, 'touch toes', and later adds the words 'O'Grady says', which increases the length but not the complexity of his utterance. The proper rules can be introduced later for older children (*see Chapter 3*).

5. The child gives teddy or dolly commands; using two dolls ensures that he has to use two words to specify both the action, and who is to perform the action, eg 'Dolly go sleep'.

6. As above, but the child can be a Circus Ringmaster, giving the model animals instructions, eg 'Tiger, jump' (Derbyshire Language Programme).

7. The child gives teddy or dolly commands involving an object. This time only one toy is used so that the child can concentrate on the action-object relation, eg 'Eat lolly', 'Wash car'. When appropriate, another toy should be included.

8. Have a tea-party with the children telling each other what to do, eg 'Orange [in] glass', 'Teddy [sit] chair'. This can be done at mealtimes, breaks and during home-corner play.

9. Take turns to be a wizard who turns everybody into animals who are in his power. 'Monkeys, jump', 'Lions, roar', etc.

Request

Use the activities listed under the one-word utterances section to elicit two-word phrases. Teach the child several ways of expressing request, eg 'Give dolly', 'Milk please', 'Want play', 'Need wee'.

The activities given for single-word and two-word utterances can also be adapted to elicit three-word phrases.

Activities to Elicit Three-Word Phrases

The child should now be capable of commenting upon his constructional play while he is playing, and using language to direct himself. He first describes what he is doing, and then what he is about to do. The adult should model this for him, by talking about the things she is doing or the child is doing.

Start by expanding the child's clause-structure to subject-verb-object sentences, such as 'lady hit man', and later to include adverbials, eg 'man goes hospital'.

Commands and Requests

1. To increase length without complexity, the child can give commands to other children, using their names. Use the ideas given in the previous section, eg 'Susan, touch table!'; 'David, play trumpet!'.

2. In a similar fashion the child gives commands to his toys, which can be given real names, or called 'horsie', 'golly' and so on, eg 'Monkey drink juice'; 'Golly wash face'.

3. 'Give me' games: the children take turns to ask each other for toys and other objects. The phrase 'give me' remains constant and the object changes. Later include other names, eg 'Give Mary puzzle'; 'Give book [to] Teddy'.

4. Introduce a fantasy element, eg three children take the roles of shopkeeper, Mummy and child. Mummy tells the child what to get at the shops, eg 'get me potatoes and the child asks the shopkeeper. This basic game can be varied by playing doctors and nurses, offices, teachers, restaurants and so on. The role-plays can be built around themes to introduce or practise related vocabulary, such as foods, household items and vegetables. More imaginative children can play at spacemen, wizards, pirates, cops and robbers, etc.

5. 'Moving house': children take turns being 'boss' while the others are removal men, putting furniture into the house, eg 'Put oven [in] kitchen'; 'Toilet goes [in] bathroom (adapted from Derbyshire Language Programme).

Commentary and Description

1. Place six very different objects, eg apple, book, hat, etc on the table. Sit opposite the child and say, 'I eat . . . . .' leaving a pause for the child to say the word or point to the appropriate object. If he does neither, do it for him, ie lift up the apple and say 'an apple'. Do this several times until the child can respond consistently and then reverse roles. Sometimes get the answer right and sometimes look blank so that the child gives you the answer, producing a three-word utterance in the process.

2. Simple action songs help the child express action relations in well rehearsed routines:

eg | Teddy Bear

Teddy Bear, Teddy Bear, dance on your toes
Teddy Bear, Teddy Bear, touch your nose
Teddy Bear, Teddy Bear, stand on your head
Teddy Bear, Teddy Bear, go to bed
Teddy Bear, Teddy Bear, wake up now
Teddy Bear, make your bow.

Pancakes

Mix a pancake, stir a pancake
Put it in the pan,
Fry a pancake, toss a pancake,
Catch it if you can.

3. The adult acts out situations with large toys while the child describes what is happening. If necessary two elements can be held constant while the third is varied, until the child is consistent in his responses, eg 'Dolly making cakes'; 'Dolly making picture'; 'Dolly kicking ball'; 'Teddy kicking ball'; 'Teddy cuddle Dolly'; 'Teddy push Dolly'.

Because the child will often respond with a one- or two-word utterance the adult must provide lots of models to give the child the idea that three words are needed. Do not correct his utterance but expand it. If the child does not produce three-word phrases after plenty of modelling, adapt the situation so that he must do so in order to make his message clear. This can be achieved by introducing a third person, a student, classroom aide or older child, who cannot see the action. The child has to describe the events to this person who can question him if he is not being specific, eg 'But *who* is falling over?' '*What* is teddy eating?' The first adult is then free to help the child with his responses.

4. The same activities can be carried out with miniature toys, *Playmobile*[4] sets and dolls' furniture.

5. Clear action-pictures can be used to elicit the same constructions.

6. Cellographs and *Uniset Boards*[1] provide an enjoyable variation on the picture-description theme, because the child can arrange and rearrange the pictures to his own satisfaction. *Uniset Boards* consist of a baseboard printed with a familiar scene, such as the house, or playground, upon which vinyl pictures can be stuck.

7. The adult and children take turns to mime activities which the others try to describe.

8. The adult draws a sequence of three pictures for the child to 'read',* eg

PICTURE SEQUENCES

man   sitting   chair

cat   eating   fish

The child starts by 'reading' the pictures as they are drawn, producing them like successive single-word utterances, and then reads the completed strip as a whole. Each picture acts as a visual reminder.

9. Split picture books (*see previous section*): paste pictures of people and animals on the top halves and objects on the bottom halves. The child flips through, making possible sentences by adding a suitable verb. This is fairly difficult because the child has to think of the actions for himself. To begin with only agent-action-object relations such as 'girl eating sweets', should be required, but at a higher level the child should be able to create a sentence such as 'girl going [down] slide', 'cat sitting [on] bed' (adapted from Jeffree and McConkey, 1976).

10. The child 'reads' picture-sentences showing contrastive word order, eg 'lady stroking cat' and 'cat stroking lady'. Amusing cartoons can be made up for this purpose. You should try to discuss with the child the plausibility of each sentence.

11. Make large floor lay-outs of a zoo, farm, a house, a park, a street-scene, a hospital, etc. The child moves model figures around the lay-out saying 'Lady go shops', 'Car drive garage'.

Three-word phrases can also be produced by expanding a constituent the child already uses, eg expanding a noun-phrase by adding a possessive or attribute.

* The Rebus Reading Scheme may also be used for this purpose. Rebus has standard pictures for each word and includes prepositions and adjectives.

1. During gross motor activities, 'Follow My Leader', 'O'Grady Says', etc the child has to be more specific in his commands, eg 'Touch Sally's toes'; 'Climb the big table'.

2. Dressing up: two piles of identical or similar clothing are placed on the floor. Two children have to race to put them on while a third child gives orders, eg 'Put on red hat', 'Put on green blouse'. If he forgets to say the whole sentence he is replaced by another child.

A variation of this for children who can cope with losing, is to have only one pile of clothing and the winner is the child who ends up wearing the most.

The other children get the opportunity to practise related language such as 'Come on', 'Hurry up', 'You're winning' etc and to support the children by calling their names.

3. Action songs that involve adjectives:

eg   My Red Engine

My red engine goes Chuff Chuff Choo, Chuff Chuff Choo.
My shiny drum goes Rum Tum Tum, Rum Tum Tum.
My Teddy Bear goes Grr Grr Grr, Grr, Grr, Grr.
My wooden bricks go pitter patter, pitter patter, rattle, bang, CRASH!

(Make up your own lines to use the adjectives you want to practise.)

The Red Engine

One red engine
Puffing down the track.
One red engine
Puffing back.

One blue engine, etc.
One dirty engine, etc.
One wooden engine, etc.

4. Hiding games: the teacher and children take it in turns to hide a collection of objects around the room. The hider then calls out which object is to be found first, and the others race to find it. Make sure that the child needs to use a possessive or attribute to specify the object, and take care that the child is familiar with the vocabulary. (*Logic People*[4] could be used in these games.)

5. Pictures are hidden around the room or stuck on to the wall. As above, the hider calls out a picture and the first to spot it brings it to him. To give everybody a chance to find a picture, each winner can sit out the next round. Ensure that there are as many pictures or objects to find as there are children playing.

6. The adult slowly uncovers a picture and the child guesses what it is. Afterwards he describes the whole picture, eg 'Man. Wearing red hat.'

7. The child tells the adult what to paint, draw or make, eg

Draw man . . . . . kicking a ball
wearing brown trousers
driving big car, etc.

8. Whispering games: the adult whispers a phrase to the first child, eg 'Susan's big nose'; 'tomatoes are red' etc. The phrase is then whispered right round the group; the last person whispers it back to the adult who says it out loud. Remember to vary the order of seating so that each child has the chance to hear the original version. This can be achieved by the adult changing places.

Beyond the Three-Word Phrase

The length and complexity of utterance can be gradually increased by continued expansion of both noun and verb phrases, and by combining whole utterances. To do this successfully the child needs to learn grammatical morphemes and new vocabulary, including prepositions and adverbs. Novel words and constructions should first be introduced in shorter, simpler utterances, eg the child should be taught 'Mummy in kitchen' before he is expected to say 'Mummy washing up in kitchen'.

Grammatical Morphemes

Most of the inflections and auxiliaries should be introduced into the activities already described, guided by the order of acquisition outlined on page 62, and by the child's readiness to learn. As many of the grammatical morphemes are redundant, adding no new meaning to the sentence, the adult needs to provide plenty of models, using slightly exaggerated stress and intonation. Elicited imitation procedures may also be useful, ie the child is required to imitate the adult's model immediately it has been given.

Progressive (-ing)

This is to be introduced into action activities as described above. Although the adult models the full structure she should not worry if the child omits the copula at this stage and produces utterances such as 'he running'. *Photo Action-cards* [5], Winslow Press *Basic Sequences* and *Children at Play Jigsaws* [1] showing children playing indoors and outdoors are useful.

Activities to Elicit 'In' and 'On'

Start with the preposition 'in' and when the child can consistently express this, introduce 'on'.

1. The children call out to each other where they are. Organise the room so that as many different places as possible can be used. Early on it is best for 'in' to refer to a definite container, eg cupboard, box, bag, (empty) dustbin, and later to more abstract places such as a ring, the classroom, a square marked out on the floor, the corner.

2. The children tell each other where to go, eg 'in the box'; 'sit on the table'.

3. Hide-and-seek: give the child a few minutes to find his friends, and then they must call out where they are.

4. Hold races that emphasise different prepositions, eg a sack-race focuses on 'in' (the sack); an egg-and-spoon race focuses on 'on' (the spoon) and so on.

5. Set up an obstacle course that mixes up the two prepositions, eg the child has to go in a hoop, on a chair, in a bin, on a bucket and on to a box. The others shout out the instructions in unison. This can be turned into a race against time (use an egg timer or alarm clock) or a race between children.

6. The child tells the adult where to place toys and objects.

7. The child tells the adult or other children where to put things away, eg 'That goes in cupboard'; 'Put cups on shelf'.

8. The children take turns to hide a soft toy, eg a Snoopy-dog, and the others try to find it. If they cannot find it the child who has hidden it has to tell them where it is.

9. Setting-up and rearranging the home-corner or dolls' house is useful for preposition work. The child and adult discuss how to arrange the furniture or the child directs the adult in what to do.

10. Act out symbolic play sequences with miniature dolls or *Playmobile* [4], and to encourage the use of prepositions, eg a dolls' tea-party; 'Pour the tea *in* the cup'; 'Put plates *on* the table, Mummy'. A 'stupid' puppet can do all the wrong things, eg pour the tea in the bath (Derbyshire Language Programme).

Other symbolic play themes can include:

(i) shopping: putting the food *in* the bag.
(ii) putting baby to bed: *in* the bed; put *on* pyjamas.
(iii) getting dressed: put *on* your jumper.
(iv) doctors: medicine *in* the bottle; *in* hospital.

11. The child tells the adult where to stick pictures on to a Cellograph or *Fuzzy Felt* [4] board, or what to draw, eg 'Put flowers *in* the garden'; 'Put roof *on* house'.

12. Make special pictures with movable parts, eg you can draw a bedroom with a cupboard that has opening doors, which reveal the clothes inside, and a duvet that comes off the bed. Ask the child questions, eg 'Where's the little girl?' as you whip off the duvet to reveal all.

PICTURE WITH MOVABLE PIECES

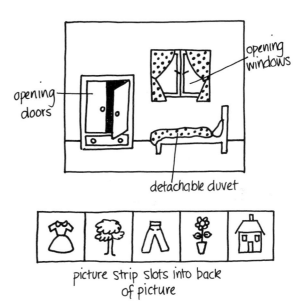

opening windows

opening doors

detachable duvet

picture strip slots into back of picture

13. The child describes what he sees in pictures (*Prepositions* [6]) in response to the adult's questions. Pop-up books, Cellographs and jigsaws make interesting variations of this.

14. Be sure to emphasise the prepositions as they occur naturally during the day's activities, eg when sticking the children's paintings *on* the wall, or mixing eggs *in* a bowl. Comment on what you are going to do and ask prompting questions, such as, 'Where shall we mix the eggs?' or 'What shall we put the eggs in?' depending upon the children's level of comprehension.

15. Tell stories emphasising the prepositions and ask the child questions such as 'and where was Goldilocks?' Answer—'*in* Baby Bear's bed'. Progress from well-known stories to inventing your own.

All these activities can be adapted to elicit more difficult prepositions later on. 'Under' is usually the next to be understood.

Examples: Washing Day: a miniature line with dolls' clothes can be put up; or draw and cut out clothes to stick on to a washing line in a book, using Blu-Tack. The child gives instructions, 'Hang the trousers *next to* the shirt'.

Tunnel He: the children play tag and when they are caught they have to stand with their legs wide apart. They can be freed if a free person crawls *under* their legs.

Obstacle courses: jumping *over* things, ducking *under* ropes, etc can be incorporated.

(*See also Chapter 4 for comprehension of prepositions.*)

Activities to Elicit the Regular Plural

1. The child can be taught the regular plural by contrasting one object with many objects. The contrast may be emphasised by making results contingent upon what the child says, eg if he asks for 'chip' at lunch-time, give him one chip. If he says, 'Do shoe up', say 'Just one shoe?', do one shoe up and wait. The same goes for 'Play with brick now', and so on. Be sure to model the correct structure when the child indicates that he wants more than one object.

2. Rhymes, songs and finger-plays encourage attention to and practice of plurals.

eg Ten Green Bottles

Ten green bottles
Hanging on the wall.
Ten green bottles
Hanging on the wall.
If one green bottle should accidentally fall,
There'd be nine green bottles
Hanging on the wall, etc.

Five Little Frogs (*a finger-play*)

Five little frogs sitting by a well,
One looked in and down he fell.
Four little frogs sitting by a well, etc.

3. Dressing-up and getting dressed and undressed are useful activities to elicit plurals because shoes, socks, stockings, gloves, sleeves and trousers usually come in pairs. The child can tell the adult what to put on herself, the child, another child, or a doll.

4. Dressing a cardboard doll with paper clothes can be used in the same way.

BOOK FOR PLURALS

5. Make a book with a picture of one object on one page, and on the facing page, many identical or similar objects. This gives the child a visual clue as he names each picture.

Using words such as 'lots of' helps to reinforce the plurality, eg 'a flower—lots of flowers'.

6. Make or buy a Noah's Ark full of animals, which of course must always travel in pairs.

Irregular Past Tense

As children learn rules they frequently apply them to irregulars that they once produced correctly, so it may not be worth directly teaching irregulars until after the child has learned the regular form.

Activities to Elicit Possessive (-s)

1. This can be introduced into the activities already described, eg 'O'Grady says—touch Nicky's knee!'

2. The adult asks questions concerning possession, eg 'Whose book is this?' Answer, 'John's'.

3. The children all take off their shoes, cardigans or coats and mix them up into a big heap. One child holds up each article of clothing in turn and asks 'Whose is this?' The others answer in unison.

4. The child sorts out other people's possessions, eg their work books, plimsolls for PE, and names them as he goes.

5. The child is in charge of the children's coats as they come in and has to hang them on the right pegs, saying 'Danny's peg', 'Sarah's peg' and so on.

6. Make a picture book with a person or animal on one side, and an object (acting as a possession) on the other. It is best to start with common associations, eg baby and bottle; policeman and helmet; dog and bone; sheriff and badge; cowboy and hat or gun.

7. Wash-Day: the child undresses his dolls and teddies and pretends to wash and iron their clothes. Afterwards he sorts them out, saying 'That's teddy's jacket; dolly's socks', etc (Derbyshire Language Programme).

8. Make a board-game divided into large squares, each with a colourful picture of an unusual dwelling-place. The children throw a dice to move their counters round the board and name the picture they land upon, eg 'I'm in the monster's cave'. The board could be made to follow a fairytale such as 'Jack and the Beanstalk' incorporating 'the giant's castle', 'the old lady's room', 'Jack's beanstalk' and 'Jack's cottage', etc. Rules could then be added to follow the story, eg each player is a character from the story and must try to get home first.

Activities to Elicit Uncontracted Copula (-is)

1. Start with a simple subject-verb-complement (SVC) structure, eg 'It is yellow'; 'It is broken'.

   (i) Use large, clear pictures or small toys and ask, 'What colour is it?'
   (ii) Lay out several pictures and take it in turns to describe one of them, 'It is furry'; 'It is long', and the other person guesses which picture it is.

2. Progress to the more complex SVC structure, 'It is a giraffe', etc. Do not worry if the child does not produce the article at this stage as he may not be able to cope with two new elements. (On the other hand, if he shows

more inclination to use the article than the copula, capitalise on this for the present.)

(i) The teacher hides a clear, large picture of an object, person or animal, and uncovers it very slowly. The child guesses it.

(ii) Take turns to draw pictures and the others guess what it is.

3. If the child is using pronouns, gradually introduce these with the copula, eg 'He is a policeman'; 'She is dirty', using the methods described. Jigsaws, play-people and story-books can also be used. *Photocue Occupation Cards* [5] are useful for the older child.

4. Miming and acting games can be used to elicit the forms 'You are (a soldier)'; 'I am (a cat)', etc.

5. Distinctive hats or clothes can also be used, eg a stethoscope signifies a doctor; a feather-headdress means an Indian.

6. Older children can try guessing impersonations. Props can be provided as necessary.

These activities can also be used for the more frequently used contracted form of the copula.

Articles

Once the child consistently uses the copula, expect him to attempt the indefinite article. However, you may find that in trying to remember the article he forgets the copula for a while. Reduce the complexity of the sentences if possible.

The difference between 'a' and 'the' is subtle and need not be overtly taught at this stage but always give the correct model.

Auxiliaries

The earliest auxiliary to elicit is the copula used as an auxiliary, eg 'he *is* running', 'I *am* sewing'. The uncontracted form, although less natural, is easier to hear and therefore may be easier for the child to learn. The form can be elicited through physical play, large and small doll play, constructional play, describing pictures, in fact in almost every situation throughout the day when the child is talking about action. There should be ample opportunity as action is the child's predominant topic of conversation (Bloom, 1978).

'Have' should be taught firstly where it is obligatory, eg in 'I have got a birthday present'; 'I have been to the shops' and 'I have done a painting'. The contracted form is much more frequently used, but, like the contracted copula, is less obvious to the listener, which may be why it is so often omitted. The omission of this auxiliary does not detract from the meaning of the sentence or prevent the child from getting his message across and may therefore prove difficult to teach and to get carry-over. The older child may be persuaded that it sounds more grown-up to use the auxiliary verbs.

Tense

Once the child can express a sense of time by talking about things that have happened or what he is about to do, he may be ready to learn the appropriate tense markers.

The Past Tense

It is easier for the child to express the immediate past (Reynell, 1977).

1. When the child has completed an activity ask him, 'What have you done/made/painted?' etc.

2. When the child has completed an activity send him to tell another adult or child what he has just done.

3. Set up play-situations with miniature dolls, eg pretend it's dolly's birthday and she blows out the candles. Afterwards ask the child what happened, keeping to open-ended questions.

4. Use any spontaneous incident to elicit the past tense, eg if an aeroplane flies overhead, tell the children to listen and ask them about it afterwards.

5. Contrast past and present in action-pictures (*Verb Tenses* [6]). A fair amount of drilling may be necessary but this can be enlivened by making the pictures amusing.

6. Tell the children a simple story or nursery rhyme (using the past tense), which they then act out to help them remember the story. Afterwards they must retell the story. Start with familiar tales and rhymes.

The child learns to talk about things in the recent but not immediate past.

7. Gradually increase the delay between the completion of an action and the child talking about it, eg when the child has made a plasticine model ask him to tidy up *before* you ask him what he has been making.

8. When the child goes back to his classroom or is collected by his Mum help him to tell her what he has been doing. Pick out the most memorable activity. (Of course if he has done nothing interesting or exciting he won't be motivated to talk about it.)

9. Make sure that children have the opportunity to do slightly different things so that they can tell each other what they've been doing.

10. Show a short film or watch 'Playschool' if you have access to the necessary equipment, and discuss it with the children afterwards. The programmes must be short and interesting. If you have a video or cine-film you can re-run the action so the children can check how much they remembered.

11. Let the children act out and talk about outings, visits and special occasions that have recently taken place. Pictures can be used as visual prompts to ease the load on the child's memory and allow him to concentrate more upon the linguistic forms.

Future Tense

The child can be taught to use adverbials such as yesterday and tomorrow to express time, before the appropriate syntactic forms are used.

1. Encourage attention to the immediate future by asking the child what he would like to play with, drink, eat, wear, etc.

2. When the child has finished a task and discussed it, ask him what he is going to do next. Teach the forms 'I'm going to; I'm gonna'; 'I want to; I wanna', etc which is less complex than using the modals 'I will' and 'I shall'.

3. Act out situations with miniature toys and ask the child 'What is going to happen next?' eg play at families with miniature dolls, setting a scenario for the child. 'Baby is getting very tired—what should Mummy do?'

4. Carry out activities with the child that must follow a particular sequence, eg 'getting dressed', 'making a cake or cup of tea' and at each stage ask the child 'What shall

I/we do now?' Do the same with other activities that the child usually carries out in a certain order.

5. Picture books can be made to show people who are about to perform actions on one page, and in the process of performing them, on the opposite page, eg a footballer about to take a penalty, and taking the penalty; a plane about to take off, and flying. The child is helped to progress from expressing the present, eg 'The plane is on the ground', to the future, 'The plane is going to fly'.

PICTURE-BOOK FOR PRESENT AND FUTURE TENSE

footballer about to take
a penalty

footballer taking
a penalty

6. Sequential stories: Winslow Press and LDA make packs of sequential stories in line-drawing or photographic form, which vary from easy to very difficult. After the child has placed the pictures in the correct order tell him the story. Once he can sequence them without error, he is ready to tell the story himself. Teach words such as 'then' and 'next' to help the sequence flow. Make sure the child sticks to the same tense throughout the story.

7. Use comic-strips and cartoons in a similar way to the sequential stories. They can be left in their strips or cut up for the child to sequence. *Self-Care Sequential Cards* [2] show familiar routines in cartoon-style.

8. Shopkeepers: the child tells you what he is going to buy from the 'shop', and this is then acted out immediately. *Market Place* [6] food photographs are very useful.

9. Rehearsal: role-plays can be used to rehearse a real situation, eg going to a real sweet shop or going to the pictures. This can lead on to planning ahead.

10. Tomorrow: the adult and children play question-and-answer drills, turned into a game or chant.

> Adult: 'What will you buy tomorrow my dear?'
> Child: 'I/we'll buy a new coat tomorrow sir.'
> Adult: 'What will you eat tomorrow my dear?'
> Child: 'I'll eat a nice apple tomorrow sir.'
> Adult: 'Who will you visit tomorrow my dear?'
> Child: 'I'll visit the Queen tomorrow sir.'

Actions can be added to the words.

11. When the child can express both past and future events all three can be contrasted in picture form. Winslow Press produce a useful *Tense Kit* [6] which consists of a flip-book divided into three parts, showing people about to do actions, doing actions,

and having done the actions. Do not expect the child to appreciate the passing of time in a fully adult way until he is much older.

Activities to Elicit Yes-No Questions

If everything is always as children expect it to be and if they never have any problems, their questions can become very stereotyped and limited. Genuine questions should not be ignored or the child may become discouraged.

The linguistic form of questions may need to be modelled many times.

1. Guessing Games:
   (i) The child thinks of something in the room and the others try to guess what it is. Their guesses will usually be fairly concrete.
   (ii) 20 Questions: as above but the children have only twenty guesses between them. At a higher level they should be encouraged to ask 'Is it big?'; 'Is it an animal?' etc.
   (iii) The children guess what is wrapped up in a parcel.
   (iv) The adult draws a silhouette of an object for the children to guess.
   (v) The children try to guess what object is being mimed.
   (vi) The children listen to a tape-recording of common everyday or animal noises and try to guess what they are.
   (vii) The children are shown common objects photographed from an unusual angle and have to guess what they are.

2. The adult acts out emotions, eg smiling, crying, shaking fist, yawning, and the children ask 'Are you happy?' etc.

3. The children pretend to be animals, and the others ask 'Are you a lion?' etc.

Activities to Elicit Wh- and Open-Ended Questions

1. Each child has an opportunity to be in charge at mealtimes and break-times and asks the others what they would like to drink and eat.

2. Similarly, a child is put in charge of sharing out the toys or equipment for arts and crafts, and asks each child what he needs.

3. Sometimes new toys and games can be introduced and not explained in detail to the children. The child who comes to the adult to find out how it works should be taught the appropriate question-forms (Berry, 1980).

4. During the hiding-games described earlier, the seeker must ask the hiders where they are, or where they have hidden the objects.

5. The child asks teddy and dolly questions during the course of his play. The adult should answer for the toys.

6. The child asks a puppet questions while the adult takes the puppet's part.

7. Action-games and rhymes such as 'Queenie, Queenie, who's got the ball?', 'What's the time Mr Wolf?', 'Ding-dong bell, Pussy's in the well', and so on, elicit questions as part of the game.

8. The adult and children have sessions where they ask each other questions, eg about their family and pets,

their favourite music, foods, stories and animals, what they did at the weekend and on outings, etc.

9. *'Why—Because'* [5] cards help the child to express causal relations. This leads on to the appropriate use and understanding of 'Why'? questions.

General Stimulation Activities for the Older Child

The following list of activities encourage language and communication between children.

1. All play activities (*see Chapter 3*).

2. Arts and crafts.

3. Physical activities such as team games, tug of war, races, Oranges and Lemons, tag, skipping, and so on.

4. Playing 'School' or 'Speech Class': children like to take the 'teacher's' role.

5. Listening to stories, discussing their content and retelling them.

6. Describing people, objects and pictures to blind-folded children—Winslow Press *ColorCards* and *ColorLibraries* and *Children of the World Jigsaws* [4] can be used here.

7. Giving running commentaries to real events or events that are mimed or acted out.

8. Giving running commentaries to silent films or television programmes with the sound turned down (if the children can tolerate this!).

9. Putting on puppet plays. *AJDA Multipurpose Composite Furniture* [1] can be used for a variety of purposes, eg a puppet-theatre, shop, kitchen, library.

10. Describing activities such as how to make a cup of tea, clean your teeth, have a bath.

11. Memory games, which can be built around vocabulary themes, eg 'My auntie went to market and bought a straw hat'. 'My auntie went to market and bought a straw hat and a guitar'. This also encourages the use of 'and' to combine utterances.

12. Continuing sentences: the child has to think of a word to finish the sentence or he is out. At a higher level the children each add a word to try and keep the sentence going for as long as possible.

13. Continuing stories: the adult starts a story and at a strategic point the child next to her takes over. This continues on round the circle and the adult finishes it off. Start with familiar tales.

14. Outings and visits to places of interest, such as zoos, parks, supermarkets, car showrooms, etc. Follow these up with paintings, projects or discussions— *Talking Pictures* [6] are very useful for this.

15. Making scrapbooks, collections and building up interest-tables.

16. Games of chance, and choosing what work to do in an unorthodox way, eg with a paper chooser or lucky dip.

17. Discussions: these can be on almost any subject, preferably something the child brings to the group, an incident observed by the children, something in the news, a child's question, a television programme you all watch, etc. Back it up with pictures (*Celebration Jigsaws* [4]) and role-play (Berry, 1980).

18. Projects.

19. 'Let's Pretend' games, with monsters, aliens, witches, giants and wizards.

20. Problem-solving: take advantage of situations that crop up, eg half the children want a story and half want to paint. (A possible solution would be to listen to the story and then paint a picture about it.)

21. Solving hypothetical situations: these must be made fairly concrete with plenty of visual clues to prompt the child. Read a story about a child who loses his money, breaks a vase, etc and ask the children what they would do in the same situation. At a higher level, ask the children before you reveal the end of the story. *What would you do?* [5] cards are also useful.

22. LDA *What's Wrong?* [5] cards. Children usually enjoy the ridiculous pictures.

23. Give the child responsibility, especially in a group or class. Children who feel useful and important will gain in confidence.

CHAPTER 6
PERCEPTION

CHAPTER 6
PERCEPTION

Introduction

Perception refers to the receiving of information by the senses—sight, sound, taste, touch and smell. We also take it to mean, "the assigning of meaning to the physical phenomena in the child's environment" (Fraser and Blockley, 1982). This chapter will concentrate upon visual, auditory and tactile perception.

The relationship between perception and language is controversial. Joan Reynell, Bloom and Lahey, and others, consider perception to be important for language learning, as cognitive developments are based on considerable preceding perceptual experience. For instance the conceptual processes involved in measuring rely on the perceptual skills of comparing and discriminating between lengths, sizes and amounts. However, exactly what form of perceptual training might be useful in language teaching is not clear, as it has not been proved that perceptual tasks involving non-linguistic materials directly influence language acquisition. It is beyond the scope of this chapter to examine these controversies in detail and therefore we attempt only to explain some of the terms that may be encountered and to mention a few of the studies the reader might like to consult.

Uses of Training in Perceptual Skills

1. Perception may form an important foundation for the growth of comprehension and cognition.

2. Perceptual tasks can direct, focus and extend the child's concentration and can therefore be used in attention therapy.

3. Auditory-perceptual tasks may enhance listening skills.

4. Many perceptual activities can be demonstrated and carried out non-verbally, which can be useful for severely language-impaired children.

5. Related language can be taught alongside perceptual skills.

6. Perception training may encourage self-organisation and orderly thinking.

7. Perceptual training may help children make good use of residual vision and hearing.

8. Children whose language deficits are believed to stem directly from their poor perceptual skills, eg 'Fraser-Blockley types'*, may benefit directly.

---

* The 'Fraser-Blockley' type of language disorder is believed to be a specific disorder secondary to a perceptual disorder. See *The Language Disordered Child*; Fraser, G.M. and Blockley, J.; NFER Nelson Publishing Co Ltd, 1982.

Assessment

The assessment of perceptual skills usually forms part of a performance test, which is administered by a paediatrician or psychologist in order to evaluate a child's general level of development. These results, together with the therapist's informal observations of the child's visual, auditory and tactile skills, would indicate whether direct teaching in these modalities was necessary. Assessment may also indicate the modality in which the child is most receptive to remediation.

Developmental check lists, such as those produced by Sheridan, Gesell and Griffiths, give an overview of the normally developing child.

1. Sheridan, M., 'Children's Developmental Progress. From Birth to Five Years'.

2. 'Griffiths Mental Developmental Scales for Testing Babies and Young Children from Birth to Eight Years of Age.'

3. 'Gesell Developmental Scales—1 to 72 Months.'

Formal Tests Used by Psychologists

1. Merrill-Palmer Scale of Mental Tests. Tests for visual matching, spatial organisation and visual construction in children aged 24 to 48 months.

2. Snijders-Oomen Non-Verbal Test of Intelligence. Tests for visual discrimination, sorting, analogies, mosaics etc.

3. Illinois Test of Psycholinguistic Abilities. Tests for auditory memory and visual association, amongst others.

4. Frostig Developmental Test of Visual Perception. Tests for eye-hand co-ordination, figure-ground perception, form-constancy, position in space and spatial relationships.

Visual Skills

"Looking—paying attention to what is seen with the object of interpreting its meaning" (Mary Sheridan, 1973). Under this heading we include visual discrimination, matching, sorting, form-constancy, spatial relationships, scanning, visual sequencing and visual tracking.

Visual discrimination is the ability to perceive similarities and differences. We may discriminate on the basis of colour, size, shape, dimension, and so on. Shape discrimination develops fairly slowly: young children find it easier to match shapes than to draw them, because the latter requires a more accurate perception of outline and good eye-hand co-ordination. Up to 2½ years old, children match shapes on a trial-and-error basis, while 3 to 4-year-olds find it helps if they can manipulate the shapes. Simple shapes are easier than complex ones, up to the age of 6 (Vernon, 1970).

Matching and sorting may be perceptual, eg sorting by colour or shape; or conceptual, eg sorting by function. According to Dr Reynell, a 2-year-old can match two identical objects, and by 2½ to 3 years old, can match two non-identical objects, according to either colour, shape or size, providing that simple shapes and primary colours are used. Shortly afterwards the child begins to sort large numbers of objects, first by one criterion, eg colour, and then by two, eg colour and size.

Figure-ground discrimination refers to the ability to distinguish an object from its background, and is an important, fundamental perceptual skill. It develops from the child's handling and appreciation of three-dimensional material.

Form-constancy refers to the consistent recognition of objects, people, shapes, etc, despite variations in size, orientation and distance from the child (Bryant, 1974). It is an important part of the object-concept (*see Chapter 1*).

Spatial relationships refers to the relative positions of objects in space, ie the angles and distances between them; whether one object is on top of another or inside it, and so on. The child first has to understand his own position in space, and as he explores his environment he learns through trial and error to judge angles, distances and dimensions by sight.

Scanning refers to the ability to locate and assimilate all the visual information that lies within the normal field of vision. Children may not scan efficiently until they are about 7 years old (Vernon, 1970) and we therefore cannot take it for granted that a child is 'looking' at everything he is 'seeing'.

(Visual sequencing is considered under the general heading of Sequencing. Visual tracking activities are given in Chapters 2 and 3.)

Auditory Skills

"Listening: attending to what is heard in order to interpret its meaning" (Mary Sheridan, 1973). Under this heading we include auditory discrimination, auditory sequencing and sound-location.

Auditory discrimination involves the perception of similarities and differences between sounds. Very early on the child distinguishes between human and other sounds, and between speech and non-speech. He also learns to discriminate between different voices, eg that of his mother and that of the next door neighbour, and different sounds, eg that the sound made by the doorbell is not the same as the sound made by the telephone. As he grows older he must learn to discriminate between the different phonemes of speech.

Sound-location is the ability to pinpoint a sound source. This is important for orienting oneself to a speaker, and for relating sounds to objects. If a child cannot tell where a sound is coming from he may have difficulty making a meaningful association between a sound and its source.

(Auditory sequencing is considered under the heading of 'Sequencing'.)

Tactile Skills

By tactile skills we mean the ability to take in information about the environment through the sense of touch. We may include tactile discrimination, matching and sorting under this heading. Small children learn much through touch and manipulation, but we are apt to forget that older children too may learn more easily if they are encouraged to use these skills.

Multi-sensory Integration

It is important for conceptual and language development that a child integrates the visual, auditory and tactile features of an input, ie that he realises that the sight, sound and feel of a drum, for instance, all refer to the same object. Children who are unable to do this often have very unstable concepts upon which to build language (Bloom and Lahey).

If lack of integration means that the child can only attend to one modality at a time, this has serious repercussions for language learning, which involves the simultaneous processing of both speech and the events that speech refers to (Reynell) (*see Chapter 2*).

Sequencing

This is the ability to perceive or predict an order, either spatially or temporally. Spatial sequencing refers to the ordering of objects according to their position in space, eg beads threaded in a red-blue-red-blue sequence, while temporal sequencing refers to the order in which they occur in time. Auditory stimuli are almost always perceived temporally. Visual stimuli may be perceived either temporally or spatially, although the latter tends to be dominant (Hermelin and O'Connor).

The relationship of language to a general sequencing ability is a very controversial issue. Some researchers have noted a general sequencing deficit occurring in language-disordered children (eg Poppon), while others have found only an auditory impairment (eg Menyuk). Still others have found no evidence for a causal relationship between sequencing deficits and language disability, eg Bloom and Lahey, who believe that the presence of both in one child could be due to some, as yet unknown, central deficit.

Consequently, there is no consensus of opinion as to the usefulness of non-linguistic sequencing tasks in language teaching. There may be direct application in the case of certain types of language-disordered children, but until research studies have proved more conclusive, we feel that therapists and language teachers should keep an open mind. The activities suggested here may be useful in encouraging ordered, logical thinking, attention and concentration in children who lack these qualities.

Memory

Many perceptual tasks involve memory and a child's failure in such tasks could be due to limits on his memory rather than an actual perceptual difficulty. Most auditory tasks have a memory load; for example, in order to discriminate between two hidden musical instruments a child must retain both the visual representations of the instruments and the sounds that they make.

Although the tendency is to divide memory tasks into visual, auditory and tactile memory, it is by no means certain that these are separate. Pre-school children may have fewer recall-strategies available to them than adults do; Conrad states that children under 5 are unable to use language to help them remember things. There is evidence that they may use 'imaging', which involves holding a picture of the object in the mind in order to recall it, eg a child is shown a picture of a cat, a ball and a chair; when one is taken away he must remember it by matching his mental image of the sequence to what he can now see. Young children may also use this strategy in auditory recall tasks.

Older children may make more use of language mediation in memory tasks, eg they may recall a missing picture by remembering its name. Verbal rehearsal may be helpful in the short-term, but experimental studies in the usefulness of naming aloud as an aid to long-term recall have been inconclusive (Hermelin and O'Connor).

Guidelines to Remediation

1. Teaching should follow a developmental sequence.

2. Verbal instructions should be appropriate to the child's level of comprehension.

3. Tasks and materials should be varied within the child's developmental level—he cannot be expected to stick to the same task for long periods.

4. Gradually increase the perceptual complexity of the task but make sure the child has consolidated each step before introducing something new. If necessary, simplify one feature of an activity when making another more difficult.

5. Keep tasks as enjoyable as possible, using materials interesting to the child.

6. A task should always be within the child's ability with a little effort on his part and help from the adult. The child should experience and be aware of early success.

7. The ultimate goal is improved language ability, so perceptual training should be used as an adjunct to language teaching and not as a substitute.

ACTIVITIES FOR DEVELOPING PERCEPTUAL ABILITIES

We have attempted to put the activities listed under each main heading in order of complexity, but each child develops differently, and what may be difficult for one may be relatively simple for another. If a child cannot complete an earlier task it does not automatically mean he won't manage a later one. If a child is not coping with an activity that should be within his reach, examine the way it is being presented. Is complexity reduced and are sufficient clues being provided? Have you helped him to find strategies? Are you using too much distracting and confusing language? Does the task involve other skills, such as manipulation and hand-eye co-ordination that the child finds difficult? Is the activity interesting enough?

Visual Skills

General Visual Awareness

For the younger child visual awareness can be encouraged through play, with the many visually stimulating toys that are commercially available, or can be made at home. Toys such as mobiles, flashing lights and colourful spinning-tops capture the child's attention. Posting-boxes and pagodas, shape-form boards, floor mosaics, plasticine and pastry cutters encourage shape perception; stacking barrels, nesting boxes, large and small toys of all descriptions encourage size perception; coloured beads, paints, bricks, cotton reels etc develop awareness of colour, while interlocking toys, pull-apart toys, hammer-and-peg sets and peg-men help the child to appreciate how things fit together.

From a very early age children should be encouraged to look at large colourful picture books. Small children should also be helped to look at what is going on around them in the environment.

For the older child games and discussions can be useful to help them appreciate the importance of vision. Blindfold games, such as 'Blind Man's Buff', 'Pinning the Tail on the Donkey' and 'Squeak Piggy Squeak', not only teach the use of other senses, but are also a reminder of how we rely on our eyes. Magnifying glasses, binoculars, microscopes, camera lenses and both ends of a telescope provide interesting visual effects (Dowling, 1980).

To Encourage Shape Perception

1. Give children a variety of natural and man-made shapes to handle and experiment with, including stones, shells, leaves, nuts, boxes, tins, screws and books (Dowling, 1980).

2. Examine the properties of shapes—whether they roll, stand up, have points or straight edges, etc.

3. Encourage the child to compare geometric and abstract shapes such as circles, triangles, rectangles and squares with similar real-life shapes such as balls, tents, doors and boxes.

4. Make real-life pictures out of drawings of shapes, eg a square becomes a house; a circle, the sun, and so on.

5. Make shapes with plasticine and dough; ready-made cutters in all sorts of shapes can be used.

6. Make print patterns with shapes (Dowling, 1980).

7. Draw around shapes.

8. Trace shapes.

9. Help the child to copy shapes, first by demonstration, then from memory.

10. On outings ask the children to find round and pointed stones; cones and round leaves, etc. But have models available for any children who may not understand the vocabulary.

11. Use different-shaped trays and buckets in sand and water play.

To Encourage Size Perception

1. Compare children and adults, marking the different heights on the wall.

2. Compare large and small toys, animals, books, clothes, etc.

3. Make sand-castles with different-sized containers.

4. Make long and short 'trains' and 'roads' with different numbers of bricks or children, etc.

5. On outings compare trees and flowers, buses and cars, blocks of flats and houses, and so on.

Remember to draw attention to all the different dimensions: high-low; tall-short; fat-thin; long-short, as well as big and little, even though the child may not have the vocabulary for these. To the 3-year-old everything may be 'big' and 'little', but he will still attend to other dimensions perceptually.

Matching

A child who does not spontaneously match identical objects may only need one or two demonstrations, or he may need careful teaching in the following hierarchy (adapted from Kiernan, Jordan and Saunders).

1. Have two meaningful identical objects, eg large red bricks; give one to the child and keep one. Be sure to emphasise their sameness.

2. Put your red brick into a red box and help the child to do the same.

3. Repeat this procedure with more pairs of red bricks until the child is imitating spontaneously.

4. Now take two bricks, one red and one yellow, but similar in all other respects. Give the child the red one and keep the yellow one. Look carefully at the yellow one and place it in a yellow box. The child should put his red brick in the red box as usual, but if he does not, help him to do so, emphasising the colour difference.

5. Repeat this procedure until the child consistently performs the correct action.

6. Now encourage the child to place the red brick in the red box and the yellow one in the yellow box.

7. Repeat, using one plain box.

8. Repeat, using two plain boxes.

9. Repeat, leaving out the boxes.

10. Try the child with the red and blue bricks, handing them to him in pairs. (If he has not generalised start again from step 3.)

11. Gradually increase the number of colours.

12. Teach simple shape matching in the same way, keeping colour and size constant. If necessary shape cues can be provided by putting squares into a square tin and circles into a round one.

Other Ideas

1. Make trains, towers and roads with bricks, for the child to match by colour. Start off with all one colour and gradually increase the number of colours. The child initially copies the adult as she is building her model, but later he must wait until the model is completed.

2. Match Noah's Ark animal pairs.

3. Match doll-sized furniture and accessories.

4. Use matching pairs of cards, showing picture, colour, shape or size.

5. Play dominoes and Snap, matching shape, colour or object. There are plenty of these on the market but they can also be home-made from robust materials. It is best to start with a few large dominoes and build up.

6. Lotto and Bingo games: the adult shows the child a picture and if he has an identical one on his card he can keep it. This is more natural if it can be played in a group.

7. Make cards that show between two and five different pictures or abstract shapes. The child has to match the whole card.

8. Collect ladybirds, matching them by their spots.

9. Match small pictures to a large composite picture, eg pictures of slides, swings, etc on to a fairground scene. The child's scanning ability and figure-ground perception will need to be fairly good.

Non-Identical Matching

1. At a simple level lift-out puzzles and posting boxes are useful for shape-matching.

2. Match cardboard shapes to plastic and plasticine shapes.

3. Make jam tarts with different-sized or different-shaped pastry cutters, and before eating, see if the child can match them back together.

4. Match a red brick to a red car; a yellow bead to a yellow cotton reel, etc.

5. Play 'croquet' by pushing coloured balls through the same-coloured hoops.

6. Make print-pictures with different shapes and silhouettes of animals, and have the child match the prints back to the templates.

7. *Sequencing Beads* [2]: the child matches wooden beads to a pattern-card. eg

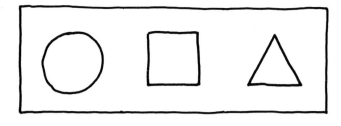

8. Board games involving the matching of colour and shape on dice to those on a board.

Sorting

Once the child is matching efficiently he is well on the way to being able to sort. Start with a few colours and use coloured sorting trays. Move on to sorting in plain trays and then in a free space. When the child has mastered sorting by one criterion and generalised this skill, progress to two criteria, eg sorting large red balls from a mixed collection of balls of different colours and sizes. Lastly, the child must learn to sort by his own chosen criterion in order to develop self-organisation skills. Eventually the child should realise that the same objects can be grouped in many different ways.

Objects can also be sorted according to their functions and characteristics, but this involves conceptual thinking and will not be dealt with here.

Start by sorting two groups of very dissimilar objects:

1. While tidying up the child can put all the teddy bears on one shelf and all the dollies on another; the pencils in one jar and scissors in another, and so on.

2. In a group, line up all the boys on one side and the girls on the other.

3. Sort boxes from bottles; stones from shells; rings from necklaces; cups from saucers; knives from forks and spoons, etc.

4. For children who have reached the symbolic stage of picture recognition, pictures can also be used.

Proceed to sorting on the basis of one difference:

1. Sort the children with dark hair from those with fair hair.

2. Tidy up by putting red bricks in one box and green ones in another, etc.

3. Sort out different-coloured beads for making different-coloured necklaces.

4. Sort different plastic shapes.

5. Make flowers out of plastic shapes by sorting out circles for the centres and triangles for the petals.

6. Separate the large toys from the miniature toys.

7. Give the child a variety of objects and ask him to post all the red things, etc.

8. Make different print-pictures, eg cover one sheet of paper with prints of red apples, another with green apples or red bananas.

9. Draw around shapes, templates or stencils, cut them out and sort them.

10. In the classroom the child can sort out the different-sized and different-coloured pencils, crayons, paintpots and sheets of paper.

Children can sort almost anything. Some further ideas are: coloured buttons, cotton reels, plastic animals, trees, *Logic People*[4], laces, buttons with different numbers of holes, picture–cards, *Slot-o-build*[1], *Disco Shapes*[1], and *Reo-click*[1].

Size Grading

Once the child is aware of different sizes he should be able to discriminate between two very dissimilar sizes. Some of the sorting activities listed above are based on size discrimination.

Teaching Hierarchy

1. Let the child sort through sets of large and small objects, eg cereal spoons from teaspoons, large and small dolls, real knives and forks from miniature ones, etc. Make sure you use only two size-contrasts at this stage.

2. When he can do this introduce a third object, again very different in size. Let the child grade two sizes as usual and then add an otherwise identical object which is either much bigger or much smaller. Draw his attention to it. Terms such as 'biggest' and 'smallest' should be avoided at this stage if the intention is to increase the number of objects to be graded.

3. Let the child grade two objects and hand him the third, encouraging him to place it in the correct sequence.

4. Give him all three objects at once.

5. Increase the number of objects.

6. Decrease the size difference.

Graded inset-boards and lift-out puzzles can help the child as he can only fit the pieces back if he puts them in the right order.

Nesting-boxes can also help the child. As he pulls each piece out he can lay it down in order, thus ending up with a graded sequence. Plastic rings that fit on a stick can be used in the same way.

Other Ideas

1. Nesting saucepans can be graded by size.

2. Grade pastry-cutters, bowls, baking tins and measuring spoons (Dowling, 1980).

3. Grade the shoes of adults, teenagers, schoolchildren, toddlers and babies.

4. Babushka dolls (Russian dolls that fit inside each other), Russian eggs and *Billie and his Barrels*[1] are size-graded.

5. Grade sets of different-sized animals.

6. Make print-patterns with different-sized blocks.

7. Draw around graded rings on separate cards and grade them.

8. Make graded footprints for the child to put in order. Afterwards make up a story about them.

9. Tell stories such as 'The Three Billy-Goats Gruff' and 'Goldilocks and the Three Bears' with accompanying graded animals or pictures (Dowling, 1980).

10. The child draws round different-sized objects and colours them in. He must check that his drawings are in the correct order of size.

11. Size-graded inset-boards and jigsaws can be used on their own without the board to help the child eg *Party Numbers Jigsaws* [4].

Discrimination

Matching and sorting, although dependent upon discrimination, tend to emphasise similarities, whilst discrimination tasks focus on differences.

Teaching

1. Place two different-coloured beakers in front of the child. Consistently hide a toy or sweet under the same beaker but randomly change the position of the beakers (Kiernan et al).

2. If he doesn't find the toy help him by showing him the right beaker.

3. When he can find the toy every time by watching you, place a screen between you and hide it out of his sight. When the child consistently chooses the correct beaker he is discriminating between them (Kiernan et al).

Other Ideas

1. Using sets of three objects, two of which are identical and one different, get the child to make pairs of the identical ones and discard the other. You may use sorting toys, such as treesorts and *Animal Allsorts* [4], miniature toys such as cars, animals, dolls and dolls furniture, and real objects.

   (i)   Present the two identical objects first, then the other.
  (ii) Present the different object then the two identical ones.
 (iii) Present them in the order – 'same, different, same'.
 (iv) Randomise the order.

2. Use sets of three pictures in the same way. Gradually decrease the difference so that the child must pay attention to details, eg two pictures of a clown's face have a smiling mouth, and one has a turned-down mouth.

3. Present pairs of objects or pictures that are either the same or different for the child to judge.

4. Give the child a whole pack of jumbled picture-cards to find identical and different ones.

5. Present pairs of cardboard or plastic shapes that are either the same or different.

6. Present a series of cards showing simple shapes, in groups of three. One card differs in a small detail, which the child must spot (Kirk and Kirk).

Missing detail, eg

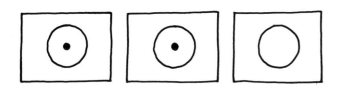

Substitution, eg

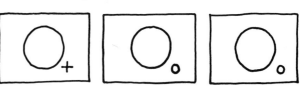

Positional change, eg

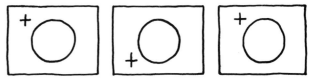

7. Present a series of cards or silhouettes of familiar animals and objects with one detail different.

Reversal, eg

Omission, eg

Orientation change, eg

(for the older child)

Size change, eg

(Kirk & Kirk)

8. Similar tasks can be given using the blackboard or a wipe-clean slate for a change. Pictures can also be put on a fuzzy-felt board, and shapes made out of matchsticks. The disadvantages with these methods are that the child cannot manipulate the pictures or shapes, but he can rub them off, break the matchsticks, etc so be wary of using them with very restless children.

9. Place two/three objects or pictures in front of the child. He must find the duplicates from a set of cards, or tin of objects. Increase the number of items.

10. Go behind a screen and remove or add a piece of clothing or jewellery. If the child doesn't spot the difference point it out to him (Kirk and Kirk). This also makes a good scanning exercise.

11. Show the child a large picture of a single toy or object, then cut it in half and help him put the picture back together. Do this with many pictures.

12. Cut lots of pictures into pairs and jumble them up so that he has several pairs to sort out.

13. Make the pictures increasingly similar, eg red apple/green apple; house/flat/shop, etc. It may be sensible to back the pictures with cardboard before cutting them.

14. Do the same with pictures cut into three, four and five pieces.

15. Show the child a stick and the child must select one of similar length from a set.

16. Show the child a stick and lay a shorter one beside it. The child must find another stick to place by the shorter one to make it up to the length of the first stick. Sets of these sticks are available commercially but can be made from lengths of stiff cardboard.

17. Spot-the-difference pictures: these abound in children's books, comics and magazines, but you can also make your own simpler versions.

18. Use *What's Missing?* [1] cards but make your own completed models.

Figure-ground Discrimination

1. Show the child a small object, eg a miniature farm animal; he must find its duplicate amongst a large tin of similar objects. To make it slightly easier he can tip them out, first on to a plain surface, later a patterned one.

2. Put objects around the room and show the child a duplicate of one of them to find. Make this harder by: hiding a red toy against a red background, etc; using two-dimensional shapes.

3. Draw a simple, familiar shape on to a white card and draw black lines over it. The child shows you the outline with his finger or traces it (Kirk and Kirk). Gradually make the lines closer together, and use coloured cards.

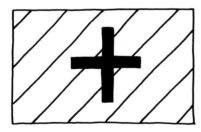

4. Draw a simple shape on a patterned background; again the child traces it with his finger or on to paper.

5. Draw outlines of animals and objects in a similar way. Make this more difficult by: making the outline less bold; increasing the number of shapes on the card; drawing dotted outlines (for children 5 to 6 years) (Kirk and Kirk).

6. Draw overlapping shapes on to a white background. The child traces each outline with his finger and then traces or copies each shape separately, and colours them in, eg

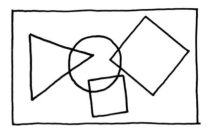

(adapted from an idea by Kirk and Kirk).
Increase the complexity of the background.

7. Use commercial products such as Frostig Figure-ground Worksheets (available from NFER-Nelson) and *Figure-ground Activity Cards* by DLM.

8. The child has to find hidden shapes, objects, flowers, letters and numbers in a large composite picture.

Spatial Relationships

The Child's Own Position in Space

The child has first to orientate himself to the objects in his world. He learns that some objects are constant, eg the walls, the fitted wardrobe, but he can change his orientation to them by moving himself. He also learns that some objects are semi-constant, eg a chair, which is usually upright and at the table, but may fall over, and may be placed in other situations. With a child who has difficulty estimating his own position relative to other objects, it is necessary to place him in those positions, and emphasise the point.

1. Help the child to walk towards or away from named objects.

2. Help the child to walk over and around objects in his way, judging the distances appropriately.

3. Show him how things look different from different positions eg from on top of a chair and under a chair; while standing up and lying down.

4. See if he can reach out and touch things from a certain distance away. Start with yourself so that you can catch him.

5. Use *Soft Shapes* [1] —large cushioned shapes that the child can crawl and roll over without hurting himself.

6. The child must follow a pathway made of *Stepping Stones* [1] or *Tac Tracks* [2] .

7. The child picks up objects whilst sitting in a chair, or standing inside a hoop (Fraser and Blockley, 1982).

8. Make an obstacle course where the child must:
   (i) Crawl under chairs, ropes or sticks balanced on skittles of varying heights.
   (ii) Jump or step over objects; manoeuvre round objects.
   (iii) Jump from a height to a defined space, eg from a chair into a hoop.
   (iv) Jump from one hoop to another.
   (v) Crawl through a *Play Tunnel* [4].
   (vi) Walk down an incline.

   Use school apparatus if this is possible.

The child then learns to orientate objects other than himself. He will discover that he can put teddy under his bed, or a chair, but not under the bath or a door. You can help the child by letting him put toys and objects on to various surfaces and relating them to constant objects.

1. Show the child how teddy or dolly can be sat on a chair or table quite happily, but what happens if you try to put it on top of a bottle or stick?

2. Experiment with inclines and bumpy surfaces.

3. Play hiding-games, placing large toys in various positions around the room.

4. Make teddies and dollies stand, sit and lie on their backs and fronts. This will lead on to the child perceiving relationships between movable objects.

5. Help the child to pile up books, clothes, etc putting one thing on top of another.

6. The child can make rows of his toys, putting them side-by-side or behind each other. If he leaves spaces you can show him how to roll balls or cars in between.

7. Make brick-models increasing in complexity for the child to copy. Start with towers and trains, pointing out the relationship of one brick to its neighbours. Bridges and steps introduce the perception of spaces. If the child does not leave spaces in his own construction show him how to put his finger through the model or push objects through, like a train going through a tunnel. It is best to start with large blocks where the relationships are more obvious. If the child still has difficulty, have him copy you brick by brick. (See a good developmental scale for the ages at which children are expected to copy these structures.)

8. Fitting shapes together: at a low level this can be done as a tidying up activity, eg the child must find the best way to fit bricks into a box, or shapes into a round tin.

More Complex Activities

1. Copying patterns on a peg-board: first the adult demonstrates the task and the child copies her model; next she gives him the finished pattern to copy without demonstration.

Using one peg-board:

(i) the child copies a horizontal line directly underneath the teacher's example.
(ii) the child copies a vertical or diagonal line.

Using two peg-boards:

(i) the child copies one horizontal line, then one vertical line, on a separate board.
(ii) the child copies a continuous horizontal and vertical line.
(iii) the child copies diagonal lines. This basic activity can be varied by: making the lines all one colour; using more than one colour; introducing spaces between the pegs; making the line longer or shorter; increasing the number of lines.
(iv) the child copies groups of four to five pegs in the same colour.
(v) the child copies scatter-patterns, ie the pegs have no immediate relationship to each other.

When using two peg-boards the child will find it easier if the master-board is placed directly above his own, so that he can see the direct comparison. Once he can copy the patterns like this, vary the position of the board.

2. Peg-board copying can be made more complex by having the child translate a paper pattern on to a peg-board, and vice versa.

(i) Stick a simple plastic or cardboard shape on to the peg-board with *Blu-Tack* and have the child place pegs around the outline. He then lifts the shape out and compares it to his outline (Kirk and Kirk).
(ii) Put another shape inside the first one, ie having made a square using the above method, place a triangle or circle inside the square and let the child make a peg outline of it (Kirk and Kirk).
(iii) Draw a horizontal line on paper for the child to copy on to the peg-board.
(iv) Increase the number of lines and introduce verticals and diagonals.
(v) Make lines on the peg-board for the child to copy on to paper (Kirk and Kirk).
(vi) The child copies more complex paper patterns. These can be obtained from LDA or home-made if using a simplified peg-board.

3. Packing the suitcase: give the child a paper rectangle representing a suitcase, and several shapes to fit into it (Dowling, 1980). (This can also be a matching game, by marking the shape on to the paper 'suitcase'.)

4. Make three-dimensional structures, using 1-inch cubes, from two-dimensional paper-patterns, either making your own, or using DLM *Plain Inch Cubes in Perspectives*.

5. Draw a series of lines, each about matchstick length and have the child copy them using matchsticks. Be careful to use dead matches!

eg (Kirk and Kirk)

6. Draw a series of curved lines which the child copies in plasticine or 'play-doh'.

eg (Kirk and Kirk)

7. Draw a series of shapes using curved and straight lines for the child to copy.

eg (Kirk and Kirk)

Scanning

Encourage scanning as part of other visual tasks by stretching out the array of items or pictures, or by pinning them up on the wall or a board. Unless encouraging left-right scanning and orderly work, the items need not be in a straight line. It may be necessary to prompt the child to scan by gently turning his head, or pointing to each item in turn, and saying 'Look'.

Some specific activities for scanning are:

1. Stick large pictures up around the walls and show the child a duplicate of the one he must find.

2. Draw a very long picture, eg a caterpillar, a snake, or an elongated dachshund, that stretches all round the room.

3. Queenie Queenie: play a version of Queenie Queenie in which children take it in turns to hide their eyes, while a small object or badge is pinned somewhere on one of the other children or the teacher. The child has to spot it.

4. Put some toys slightly outside the child's immediate visual field while he is playing, and draw his attention to them.

5. Draw the child's attention to all the details of a simple picture or all the aspects of a room or toy.

6. Ask the child to look around the room or playground and point to classmates or objects that the teacher names.

7. Draw the child's attention to all the details of a composite picture and help him to understand it as a whole (*see Chapter 1*).

8. Dot-to-dot pictures and patterns, found in many shops, encourage the child to scan efficiently in order to join up all the dots to form a picture. A finished version may be given to the child as a model.

9. See also Visual Sequencing activities in the next section, as these encourage left-right scanning.

Visual Sequencing

Encouraging the Child to Perceive Order in Everyday Life

1. Many everyday activities help the child to become aware of order, eg when a child gets dressed he must put on his underwear first, followed by his top clothes and then his outdoor clothing. Help the child to carry out self-care and household tasks by himself, thinking about each stage of the procedure. This will make him aware of sequences in real life. You can also make pictures of each stage of a routine for the older child to put into the correct order, to emphasise how one action follows on from another, eg make pictures showing the child:

   (i) taking the top off the toothpaste.
   (ii) squeezing the paste on to the brush.
   (iii) putting the top back on the toothpaste.
   (iv) brushing his top teeth.
   (v) brushing his bottom teeth.
   (vi) rinsing his mouth
   (vii) drying his mouth.

2. Establish daily and weekly routines for the child, eg parents could take their pre-school child for a walk each weekday after breakfast or lunch, or have a special time set aside for reading him stories. Weekends should involve a little 'treat' to set them aside from weekdays. Routines not only help children to feel secure, they help them to become aware of, and predict, order in life.

3. Children's games can also involve sequencing, eg when a group of children play skittles, they must learn to do things in a certain order. Each child must throw the ball, go to pick up the fallen skittles, retrieve the ball, give it to the next child and take his place at the end of the queue.

Specific Sequencing Activities

The child's work with advanced matching activities prepares him for the more complex skills of sequencing.

(See page 83 for some examples of matching activities with a series of items. Also use *Sequencing Beads*[2].)

Teaching

Start with a simple sequence, using colours, shapes or pictures, which you may have to build up for some while before the child gets the idea. If he doesn't, use the following procedure.

1. Using two primary colours, eg red and yellow, place large bricks in a simple ry-ry-ry sequence, making sure there are an equal number of colours. Leave one yellow brick for the child to complete the sequence.

2. Encourage the child to add more and more bricks to complete the sequence. Eventually placing ry-ry should be enough for the child to perceive and continue the order.

3. Repeat the procedure using red and a new colour, eg blue. If the child continues the sequence straight away, he has learnt the task. If not, repeat steps 1 and 2.

4. Repeat, using two colours as before but give the child three colours to choose from.

5. Increase the number of colours to choose from.

6. Build up the following sequences: ryb-ryb-ryb; rry-rry-rry; ryy-ryy-ryy, etc.

To make a sequencing task more difficult, introduce the memory factor by starting the sequence off in the child's sight, and then hiding it.

Other Ideas

1. Thread large coloured beads on to a string.

2. Draw a large flower and colour the petals according to a sequence.

3. Draw or build a train with lots of trucks sequenced by colour or size.

4. Sequence different sized bricks.

5. Sequence pictures of toys or objects (use Snap cards or similar).

6. Use plastic shapes in the same way.

7. Sequence lines of coloured pegs, on a peg-board, horizontally, vertically, diagonally. Use the spaces as part of the sequence.

8. Use the whole pegboard to make a sequence of pegs (Kirk and Kirk), eg

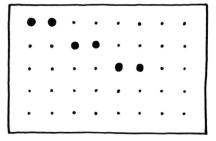

9. Draw or construct a sequence with an odd man out for the child to spot. This can be varied from a very obvious error to a subtle change in orientation, eg

$$++ \quad + \quad ++ \quad \times \quad ++ \quad +$$

etc (Kirk and Kirk).

10. Draw shapes or dots on paper for the child to continue (Kirk and Kirk), eg

. . : . . : . . :

etc. (This is a fairly abstract task for older children only.)

11. Logical sequencing tasks can be given to the older child, but they do demand both perceptual skills and logical thinking. You can invent your own, eg.

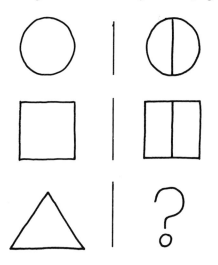

Auditory Skills

General Auditory Awareness

There are plenty of sound-making toys for very young children. They should also be encouraged to explore environmental sounds, relating them to objects and events, by trying things for themselves, eg switching on the hoover, flushing the toilet.

Older children can be encouraged to examine sound by:

1. having a few minutes' quiet time to listen to the sounds around them, and their own breathing (Dowling, 1980).

2. listening to and comparing soft and loud noises.

3. listening to music and sounds with their hands over their ears, wearing woolly hats or headphones, and through ear-trumpets.

4. using a stethoscope.

5. playing shouting and whispering games.

6. comparing pleasant and horrible sounds (Dowling, 1980), eg piano music with nails scraping on a blackboard.

7. listening to music, rhymes, stories and songs.

8. collecting different sound-makers for a sound-table.

9. *Fun with Sounds* [1] set: this presents the concepts of high and low; loud and soft; long and short sounds.

Discrimination

Make sure that the child can associate a sound to a sound-maker through lots of demonstration and play. Always let the child see what you are doing when introducing a new activity. When he can successfully discriminate between sounds using both visual and auditory skills, let him attempt a purely auditory task.

If the child is unsuccessful at his first attempt, it is essential to repeat the task exactly, as a purely auditory task.

If the child is unsuccessful at his first attempt, it is essential to repeat the task exactly, as it is all too easy to confuse the child by changing the original stimulus.

1. Show the child two dissimilar sound-toys or musical instruments, eg a whistle and a rattle. When he is settled, demonstrate each sound until he knows which sound belongs to which toy. Ask him to shut his eyes or hide the instruments behind a screen. Make one of the sounds and he must either point to the correct toy or make the same sound. A duplicate set of sound-makers will make this task easier to control.

2. Vary the above activity, using familiar sound-making objects, eg a spoon rattled in a cup, a music-box, a tube of Smarties!

3. Gradually increase the number of dissimilar sound-makers, or keeping to two objects, make the noises more alike. The child should eventually be able to discriminate between several fairly similar sounds.

4. Lay 2 or 3 dissimilar shakers in a row and repeat activity 1 (above). The shakers can be made by filling similar containers with different substances, such as dried peas, sugar, small pebbles, paper-clips, coffee-beans, etc. To aid memory a detachable coloured tag could be fitted to each shaker.

5. Ask the child to shut his eyes. Make a familiar noise in the room, eg shut the door, cough, use a pencil-sharpener, and the child has to make the same noise.

Children are notorious cheats when it comes to keeping their eyes shut, which is a difficult thing for little ones to do. Be warned!

6. Place several identical pairs of shakers before the child and ask him to choose one and shake it. He must then shake all the others until he finds the one he thinks sounds the same. He can check if he is right by opening them to see if the contents are the same. This can be extended into a pairs collecting game.

7. Pass-the-parcel: the child unwraps a parcel when the music stops and must pass it on when it starts again.

8. Ask the child to walk around the room while you play two instruments, eg the recorder and the drum. He must march like a soldier to the drum and dance like the Pied Piper of Hamelin, to the recorder. Tell him stories to illustrate these characters.

9. The child walks around the room while you play on the drum. He takes giant steps when he hears a loud beat, and pixie steps when he hears a soft one.

10. Play all the notes on a chime-bar. When the child has turned his back play two notes and ask him if they are the same or different.

11. Play one high and one low note on the chime-bars as the child watches. Ask him to turn his back and replay one of the notes. The child must copy or point to the correct bar.

Sound-Location

1. Roll a sound-making ball, eg *Roll and See* [3] and *Touch–'ems Clutch Ball* [3], between the adult and child. The child tracks it both visually and auditorily.

2. Mum and Dad sit on either side of the child and call his name or shake a rattle. When he turns to the sound let him play with the toy.

3. Shake or squeeze a sound-making toy in front of the child and allow him to take the toy and play with it. Encourage him to turn to the sound by shaking it first to one side of the child, then behind him and then slightly above his head. Gently turn the child if he does not respond spontaneously.

4. Use mobile sound-making toys to pass between parent and child, or between Mum and Dad, across the child's line of vision. Suitable toys are *Clatterpillars*[4], *Clatterclowns*[4] and *Baby's First Car*[4].

5. Call the child from different parts of the room and see if he can turn to you.

6. Mum and Dad hide in different places and call the child. Tell him to find either Mum or Dad first.

7. Make interesting sounds from different parts of the room.

8. While the child shuts his eyes, hide a loudly-ticking clock or music-box. The child has to find it by following the sound (Jeffree, McConkey and Hewson).

9. Blindfold the child and make a noise fairly close to his head. Ask him to point to the noise and hold his hand, so that he can see how close he was, when the blindfold is removed. Gradually increase the distance and angle, ie make the sounds from higher or lower than ear level. (This game may need two adults—one to make the sounds, and one to hold the child's hand and remove the blindfold.)

10. As for 9 but make two noises, one of which acts as a distractor.

11. Squeak Piggy Squeak: a blindfolded child stands in the middle of a group of seated children. One of the children shakes a rattle and the blindfolded person either points to him or sits on him. When he has found the right person he can say, 'Squeak, Piggy, Squeak', whereupon the other child must say something and the first child guesses who it is.

12. Blindfold a child and turn him round. He must then follow you as you walk around the room, calling his name.

Auditory Sequencing

Auditory stimuli could be sequenced in a similar way to visual stimuli, but most auditory sequential tasks consist of asking the child to recall auditory information in the order in which it was presented. Therefore games and activities are listed under the heading of auditory memory.

Memory

Helping the Child to Remember Everyday Activities

Memory involves an awareness of past events. This can be developed using the activities given in Chapter 5. The best way to help the child to remember everyday events, is to talk about them beforehand, while they are taking place, and then again afterwards. By talking about an outing or event beforehand you alert the child and help him to take in subsequent information and make sense of what he sees. Scrapbooks, projects and role-play can help the child to relive and remember incidents. Imaginative use of video and cine-film can also help the child's memory. Next time he goes to the park or zoo, take a film of the different rides or animals he encounters, and afterwards play it back to him and talk about it.

Specific Activities

Some factors are basic to both visual and auditory memory activities:

1. Vary the materials used, eg toys, dolls, miniature furniture, vegetables, pictures, classroom objects, clothing, family photos, etc.

2. Some children may have to be taught how to fetch objects. In this case another adult should demonstrate what is required, and take the child through the motions until he grasps the idea.

3. Use strategies to help children who have difficulty recalling information. These may be either external prompts, such as saying to the child, 'Tell me all the animals you saw' (Jeffree and McConkey), or devices that the child can learn to use as self-cueing strategies. Cues can gradually be faded out, or if necessary, they can be employed by the child in his everyday life.

4. All memory tasks can be made harder by:

  (i) increasing the number of items to choose between.
  (ii) increasing the number of items to recall.
  (iii) increasing the perceptual or conceptual similarity of the items used.
  (iv) requiring that the child remembers items in the right order.
  (v) introducing a delay before the child responds.
  (vi) introducing a distracting task before allowing the child to respond.
  (vii) increasing the complexity of any verbal instructions.
  (viii) putting a time-limit on the activity.

Visual Memory

Always refer back to the model so that the child can check that he is right. Strategies such as pointing to each item the child has to recall, allowing him to handle it, telling the child to keep a picture of it in his mind, encouraging him to say the name of each item out loud, or doing this for him, and giving him plenty of time to look at each item, may all help him.

Many of the visual discrimination tasks already described can incorporate a memory factor by hiding the model so that the child has to remember what it is he must copy, match or find.

1. Hide a small toy in one of your hands—see if the child can remember which hand it is in. When he can do this, put your hands behind your back for a moment and see if he can still remember where it is.

2. Do the same with a toy and two large boxes.

3. Place two beakers in front of the child and put a toy under one of them, which he must find. When he can do this:

  (i) increase the number of beakers
  (ii) change the position of the beaker with the toy.
  (iii) hide two animals under different beakers and show the child a duplicate of the one he must find.

4. Hide-and-Seek: let the child see where you hide and then come and find you. Gradually make him wait longer before he comes to seek.

5. Some of the object-permanence activities suggested in Chapter 1 are useful for early memory tasks.

6. Show the child two objects or different-coloured bricks. Hide them and have the child find duplicates.

7. Show the child two toys: produce a duplicate of one of them, hide it and ask the child to point to the correct original.

8. Place three toys or pictures in a row: ask the child to shut his eyes and take one away, leaving the gap as a positional clue. The child names the missing item or finds a duplicate. Lotto, Snap and Pelmanism cards are useful for this game.

9. Repeat activity 8 but remove the positional clue by moving the objects together, or jumbling them up.

10. Show the child three objects in a row. With his back turned, shuffle them round and ask the child to put them back into the correct order. (It is best to have a model available so the child can compare his effort.)

11. Show the child three pictures: turn them over and ask him to say what they are.

12. 'Postman Pat': you or the child post objects into a postbox (made from a converted shoe-box). The child recalls what they are by naming them or finding duplicates. He can then lift the box-lid to check that he is right (Jeffree and McConkey).

13. 'Shopkeepers': show the child pictures of things he has to 'buy' from the 'shop'. He may either fetch these from a table acting as a shop, or he has to ask for them from another child, who is shopkeeper.

14. Hide toys around the room as the child watches; then he must find them. Build up from one to six toys.

15. 'Kim's Game': place several objects on a tray and allow the child as long as he likes to memorise them. Cover with a cloth and ask him to remember as many items as possible. It may help to trigger his memory if the objects are all in the same category, eg toys or utensils.

16. As for 15 but remove one or two toys and the child must say what is missing.

17. 'Pairs', or 'Pelmanism': lay several pairs of picture-cards face down and take turns to collect identical pairs, by turning them over, two at a time, and remembering their positions.

18. 'Snap': use shape, colour or picture-cards and lay them face down as they are played, so that the child has to remember what they are.

19. Show the child one of a pair of objects or pictures. Hide it and show him a second item, asking him if it is the same or different (Kirk and Kirk).

20. Make a picture-book with a large picture of an animal or toy on each alternate page. On the intervening pages stick a number of smaller pictures, including a

MEMORY PICTURE BOOK

small version of the large picture on the preceding page. The child has to find the smaller version without referring back (Kirk and Kirk). Silhouettes can also be used for this.

21. Play a simple board game and ask the child to remember what colour, shape or number was on the dice each time he throws it.

22. *Visual Recall Flash Cards* [5]: the child remembers an increasingly long sequence of shapes or pictures, which has been hidden.

23. Use coloured Unifix cubes that fit on to the finger, to build up the child's memory in the following hierarchy:

2 cubes the same colour	red red
2 cubes of a different colour	red yellow
3 cubes the same	red red red
2 cubes the same, 1 different	red red yellow
1 cube the same, 2 different	red yellow yellow
1 cube the same, 1 different, 1 same	red yellow red
3 cubes different	red yellow blue
4 cubes the same	red red red red, etc.

Present these combinations, hide them and have the child reproduce them from memory. They make good quick-fire group tasks too.

24. Repeat 23 using different materials, eg pegs, threading-beads and cotton reels, daubs of paint, building-bricks, coloured sticks or pencils, etc.

Auditory Memory

Ensure that the child is familiar with both the objects and the vocabulary being used. Again, help him to find strategies to cope with the complexity of auditory memory tasks. Encourage the child to gesture the object or trace its outline in the air, or do these for him, or tell him to make a picture of the object and keep it in his mind. He may be helped by repeating the items after you or fixing his visual attention as he listens to you, eg if you want the child to remember and fetch a ball, a book and a shoe, point to blank index-cards as you name these items. This device has been known to aid the memory of children as young as three, although we do not know exactly why. It may help the child to picture the items by projecting their image on to the blank cards, or it may focus the child's visual attention, thus cutting down on possible distractions.

Remember that it is easier for a child if he can see the things that you want him to remember, as he may then use visual clues to help him. If you want him to rely on auditory clues alone he must not be able to see the items you are naming.

1. Fetching games: two or three objects are laid on the table and the child is asked to fetch one of them.

2. There are many variations on this game:

(i) The Shopping-list: read out the items on a shopping list. Real vegetables and canned foods can be used.

(ii) Draw a large Christmas Tree and stick pictures of toys on it with *Blu-Tack*. Name the toys the child must remove.

(iii) Father Christmas's Sack: pretend that miniature toys are presents and ask the child to put two or three of them in the sack or the sleigh (represented by a box).

(iv) Treasure-hunts: ask the child to collect various items from around the room or while on an outing.

(v) Name two or three objects the child must find in a tin of similar objects.

(vi) Dressing-up: have a pile of clothes and ask the child to put on 'a hat and one sock', etc. If numbers are to be used be sure he understands them.

(vii) Have a large picture of a farm, zoo, street, park, etc and ask the child to put on toys or pictures in the order they are named. Use *Cellograph* (produced by Philip and Tacey), *Fuzzy felt* [4], *Play-Mats* [4], *Uniset Boards* [1] and *Magnetic Story Boards* [4] or make your own. An older child can listen to a short story woven around the scene. Afterwards he retells the story using the pictures to help him.

(viii) Hunt the thimble: prior to the session hide several objects around the room. Ask the children to find the ones you name.

(ix) Cooking: if possible make real cakes and tarts, and name the ingredients the child must fetch. Lots of infant and nursery classes have cookery sessions and could incorporate this activity.

(x) During the normal course of the day the child can be asked to fetch things for his teacher, parents, etc. This can also be practised in therapy, using similar objects. He can also be sent to 'borrow' things from other people in the school or clinic; warn them first to expect the child.

3. Following commands: these must be kept within the child's comprehension limits.

(i) In a group, ask each child to give something to another child, eg 'Give the book to Michael'.

(ii) Pointing to body parts: if the child understands 'my' and 'your', give commands such as, 'Point to *your* ear, *your* knee and *my* neck', emphasising the possessives. Otherwise use the children's names and make it a group activity.

(iii) Posting pictures: have one to four coloured post-boxes and several toys or pictures. Start off with simple commands, eg 'Post the sock'. Gradually increase the length of the commands, eg 'Put the ball in the yellow box'; 'Post all the red toys in the blue box'.

(iv) Ask the child to hand you named pieces from an inset-puzzle.

(v) Obstacle Race: tell the child a series of actions to perform, eg 'Jump over the brick, crawl under the chair and touch the wall'. In a group this can be made into a race.

(vi) Practise the sorts of commands that the child will have to follow in his nursery or infant class, eg 'Hang up your coat and fetch the peg-boards'.

4. Copying rhythms, using musical instruments: make a simple rhythm, eg one short and one long blast on a whistle, which the child copies.

5. Clap or tap out a rhythm for the child to copy.

6. Repeating digits, words or sentences: repetition of digits is useful for a quick-fire memory task in a group and for keeping children alert. Otherwise make such exercises as useful as possible by sending children to ask questions or make requests of other teachers. It will be necessary to prime the other adults so they know what is expected of the child.

7. Spotting the Odd Man Out: eg

dog cat orange (semantic difference)
cake make tock bake (rhyming difference)
ball bush bone toy (initial phoneme difference).

8. Read or tell the child a simple story which mentions objects, animals or actions. Afterwards list the ones the child can recall, and re-read the story or let him see the pictures to find out how many he got right. Stories such as *The Golden Goose* and *Chicken Licken* which slowly build up the list of characters, are easier to remember.

9. See also the suggested activities for listening-skills in Chapter 2.

Tactile Skills

General Tactile Awareness

Small children can be helped to develop their tactile skills by giving them lots of different substances and materials to touch, feel, taste and play with. Talk about these materials, modelling the vocabulary that accompanies tactile experiences.

There are several suggestions of things to do in Chapter 3, on Play. Also use sand and water play, soap and bubbles, touching and tasting hot, warm and cold things, wrap the children in soft and hard materials and have them roll over cushions, grass, the hard floor, sand, and so on. Experiment with face-paints and make-up, finger-painting, hand and foot printing, nail-varnish, clay and plasticine. If you have the opportunity, supervise the child while he discovers the texture of different animals, eg stroking kittens, dogs, frogs and snakes.

Encourage older children's awareness of touching by:

1. touching things with different parts of the body and trying to identify them with the eyes closed.

2. helping the child to feel round shapes or objects to discover their contours.

3. cutting shapes from sandpaper and other materials.

4. making collages.

5. trying out activities without using the hands, eg drinking your tea (without a straw).

6. going for a 'touching-walk', exploring different surfaces and collecting things with an interesting feel.

7. setting up a 'touch-table' with lots of different textures (Dowling, 1980).

8. cooking, with different doughs and mixtures.

Tactile Discrimination

1. Feelie-bag: place objects in an opaque bag and the child must recognise what they are by feeling them.

(i) Show him an object and have him find its duplicate in the bag.

(ii) Introduce themes, highlighting the shape, texture or size of objects in the bag.

(iii) Describe one of the objects in the bag and the child has to find it.

2. Feelie-box: the same principle but a box is more versatile and the child has less opportunity to cheat. Simply cut a hole in a large box and place inside it wet things, dry things, furry things, rough and smooth things, things to eat, etc.

3. The child can identify things by feeling them when he is blindfolded. This can be extended to people's faces, furniture, large toys, articles of clothing, etc.

4. The child feels somebody's face and names the part he is touching.

5. Scavenger-hunts: pass round various objects in a group of children and each child has to collect other things that feel the same, eg all soft objects, sharp objects, warm or cold things.

6. Make picture-books out of textured materials.

7. Sort materials for collages.

8. *Texture Shapes Set*[1]: two matching sets of ten different textured squares.

9. Put two or three materials on a table and allow the child to handle them. Then place a duplicate of one into his hands behind his back. Remove it and ask him to point to the correct material on the table (Dowling, 1980).

10. Make feelie dominoes, using felt, satin, velvet, sandpaper, straw, wood, etc.

11. Collect pairs by feel: these can be made out of different textured sandpapers, emery-boards, materials, wood, cardboard, etc.

12. *Tactile Buttons*[4] have a matching board; *Touch Cards*[4] discriminate by feeling both texture and size.

Integration of Multi-sensory Input

Many of the games described above rely on sensory integration to a certain extent, eg the auditory memory tasks demand that the child relate a verbal label to an object or a sound to an instrument, etc. If the child cannot do this he must be taught to match objects across modalities. This can only be done by lots of demonstration by the teacher, and, even more crucial, plenty of first hand exploration by the child. He will learn that a chime-bar makes a specific noise, by striking it over and over again, that a ball is round, by rolling it and feeling it, that a verbal label relates to an object, by looking and listening, and later, articulating.

Some games that you might like to play to help cross-modality identification, are:

1. Sound-picture matching and *Photo Sound Lotto*[5].

2. Picture-gesture matching and vice versa.

3. Telling a story that involves sounds, and helping the child to make the appropriate sound at the right time.

4. Telling a story that emphasises touch, and passing round the items described, for the children to handle.

5. I spy, eg 'I spy something red'; 'I spy something furry'; 'I spy something that plays music'.

6. Play auditory-discrimination games with a matching set of pictures, ie the child listens to the sound and then points to the picture of its sound-maker.

Appendix 1
TOY LIST

Listed below are the toys mentioned in this book and their manufacturers. Numbers against toys in the text indicate the manufacturer—their numbers are as follows:

Manufacturers and Retailers

1. NES Arnold Ltd
2. Taskmaster Ltd
3. Early Learning Centres
4. Galt Educational
5. Learning Development Aids (LDA)
6. Speechmark Publishing

1. NES Arnold, Findel House, Excelsior Road, Ashby Park, Ashby de la Zouch, Leicestershire LE65 1NG, United Kingdom www.nesarnold.co.uk

AJDA Multipurpose Composite Furniture: made to order versatile furniture units can be shops, theatre, kitchen, library, etc.

Asian Cooking Sets: include place-settings and serving utensils.

Billie and his Barrels: 6 nesting barrels.

Chapati Pan: for pretend cooking

Children at Play Jigsaws: Indoors and Outdoors – seven 12-piece puzzles showing children of various ethnic backgrounds at play.

Disco-shapes: Interlocking plastic discs.

Duplo World People.

Educat: take-apart felt cat.

Equal Opportunities Jigsaws: four 30-piece puzzles, depicting men and women as train-drivers, chefs, doctors, pilots.

Fun with sounds set.

Jack-in-the-Ball: Jack pops out when a button is pressed.

Loddy: for riding and transporting earth, etc.

Occupation Inset Trays: three seven-piece puzzles, depicting footballer, doctor and teacher.

Reo-click: plastic tubes, wheels, rings, etc that fit together.

Rotello: construction toy with 90 bright, unbreakable pieces, for making pull along vehicles.

Slot-o-build: slotting plastic shapes.

Soft Shapes: very large soft blocks, for active play.

Stepping Stones: different shapes for the children to step on.

Texture Shapes Set: matching sets of ten different textures.

Uniset Boards: printed baseboard with self-sticking vinyl cut-outs.

What's missing? cards: simple line-drawings.

2. Taskmaster Ltd, Morris Road, Leicester LE2 6BR, United Kingdom. www.taskmasteronline.co.uk

All-purpose Photo Library: coloured pictures of many different objects.

Dyna-Balance Walking Board/Rocking Platform: encourages balance, foot-positioning and self confidence.

Figure-ground Activity Cards: for perceptual activities.

Pegboards: with design cards for perceptual activities.

Self-Care Sequential Cards: in cartoon style.

Sequencing Beads/Sequencing Bead Patterns: wooden beads and pattern-cards.

Tac Tracks: two-coloured footprints for encouraging left-right recognition.

3. Early Learning Centres (ELC Direct), South Marston Park, Swindon SN3 4YJ, United Kingdom www.elc.co.uk

Activity Bear: ten rewarding activities.

Activity Bear Play Centre: over 40 play activities, including telephone, mirror, shape-sorter, which grows as baby grows.

Animal Pram Toy: these colourful animals bounce, turn and rattle at every touch.

Brio Passenger Train: engine and three carriages fit together magnetically.

Bubble Balls: colourful pictures spin inside the bubbles.

Digger: tough, working toy, which digs sand and earth.

Elephount: bath-toy, squirts water from his trunk.

First Lift-Out Puzzle: 14 familiar objects.

Hammer and ball set: knock the balls through the holes and see them reappear.

Hippo Shape Sorter: also a pull-along toy.

Humpty-Dumpty: press the lever and Humpty-Dumpty 'has a great fall'.

Musical Bear: pull the string and watch the bear lick honey from the jar.

Musical Mobile: four removable soft toys revolve to the music.

Musical Rabbit: pull the string and watch the rabbit rub his eyes and yawn.

Musical Turtle: pull the string and the mummy turtle waddles off pulling her baby behind her.

Pull-along Ladybird: ladybird's wings flap and a bell rings.

Ready-Teddy Go-Boat: watch him go round the bath.

Roll and See: soft, inflatable roller, with tumbling balls inside.

Rolling Bells: roll-along vehicle with four wheels containing bells.

Soft Cat Rattle: ideal for a new born baby.

Soft Stuff: versatile modelling material.

Super Helta Skelta: set of interlocking pieces to make an endless variety of marble runs.

Toddler Truck.

Touch-'ems Clutch Ball: easy-grip ball with six different textures.

Webster: pull-along wobbly spider.

Wooden Trike.

4. Galt Educational & Preschool,
Johnsonbrook Road, Hyde,
Cheshire SK14 4QT, United Kingdom
www. galt-educational.co.uk

Animal Allsorts: 144 different-coloured animal shapes.

Baby's First Car: action-car with moving eyes, ringing bell and squeaky button.

Basic Builder System: wheels, baseplates, spacers, nuts and bolts.

Catch-a-mouse: board game.

Celebration Jigsaws: come in three sizes – 42, 63 and 99 pieces, and show many special occasions: weddings; christmas; etc.

Children of the World Jigsaws: six puzzles of Asian, Black and White children's faces and bodies.

Chunky Wooden Inset Boards: five giant insect-boards with easy-grip chunky handles.

Clatterclowns: rolling toy with clicking clowns.

Clatterpillar: pull-along toy.

Construct-o-Straws: flexible straws to make designs.

Duplo Sets: an enormous range of construction toys, including people, animals, vehicles, furniture, and building sets.

Ethnic Dolls' Clothes: African suit and Indian sari.

Ethnic Dressing-up Clothes: Indian, Japanese, Pakistani, and Arab clothes for 4–9 year olds.

Ethnic Serving Utensils: Asian set, including bowls and pickle tray.

Friends Jigsaw: large 32-piece puzzle, featuring children from different cultural backgrounds.

Fun Barrels: giant barrels for energetic play.

Fuzzy-felt: cards and pieces to make pictures and patterns.

Galt Creative Templates: seven topics – including space, vehicles, and different kinds of animals.

Glug-glug Tug/Plane: fill with water and watch them go.

Hammer-Balls: disappear momentarily before reappearing.

Inset Puzzles: Playground/People at Work.

Jack-in-the-Ball: east peep-bo toy.

Large Baby Dolls: soft-bodied Black and White baby dolls.

Lego: building bricks, figures and accessories.

Logic People: an assortment of different-coloured people performing different actions.

Magic Man: push-along clown which wobbles and rattles.

Magnetic Story Boards: two story-books with matching magnetic picture-sets.

Miniature Doctors and Nurses: six flexible dolls of mixed ethnic origins.

Noughts and Crosses: traditional game with large pieces on a board.

Party Numbers Jigsaw: 20-piece puzzle showing children aged 1–10.

Pegmen: and various accessories.

Penny Felt Puzzle Pictures: practise various fastening skills.

Photographic Language Lotto: colour photos of people who vary in age, sex and appearance, expressing different emotions.

Photo Resource Pack: Food: four themes – Shops, Restaurants, Food Preparation and Eating, in different cultural settings.

Play Boat: bath toy that can also be pulled along the floor.

Playmats: including farm and railway scenes.

Playmobile: playpeople with lots of different accessories; also Ethnic Playpeople and children.

Playmobile Swing: part of the Playground Set.

Play Tunnels: nursery and adventure-playground size.

Puppet Families – Black, White and Asian: large hand-puppets featuring grandparents, children and babies.

Ring Figures – policeman and guardsman: bright wooden pieces fit onto a central pole.

Rocking Boat: for active play.

Sand Wheel: discovery toy for the sand-tray.

Seesaw for 3: three little figures on a miniature seesaw.

Single Figure Jigsaws: people from different ethnic backgrounds as policeman, engineer, doctor and nurse.

SoftBlocks: soft picture-cubes.

Space Hopper: sit-upon, bouncing toy.

Space Horse: sit-upon rocking horse.

Stacking Figures: wooden clown and caterpillar.

Steps: soft-play steps.

Superstore: shop complete with striped canopy.

Tactile Buttons: with matching board.

Tap 'n Turn Bench: hammer the six little men – turn them other and hammer again!

Touch Cards: 34 cards demonstrating different tactile sensations, eg large/small; rough/smooth.

Water Pump: see it draw up water through the clear barrel.

Worm-in-the-Apple: the worm pops out of the apple when someone talks to him.

5. **LDA**, Abbeygate House, East Road, Cambridge CB1 1DB, United Kingdom
www.LDAlearning.com

Picture-Clues: 35 simple pictures and a holder with a series of flaps. The child lifts the flaps to reveal more and more of the picture.

Photo Action Cards: photos of people performing various actions.

Photocue Occupation Cards: photos of different jobs.

Photo Sound Lotto: real photographs in four topics with matching sounds.

Visual Recall Flash Cards: stretch visual memory with pictures or shapes increasing in number.

What would you do?: eight large cards showing a hypothetical situation. Smaller cards show possible solutions.

What's Wrong? cards: pictures showing such absurdities as a bicycle with square wheels.

Why-because cards: these stimulate the appreciation of cause and effect in everyday situations, eg if someone breaks a window he must pay for it.

6. **Speechmark Publishing Ltd**, Telford Road, Bicester, Oxon OX26 4LQ, United Kingdom
www.speechmark.net

ColorCards®: Designed to help develop both language and social skills of children and adults of all ages. *Adjectives, Basic Sequences, Basic Verbs, Emotions, Everyday Objects, What's Different?, Objects & Owners, Odd One Out, Prepositions, What's Added?, What's Inside?, What Is It?, What's Missing?, What's Wrong?*

ColorLibrary: Divided into six categories and designed to create a rich resource of essential vocabulary: *Home, Food, Animals & Birds, Occupations, Sports & Leisure, Possessions, Transport & Vehicles.*

Pocket ColorCards®: Set of language flashcards: *How's Teddy?, How Many?, Heads & Tails, Fun Pictures, Snack Time, Early Objects, Match Up, Early Actions, Early Opposites, Early Sequences, Guess What?*

Sequencing ColorCards®: Story sequences in photographic form from simple to complex: *Daily Living, Problem Solving, Basic Sequences, Social Situations, Cause & Effect, Simple Sequences, Activities & Events.*

Verb Tenses: Strip booklet of pictures illustrating past, present and future tenses.

Skills for Daily Living: Illustrated ColorCards®: Complex and potentially dangerous situations in full-colour illustrated format to be used for a range of clients with various needs: *Social Behaviour, Personal Safety.*

Listening Skills: Sound and picture matching activities for individuals or groups: *Indoor Sounds, Sequencing Sounds, Outdoor Sounds.*

Multi-Match: Two sets of identical pairs of cards designed for a variety of matching tasks and activities: *Categories, More Categories (Colours, Patterns & Shapes).*

Find the Link: Photographic game cards suitable for individuals or groups of up to five players from children to adults. This versatile board game is aimed at developing word-finding and categorisation skills.

Everyday Objects Interactive: Using images from *Everyday Objects ColorCards®* this software program contains a range of activities that reinforce a variety of developmental skills with audio and visual assistance. Fully configurable to suit the needs of individuals, this program has a record-keeping facility to monitor progress.

Resource Materials

Other useful addresses from which to obtain toys, materials, equipment and advice are:

Winslow Catalogue (ROMPA), Goyt Side Road, Chesterfield, Derbyshire S40 2PH, United Kingdom
www.winslow-cat.com

Invicta Plastics Ltd, Educational Aids Division, Oadby, Leicester LE2 4LB, United Kingdom
www.invictagroup.co.uk

NferNelson, The Chiswick Centre, 414 Chiswick High Road, London W4 5TF, United Kingdom
www.nfer-nelson-co.uk

NES Arnold, Findel House, Excelsior Road, Ashby Park, Ashby de la Zouch, Leicestershire LE65 1NG, United Kingdom
www.nesarnold.co.uk

Philip and Tacey Ltd, North Way, Andover, Hampshire SP10 5BA, United Kingdom
www.philipandtacey.co.uk

Jack Tizard School, Finlay Street, London SW6 6HB, United Kingdom
www.lbhf.gov.uk

APPENDIX 2
USEFUL ADDRESSES

General

The Royal College of Speech & Language Therapists, 2 White Hart Yard, London SE1 1NX, United Kingdom
www.rcslt.org

The Association for All Speech Impaired Children (AFASIC), 2nd Floor, 50–52 Great Stutton Street, London EC1V 0DJ, United Kingdom
www.afasic.org.uk
An association of parents and professionals formed to promote the interests of children and young people with specific speech and language disorders.

National Children's Home, Chief Office, 85 Highbury Park, London N5 1UD, United Kingdom
www.nch.org.uk
Care of children and young people through homes, special schools, family-centres, foster care, day nurseries, aid to families and help to community projects.

National Council for One-Parent Families, 255 Kentish Town Road, London NW5 2LX, United Kingdom
www.ncopf.org.uk
Free help and advice to lone parents; information service and pressure group.

National Society for the Prevention of Cruelty to Children (NSPCC), Weston House, 42 Curtain Road, London EC2A 3NH, United Kingdom
www.nspcc.org.uk
Provides a casework service, playgroups, Day Care Centres and Special Units offering family treatment, education and advice.

National Association of Toy & Leisure Libraries, 68 Churchway, London NW1 1LT, United Kingdom
www.natll.org.uk
Co-ordinates over 1,000 Toy Libraries, publishes *The Good Toy Guide* annually, and in association with ACTIVE, designs and produces individual aids for the profoundly disabled.

Disablement

Access Travel, 6 The Hillock, Astley, Lancashire M29 7GW, United Kingdom
www.access-travel.co.uk
Specialising in holidays for disabled people.

Department of Health and Department of Social Security
www.dss.gov.uk, www.dhssni.gov.uk
For advice on aids and benefits for the disabled, contact local offices.

Disabled Living Foundation (DLF), 380–384 Harrow Road, London W9 2HU, United Kingdom
www.dlf.org.uk
Information service on aids, equipment and services for disabled people.

Holiday Care Service, 2nd Floor, Imperial Building, Victoria Road, Horley, Surrey RH6 7PZ, United Kingdom
Advice on holiday arrangements for disabled people, single-parent families, the elderly and unemployed people.

Mental Disability

Down's Syndrome Association, 155 Mitcham Road, London SW17 9PG, United Kingdom
www.dsa-uk.com
Promotes care and education of Down's Syndrome children and conducts research into the causes and effects of this condition.

National Autistic Society, 393 City Road, London EC1V 1NG, United Kingdom
www.nas.org.uk
Advice and information about autism; the provision of homes, education, training and welfare for autistic children.

Royal Society for Mentally Handicapped Children and Adults (MENCAP National Centre), 123 Golden Lane, London EC1Y 0RT, United Kingdom
www.mencap.org.uk
Advice, counselling and information on a variety of matters to do with mentally handicapped people.

Physical Disability

Association for Spina Bifida and Hydrocephalus, 42 Park Road, Peterborough PE1 2UQ, United Kingdom
www.asbah.org
Support and advice to sufferers and their families and the promotion of research into causes and treatment.

'I CAN' (Invalid Children's Aid Nationwide), 4 Dyer's Buildings, Holborn, London EC1N 2QP, United Kingdom
www.ican.org.uk
Information and advisory service to children with disabilities and their families.

Muscular Dystrophy Group of Great Britain and Northern Ireland, 7–11 Prescott Place, London SW4 6BS, United Kingdom.
www.muscular-dystrophy.org
Raises funds and directs research projects into muscular dystrophy and allied diseases.

SCOPE, 6 Market Road, London N7 9PW, United Kingdom
www.scope.org.uk
The care, education, training and treatment of cerebral-palsied men, women and children; advice, information and research into all matters relating to cerebral palsy.

Hearing Impairment

Hearing Concern, 7–11 Armstrong Road, London W3 7JL, United Kingdom
www.hearingconcern.org
Promotes the interests of the deaf and hearing-impaired people through encouraging the provision of services, clubs, classes and other local facilities.

National Deaf Children's Society, 15 Dufferin Street, London EC1Y 8UR, United Kingdom
www.ndcs.org.uk
Represents deaf children's interests and supports parents through self-help groups.

Royal National Institute for the Deaf (RNID), 19–23 Featherstone Street, London EC1Y 8SL, United Kingdom
www.rnid.org.uk
Aims to promote, safeguard and protect the interests of deaf people and offer help, information, and advice, including a comprehensive library service on all matters concerning deafness.

Visual Impairment

Royal National Institute for the Blind (RNIB), 105 Judd Street, London WC1H 9NE, United Kingdom
www.rnib.org.uk
Promotes the education, welfare and employment of blind people and sponsors research into the prevention of blindness.

BIBLIOGRAPHY

Baldwin, A & Baldwin, C B, 'The Study of Mother-Child Interaction', *American Scientist* No 15, 1973.

Bee, Helen, *The Developing Child*; 3rd edition; Harper International Edition; Harper & Row, New York, 1981.

Berry, M F, *Teaching Linguistically Handicapped Children*; Prentice-Hall, USA, 1980.

Bloom, L, *Language Development: Form and Function in Emerging Grammars*; The M.I.T. Press, 1970; Cambridge, U.S.A.

Bloom, L, *One Word at a Time: the Use of Single-Word Utterances before Syntax*; Mouton, The Hague, 1973.

Bloom, L & Lahey, M, *A Proposed Program for the Treatment of Language-Disordered Children*; unpublished dissertation, Teachers College, Columbia University, 1972.

Bloom, L & Lahey, M, *Language Development and Language Disorders*; John Wiley & Sons, USA, 1978.

Bloom, L, Lightbown, P & Hood, L, 'Structure and Variation in Child Language'; Monographs of the Society for Research in Child Development 40; Cambridge University Press, USA, 1973.

Braine, M D S, 'On Learning the Grammatical Order of Words'; *Psychology Review* 70, pp 323-348, 1963.

Broen, P, 'The Verbal Environment of the Language-Learning Child'; Monographs of the American Speech & Hearing Assoc, No 17, p72, 1972.

Brown, R, *A First Language: The Early Stages*; Allen & Unwin, London, 1973.

Brown, R & Scanlon, C, 'Derivational Complexity of Acquisition in Child Speech'; in *Cognition and the Development of Language* edited by J R Hayes; John Wiley & Sons, New York, 1970.

Bruner, J, Jolly, A & Sylva, K (Editors), *Play*, Penguin, 1976.

Bruner, J, 'The Ontogenesis of Speech Acts'; *Journal of Child Language*, 2, 1975, pp 1–19.

Bryant, Peter, *Perception and Understanding in Young Children*; Methuen & Co, 1974.

Carter, A L, 'Pre-speech Meaning Relations: an outline of one infant's sensorimotor development'; in *Language Acquisition*, edited by Fletcher & Garman; Cambridge University Press, 1979.

Clark, E, *Cognitive Development and the Development of Language*, pp 65-110; Academic Press, 1973.

Clark, E, 'Semantics and Comprehension'; in *Current Trends in Linguistics*, Vol 12, edited by T A Sebeok; Mouton, The Hague, 1974.

Clarke, E V, 'Building a Vocabulary: words for objects, actions and relations'; in *Language Acquisition*, edited by Fletcher & Garman; Cambridge University Press, 1979.

Cole, Patricia, *Language Disorders in Children*; Prentice-Hall, USA, 1982.

Cooper, J, Moodley, M & Reynell, J, 'Intervention Programmes for Pre-school Children with Delayed Language Development'; *British Journal of Disorders of Communication*, 9(2), 1974, pp 89-91.

Cromer, R, 'The Development of Language and Cognition: the cognition hypothesis'; in *New Perspectives in Child Development*, edited by B Foss; Penguin, New York, 1974.

Crystal, D, Fletcher, P & Garman, M, *The Grammatical Analysis of Language Disability: a procedure for assessment and remediation*; Edward Arnold, 1976.

Delack, J B, 'Aspects of Infant Speech Development in the First Year of Life'; *Canadian Journal of Linguistics* 21, 1979, pp 17-37.

de Villiers, J and de Villiers, P, *Language Acquisition*; Harvard University Press, USA, 1978.

Dodd, B J, 'Effects of Social and Vocal Stimulation on Infant Babbling'; *Developmental Psychology* 7, pp 80-83, 1972.

Dore, J, 'A Pragmatic Description of Early Language Development'; *Journal of Psycholinguistic Research*, pp 343-350, 1974.

Edwards, M L, 'Perception and Production in Child Phonology: the testing of four hypotheses'; *Journal of Child Language*, pp 205-219, 1974.

Eimas, P D, 'Developmental Studies of Speech Perception'; in *Infant Perception*, edited by L B Coke & P Salapatch; Academic Press, New York, 1975.

Eimas, P D, 'Linguistic Processing of Speech by Young Infants'; in *Language Perspectives: acquisition, retardation and intervention*, edited by R L Shiefelbusch & L L Lloyd; University Park Press, Baltimore, 1974.

Eimas, P & Corbit, J, 'Selective Adaptation of Linguistic Feature Detectors'; *Cognitive Psychology* 4, pp 99-109, 1973.

Fletcher, P & Garman, M (eds.), *Language Acquisition*, Cambridge University Press, 1979.

Fraser, G M & Blockley, J, *The Language Disordered Child*; NFER-Nelson, 1982.

Fry, D, 'How Did We Learn to Do It'; in *Homo Loquens*, pp 101-124; Cambridge University Press, 1977.

Garnica, O K, 'The Development of Phonetic Speech Perception'; in *Cognition and the Acquisition of Language*, edited by T E Moore; Academic Press, 1973.

Gillham, B, *The First Words Language Programme*; Croom Helm, 1979.

Gratch, G, 'Perception of Space, Speech and Sound'; in *Infant Perception: from sensation to cognition*; edited by L Cohen & R Salapatch; Vol II; Academic Press, 1975.

Greenfield, P & Smith, J H, *The Structure of Communication in Early Language Development*; Academic Press, New York, 1976.

Grieve, R & Hoogenraad, R, 'First Words'; in *Language Acquisition*, edited by Fletcher & Garman; Cambridge University Press, 1979.

Griffiths, D, 'Speech Acts and Early Sentences'; in *Language Acquisition*, edited by Fletcher & Garman, *ibid.*

Halliday, M A K, *Explorations in the Functions of Language;* in the series Explorations in Language Study; general editors P Doughty & G Thornton; Edward Arnold, 1973.

Halliday, M A K, *Learning How to Mean: Explorations in the development of language*; Edward Arnold, London, 1975.

Hermelin, B & O'Connor, N, 'Remembering of Words by Psychotic and Normal Children'; in *British Journal of Psychology* 58, pp 213-218, 1967.

Herriot, P, *Attributes of Memory*; Methuen & Co, 1974.

Holt, J, *How Children Learn*; Pelican Books, Penguin, 1967.

Hood, L, 'A Longitudinal Study of the Development of Expression of Causal Relations in Complex Sentences'; unpublished doctoral dissertation, Columbia University, 1977.

Hunt, J, *Intelligence and Experience*; Ronald Press, New York, 1961.

Jakobson, R, *Child Language, Aphasia, and Phonological Universals;* Mouton, The Hague, 1968.

Jeffree, D, McConkey, R & Hewson, S, *Let Me Play*; Human Horizons Series; Souvenir Press, 1977.

Lee, V (ed), *Language Development*; Croom Helm in association with Open University Press, 1979.

McDade, H L, 'A Parent-Child Interactional Model for Assessing and Remediating Language Disabilities'; *British Journal for Disorders of Communication*, Vol 16, No 3, 1981, pp 175-183.

Menyuk, P, 'Comparison of Grammar of Children with Functionally Deviant and Normal Speech'; *Journal of Speech and Hearing Research* No 7, 1964, pp 109-121.

Menyuk, P & Menn, L, 'Early Strategies for the Perception and Production of Words and Sounds'; in *Language Acquisition*, edited by Fletcher & Garman; *ibid.*

Mittler, P, 'Psychological Assessment of Language Abilities'; in *The Child with Delayed Speech*, edited by M Rutter and J Martin; William Heinemann Medical Books, 1972.

Moerk, E, 'Process of Language Teaching and Training in the Interaction of Mother-Child Dyads'; *Child Development* 47, 1976, pp 1064-1078.

Nakazima, S, 'Phonemicisation and Symbolisation in Language Development'; in *Foundations of Language: a multidisciplinary approach*, Vol 1; edited by E H Lenneberg & E Lenneberg; Academic Press, New York, 1975.

Newson, J & Newson, E, *Toys and Playthings*; Penguin Books, 1979.

Piaget, J, *The Child's Conception of the World*; first published by Routledge & Kegan Paul, 1929; now published by Paladin, Granada Publishing, 1973.

Piaget, J & Inhelder, B, *The Psychology of the Child*; Routledge & Kegan Paul, 1969.

Reynell, J, *Language Development and Assessment*; MTP Press, 1980.

Rieke, J, Lynch, L, & Soltman, S, *Teaching Strategies for Language Development*; 1st edition, Grune Stratton, 1977.

Rutter, M & Martin, J (eds), *The Child with Delayed Speech*; Spastics International Medical Publications, William Heinemann Medical Books, London, 1972.

Schiff, N, 'The Development of Form and Meaning in the Language of Hearing Children of Deaf Parents'; unpublished doctoral dissertation, Columbia University, 1976.

Shatz, M & Gelman, R, 'The Development of Communication Skills: Modifications in the speech of young children as a function of the listener'; *Monographs of the Society for Research in Child Development*, 38, 1973.

Sheridan, M D, *Children's Developmental Progress: from birth to five years*; NFER-Nelson, 1973.

Sheridan, M D, *Spontaneous Play in Early Childhood: from birth to six years*; NFER-Nelson, 1977.

Shiefelbusch, R L (Ed), *Bases of Language Intervention*; University Park Press, USA, 1978.

Shiefelbusch, R L (Ed), *Language Intervention Strategies*; University Park Press, USA, 1978.

Sleigh, G, 'A Study of Some Symbolic Processes in Young Children'; *British Journal of Disorders of Communication*, Vol 7, October 1972, p 163.

Snow, C, 'Mother's Speech to Children Learning Language'; *Child Development* 43, 1972, pp 549-565.

Snow, C, 'The Development of Conversation between Mothers and Babies'; *Journal of Child Language*, Vol 4, 1977, pp 1-22.

Soderburgh, R, 'The Fruitful Dialogue: the child's acquisition of his first language: implications for education at all stages'; Project Child Language Syntax, reprint No 2; Stockholm University, 1974.

Stark, R, 'Pre-speech Segmental Feature Development'; in *Language Acquisition*, edited by Fletcher and Garman; *ibid.*

Stern, D, 'Mother and Infant at Play: the dyadic interaction involving facial, vocal and gaze behaviours'; in *The Effect of the Infant on Its Caregiver*, edited by M Lewis & L A Rosenblum; John Wiley & Sons, New York, 1974.

Tallal, P & Piercey, M, 'Defects of Non-verbal Auditory Perception in Children with Developmental Aphasia'; *Nature*, 241, 1973, pp 468-469.

Thompson, J R & Chapman, R S, 'Who is "Daddy"? The status of two-year-olds' over-extended words in use and comprehension'; *Journal of Child Language*, 4, 1975, pp 359-375.

Vernon, M D, *Perception Through Experience*; Methuen's Manuals of Psychology; Methuen & Co, 1970.

Weisburg, P, 'Social and Non-social Conditioning of Infant Vocalisations'; *Child Development*, 34, 1963, pp 377-388.

Weiss, C E & Lillywhite, H S, *Communicative Disorders: Prevention and Early Intervention*; 2nd edition, C V Mosby Company, USA, 1981.

Practical

Berry, M F, *Teaching Linguistically Handicapped Children*; Prentice-Hall, USA, 1980.

Cole, Patricia, *Language Disorders in Children*; Prentice-Hall, USA, 1982.

Cox, D E & Pearson, J, *Material for Language Stimulation*; The College of Speech Therapists.

Dowling, M, *Early Projects*; Longman Early Childhood Education, 1980.

Fawcus M, Robinson M, Williams J & Williams R, *Working with Dysphasics*; Speechmark Publishing, 1983.

Fraser GM & Blockley J, *The Language Disordered Child*; NFER-Nelson, 1982.

Hastings P & Hayes B, *Encouraging Language Development*; Croom Helm, Special Education Series, 1981.

Holt J, *How Children Learn*; Pelican Books, Penguin, 1967.

Jeffree DM & McConkey R, *Let Me Speak*; Human Horizons Series, Souvenir Press, 1976.

Jeffree D, McConkey R & Hewson S, *Let Me Play*; Human Horizons Series, Souvenir Press, 1977.

Kiernan C, Jordan C & Saunders R, *Starting Off*; Human Horizons Series, Souvenir Press, 1976.

Kirk SA & Kirk WD, *Psycholinguistics, Learning Disabilities, Diagnosis and Remediation*; University of Illinois Press, Urbana, Chicago, London 1971.

Knowles W & Masidlover M, *Derbyshire Language Programme*, 1979.

Newson J & Newson E, *Toys and Playthings*; Penguin, 1979.

Pre-School Playgroups Association, *Action Songs and Finger-Plays for Under-Fives*; compiled by Sarah Williams & Judy Hunt, Kingston Press.